Sex, Drugs and
Football Thugs

Sex, Drugs and Football Thugs

On The Road With

The Naughty Forty

Mark Chester

MILO BOOKS

Published in December 2005 by Milo Books

This edition published January 2007

ISBN 1 903854 56 3
13-digit ISBN 978 1 903854 56 3

Typeset by Avon DataSet Ltd,
Bidford on Avon, Warwickshire, B50 4JH

Printed in Great Britain by CPD

MILO BOOKS LTD
The Old Weighbridge
Station Road
Wrea Green
Lancs PR4 2PH

This book is dedicated to honesty, freedom of speech, and to those who have got the bollocks to use it.

It is for those who fell along the wayside, and those who came back fighting.

It is dedicated to a unique culture, and a way of life detested by many and loved by more.

This book is dedicated to us, and we all know who we are.

Contents

Introduction

"NAUGHTY BUT WELL behaved," read the headline in the *Sentinel*. The North Staffordshire tabloid had been running stories for weeks after a poster featuring more than seventy-six known Stoke City hooligans appeared for sale on the Internet auction site eBay.

It was August 2003, several weeks before my intended launch of *Naughty*, my story of life with the Naughty Forty football firm. I'd had the poster designed to coincide with the book launch, a celebration of "terrace culture" to be held at one of Stoke's oldest landmark buildings, the Kings Hall, the civic centre in the heart of our community. MPs and councillors were outraged not only by the slur that this book would bring once again on the city and football club, but the fact that it was being launched in their premises, under their noses. Some were sufficiently seething to demand the event's immediate cancellation.

The initial outrage over the poster auction turned to a full outcry of anger and disbelief when the authorities discovered my intended launch venue and so a media campaign against the book gained momentum. Despite once being a fiercely private person, I had spilt my guts on to the keypad of a laptop

1

over the previous twelve months and I now found myself toe to toe with the media, the police and Stoke City Council.

I was already drained and mentally exhausted and I'd lost more than a stone in weight during the final months of writing *Naughty*. Now I had to dig in on a new front and prepare myself for what might lie ahead. A cancellation would be a nightmare, as that launch had to take place, whether it be inside the Kings Hall or in a circus tent in the arse end of nowhere. The Naughty Forty had spent the best part of two decades pulling off what they did best and this was to be no exception. The firm was buzzing and, as always, it was one in, all in, as preparations for the biggest launch of a book of this kind went ahead with dogged determination.

Several media interviews later and more front-page propaganda left the authorities and the North Staffordshire public in no doubt of our intentions. The fact that I was one of those "mindless thugs" who could actually hold an intellectual conversation instead of frothing out abuse and foul-mouthed obscenities, meant the council raised no objection, so the final decision as to whether the event would take place was left in the hands of the police.

Staffordshire police played their hand very well indeed in giving the event the go ahead. They were prepared to rely on in-house respect to keep the day in order, despite the fact that known members from other notorious firms would be attending the bash. The truth of the matter was that they much preferred to know where we were at all times, making a softly-softly approach to the event work in their favour. That way they could keep some sort of an eye on the day's proceedings without upsetting the mood and creating a possible flashpoint. I'm glad to say it worked, and all the "I told you so" types had nothing to get their teeth into and chew on in the following day's media reports.

The event was something a bit special even by our standards. The Kings Hall in its heyday was a concert venue, and that's exactly what we had, a rowdy concert. In excess of 1,300 people crammed into the venue from two in the afternoon until midnight. The UK Subs headed a line up of punk bands which included the Skeptix and Head the Ball. John Mac's up-and-coming The Casual Terraces came down from Leeds and hooli-rap band Acarine lent a more casual-culture approach to the afternoon. Between bands, DJs kept the mood moving with guest appearances from the author of *Casuals*, Phil Thornton, and Farm front man Peter Hooton. The whole place was enveloped in testosterone as ninety percent of the congregation was male and most full-on football hooligans of all ages and experience. The book had given us a reason for one of the biggest reunions we'd ever had and lads travelled back home from Australia, Thailand and the States to be amongst their football family. Nobody wanted to miss out on this one.

The West Ham and Chelsea supremos, Cass Pennant and Martin King, travelled up from London with Rob Silvester of the Portsmouth 6.57 Crew. Steve Cowens from the Blades Business Crew stood chatting with Shaun Tordoff and a burly crew of five from Hull, while Neil and the Wrexham lads looked lively as usual. Other firms represented were Port Vale, which surprised me a bit. Well, if you want the truth a couple of their lads are quality geezers but . . . well, I won't harp on about it. Huddersfield came across the Pennines, Wolves youth made the short trip up from the Black Country and a couple of Middlesbrough lads made the much longer trip from the northeast. As I sat behind my book-laden table observing a line of several hundred people queuing to purchase a copy for me to sign, I absorbed the intensity of the whole occasion. I was responsible for bringing this gathering together, and what might lie ahead was firmly on my toes. With so many volatile individuals under one roof with alcohol and whatever else was their preference in abundance, I could see where people's concerns had come from.

After seeing it first hand, my thoughts were as resolute as they had been in the weeks leading to it. *Our lads are quality, I know that, and every guest that has taken the time and respect to show up here today is a top boy in his own right.* There was never going to be anything other than a celebration of terrace culture, and for that reason I allowed the delightful Laura McMullen of the BBC to come along and film us. *Naughty*, but well-behaved. Observation over, I chilled out, leant back in my chair and accepted a book handed to me with a huge red-faced grin. It was Big Stevie from the Dundee Utility Crew, who have their own affiliation with Stoke. It was that kind of day.

Back in 2003, when I handed in my work for *Naughty*, I had originally included some stories of trips abroad with England and with the Stoke lads, and from my years on the run. Unfortunately, the sheer number of words made it impossible to include them, so they were shelved – until now. *Sex, Drugs and Football Thugs* covers roughly a decade, from the mid-Eighties to the mid-Nineties, after which I effectively "retired" from the scene that had been so integral to my life. It will show you a side of me that my close friends have always loved in me the most; my sleazy, uninhibited nature, the part of me that tastes of stale vodka and smells like the cold, drying semen that's been left as nothing more than a reminder. Everybody has a dark side and I'm no different.

What I'm saying is, if you're not that partial to the odd line of powder, don't enjoy filthy, unadulterated sex and then having your head kicked in at a match and laughing about it later in the pub with your mates, then this book is not for you. On the other hand, you might well be a dirty, sleazy bastard just like me, so go on, see for yourself.

This time we will leave Stoke at home and journey overseas as this time the Naughty Forty go on tour. It is best read as a companion book to *Naughty*, so if you haven't already read that, get down your local bookstore and invest the best £7.99 you'll ever spend. It fills in the gaps in that book, mysterious periods when I and others like me left Blighty's shores and got up to . . . well, read on and find out.

Chapter One

A Well-Deserved Break

LOOKING BACK, I put it down to a number of things. There was the fact that I had missed out on my irreplaceable drunken teenage years of beer-swilling sexual frivolity while serving as a soldier, and desperately wanted to participate in some now. There was also the tour of South Armagh I served and the dishonourable discharge that had me wallowing in an attitude of, *I don't give a fuck what happens to me today, never mind tomorrow*. After Ulster, I knew I was going to be a little crazy for a few months. What I did not realise was that the madness would last for over a decade.

I was twenty years old, had been in Civvy Street for just over seven weeks and already hated it. Hated everything about it, the whole fucking lot. Well, everything except for Stoke City Football Club and the hooligans who followed them. That was different. They were different. *We* were different, and everything that we did and lived by was different. Being different was all-important. It kept me alive.

I had just about enough money for the flight but that was it.

Scallying to survive was the only option or we couldn't go. So my childhood mate Eddie and I got to selling the odd illicit bits and bobs that we'd recently acquired. We got a couple of quid together, booked two seats and flew that night. Neither of us wanted to miss out on Stoke's first-ever "firm holiday" abroad. It was all anyone had been talking about since the season had finished.

"Club Tropicana's drinks are free," George Michael sang. Good job then, because we had no intention of paying for fuck-all when we got there. Why should we? We were Stoke City and for the next two weeks any cunt in Magaluf who wanted it could have it. There were 160 of us coming on three planes and we filled two hotels. Our average age was nineteen. Most of us worked, but the majority were still serving shitty apprentice-ships. We were bored most of the week, bored shitless. Then we'd go to the match. That was our identity.

English football hooligans we are, and no, we have not forgotten your allegiance to those wankers during the Falklands War. So, for the next fourteen days we want to get pissed-up in your resort and shag as many filthy women as we can. We are also hoping that, with a bit of luck, some other football hooligans will be out there on holiday too. Manchester United or Birmingham would be nice, but we're not bothered, we'll have it with anyone as long as they want it with us. Now we mostly want it with "them", that is, our kind, but we certainly don't mind having it with any foreigners, especially the Germans or the Spics. Just let one of them dirty bastards mention the HMS Sheffield or the Sir Galahad to me, I'll fucking do 'em!

With that mindset, it was always going to be an eventful fortnight on the Balearic island of Majorca. It was 1984 and I was a cocksure youth with sparkly eyes and a cheeky grin. I preferred doing it doggy but didn't mind letting her get on top, as long as I could still see the football on TV. Of course I'd been there, seen it and done it all, and had the medal to prove it. But I was still really a lost kid looking to make up for lost time. My behaviour on our first-ever firm holiday was atrocious, as was everyone's. It seems bizarre recounting juvenile anti-social behaviour in a day and age where brutal happy-slappings of innocent people are recorded by youngsters for entertainment. In our time, we were all obviously very immature but in our minds we really did believe that we were representing the true spirit of our nation by behaving the way we did in Majorca, or for that matter anywhere outside England.

Apart from the vicious bar brawls and street fighting, it was mostly mischief. I just saw it as a well-deserved break. It was a time for some reflection on my recent past and time to be spent with this new family of foot-soldiers that had replaced Her Majesty's own. No matter where this life with these people was going to lead me, I wanted to be there and always would. Life outside the firm did not bear thinking about.

Potters' Fortnight, a traditional Staffordshire holiday period, was the last week in June and the first in July, and anyone who could afford to travel went abroad. Those that couldn't went to Blackpool or "our gate" – a local term for people who couldn't afford a holiday – for the day, weather permitting. Nobody is sure who originally organised this 1984 trip, it just turned out that everybody headed to Palma Nova, a mile or so from Magaluf. That might not seem strange, but it is when you take into consideration that we were joined by twenty of Port Vale's Casuals – at the time well ahead of the rest of their firm. They were mostly from the Norton area in the east end of Stoke-on-Trent, a roughneck area and staunch Vale territory.

After I wrote my football hooligan memoir *Naughty*, people asked, "How come you didn't mention the Vale?" My first answer was, "How many times do people want to read about us doing them again?" But that wasn't really the case. The truth is that for many years we Stoke lads actually used to look out for them. We were never invited, far from it, but we did occasionally turn out if they had a big cup game against Man Utd or Spurs or a pre-season friendly with Birmingham. We turned up, got stuck in and got some nicked at all of those fixtures. The way we saw it was that those firms would be on the streets of our city, regardless of who they were playing, and we weren't having it.

It was only in the late Eighties, when Stoke slipped down a couple of divisions and they went a division above us, that we saw for the first time how much it meant to them and what a delight it was to see us briefly below them. They were cocky, and that was when our hatred for them started to develop in earnest. We violently reciprocated their hatred for us, only a hundred times worse than anything they were ever prepared for. Going back to that question about leaving them out of the book; what greater snub could I give them than simply not mentioning them at all. Get my point? That's how easy it is to do the Vale.

As you will gather from this short story, Port Vale do have some game lads and a couple of them are genuinely classed as mates. In particular, Rhino, Gazza Mellor, Ginger Bri, Stanner and Cocky were a credit to their firm on this crazy, coming-of-age fortnight, and at times nearly as mad as us.

We needed to find a nightclub to use as a base, one that was full of slappers. Then we needed to find out who else was in town and where they were firming up each night. We could do with a couple of those yellow mopeds, too. We all arrived during one hot and sweaty day, and by two o'clock in the morning Tokyo Joe's nightclub had now been aptly renamed Stokyo Joe's and designated as our new HQ, our gaff, our own place to hang out and do what we wanted. As far as we were concerned, especially as the manager gave us handfuls of free drinks tickets with a nod and a smile, we had claimed an outpost in a far-off land. It was a territory captured for Her Majesty and handed to us as a reward to protect for her and the realm. It was absolutely fucking mad but that's what happens when the English travel abroad, and make no mistake, it does not matter what sort of background you come from. We're all the same, inbreds. That's the mindset of the fiercely proud Anglo-Saxons amongst us. That is something that will never change, ever. Stokyo Joe's was now Stoke territory and if need be it would be defended to the hilt every night . . . *Fucking hell. Have you seen the arse on that?*

The first night it was always going to go off. And it did, against a mature firm of Tottenham in the Green Parrot around one o'clock in the morning. It was all over us showing a bit of bravado with some American sailors off the USS *Nimitz*. The ship had been anchored in the main port at Palma and dozens of the Yanks had headed into Magaluf looking for some European pussy. Our pussy.

A drink was spilt. You know the score. He's unhappy his uniform is soiled and you don't like his aggressive stance about it. In an instant the sailors get up from their table ten-strong. They are confident and it shows. You can read their minds.

"Who the hell do these kids think they are fucking messing with? We're the goddam United States Navy."

"Who the fuck do you think you're fucking with, Yank? We're Stoke fucking City from England."

We stood up fifty-strong and crowded in tight, immediately strangling the Yanks and causing a massive change of heart amongst their ranks. We had sunk them with a broadside of overwhelming unity and a willingness to stand together, no matter who or how old the opposition. With no punches thrown, we allowed the sailors to drink their beers and leave at their own discretion. Quickly.

We had all clocked the Tottenham lot clocking us with the Yanks, so it was now becoming a moral issue for us. We could not leave that bar after what we had just done, especially as now some of the Cockneys were becoming leery and throwing comments in our direction. Then, as always, it happened.

"Fuck it, lads. Are we in, eh? Are we fucking in these or what? Brass, are we fucking having this, they're trying to take the fucking piss out of us. C'mon Stoke. Fucking c'mon."

And off it duly went, Western style. Stoke v Tottenham in a Spanish bar. No Old Bill, no cameras. Stoke easily shade the numbers. Tottenham have the age and experience. We see it as a major scalp. They see it as a northern nuisance that needs putting in its place. BANG! It went off mental as both sides tore into each other, using tables and chairs as the preliminary assault weapons, then bottles and coshes for the hand-to-hand stuff. It was a sixty-second affair with much of the pub completely trashed in the exchange of weaponry. It went Tottenham's way for most of that minute, with Stoke fighting backwards towards a wall.

With backs against that wall Stoke made their charge, screaming as one, and moved the Cockneys out of the bar on to the terrace. Outside the fight continued as a mass chair-and-table brawl, with pockets of two-on-two exchanges. Missiles rained down from a rooftop bar, causing injury to several of our number. Brasso, Rhino and four or five others charged up a set of stairs under fire and took it to the fleeing Cockneys, slugging it out amongst the tables, chairs and overturned parasols.

The sound of Spanish sirens. Thoughts of Spanish police, Spanish courts, Spanish jail. *No thanks.* Both sides hit the streets. All of a sudden it was every man for himself or face a

12

severe beating and a stiff prison sentence.

"Fuck OFF! Get the fuck off me, you Spanish bastard." I could not detach that waiter from my shirt-sleeve. He was hanging on, determined to see me arrested. *Shit!* Now another one of them was on me. It started to sink in that I was in a lot of trouble. I was on my own, no-on else had been caught and not a soul was left except me. I struggled wildly as they pulled me inside the Green Parrot. All the time one of them was trying to kick my legs from under me and it was starting to get right on my fucking nerves. I blew and basically ripped my shirt from my body and pulled the two Spaniards in a wrenching motion towards me. I butted one and gouged my fingers into the other's eyes. It gained me a couple of seconds and that was when the panic hit me.

Outside, to my right, I could now see the flashing lights of the police vehicles and hear people shouting and a dog barking in a van. These two Spanish bastards in front of me were starting to come round and I couldn't get out through the front of the place without getting nicked. With no choice I ran blind through some swing doors into the kitchen. I scanned it quickly and saw my way out was through another door that led to a waste area below street level. The only real problem I could see was that the wall leading up to the street and my escape looked about seven feet tall and the only things visible to climb up on were dustbins full of vegetable peelings and raw fish slops.

Fuck it. I bolted towards the door just as several Spaniards crashed through the swing doors into the kitchen behind me. One lunged forward in an attempt to collar me. Dodging him, I vaulted a work surface and slid hopelessly on the greasy floor. At that point I thought the game was up, as my fall had lost me valuable seconds. I picked up a large ladle as I rose and flung it at the nearest Spaniard. He cowered and I continued to run.

As soon as I had made it into the waste area, I pretty much accepted my dire situation and chose to make a fight of it. There was no way I would be able to climb out with that lot on my back. I picked up a garbage bin, raised it above my head and hurled it at the two men, who were now armed with knives they had picked up from the kitchen. After the bin hit them, they brandished their weapons at me with intent. My only hope was to hold them off until the police came and arrested me. At least I'd only get a beating off them. I was gutted. I hadn't even seen the sea yet and my well-deserved break was nearly over.

"Jasp, hang on mate."

My back-up team came climbing down from the rooftop bar as they fled their own situation. A billboard crashed down from the street above and landed right on top of the unsuspecting Spaniards' heads, sending them reeling. Next, a bicycle was hurled down on the recovering duo. *Bloody hell!* I was expecting a taxi next.

Brasso, loyal as ever, was standing up above me, frothing at the mouth and going berserk. Anything that came to hand was hurled down with venom as he brought me the much-needed time I thought I had run out of. I reached up to grab hold of something that would take my weight but kept slipping back down into the slops. It was frantic stuff because the police had now reached inside the kitchens and could probably see me attempting my escape. Rhino appeared next to Brass and told him to take his weight. The two stood firm and reached over. With everything I had I jumped hard and Rhino's clasped hand pulled firmly enough for me to get a leg up. Then all three of us were gone, laughing into the pitch-black, crazy nightscape.

Back at the hotel we summed up the injuries. Bri had lost his front teeth and Eddie had broken his hand, but they were still laughing about it, and everyone was buzzing. That first night had delivered everything they had wanted, and with the right type of people as well. I had a laugh too, but later on it did dawn on me that I had come extremely close to getting badly cut up or even nicked and locked up. On this particular night I owed it to my old mate Brasso and Rhino from the Vale for saving my neck. It just goes to show, no matter how far you push it, if you're with the right set of lads there is always a good chance you will get through any kind of situation, even one you think is beyond desperate. It doesn't half bring you closer together as well.

Because we had booked only flights and not accommodation, Eddie and I had split up and bunked into other people's rooms in a hotel we called the Don Bigote. I was in with Turney and Thommo, and Eddie was with Stiko and Quinney, while Brasso was bunked into the Hotel 33. Neither hotel was suitable for us lot really and the staff and other holidaymakers were visibly gutted when we showed up. Mainly filled with Germans and Scandinavians, they were both quiet and relaxed places – until we all got round the pools late in the afternoons and had bombing competitions. How many Bulldog tattoos around that patio? Unbelievable. If I'd been one of those guests I'd have hated us too.

Eddie and I went looking for Brasso and walked together along the parched road, crossing over towards what we hoped was the Hotel 33 reception. Outside, lying unconscious and face-up in the gutter, was Psycho Johnson, an eccentric, over-intelligent flat-top who drank with us in Hanley and who had without doubt earned his reputation of being a full-bore loon. He was barefoot, wearing combat shorts and a white Bundesliga vest and dog tags. In one hand was an empty bottle of vodka, in the other, which was across his chest, was clenched his soggy passport.

We stepped over Johns and walked into the hotel, agreeing that this must be the right place. Brass was coming out as we were going in, highly amused that he had just seen Rhino plant a huge diver's knife in the reception desk and place his shades on top of the handle while he waited for his key. *Fucking hell, these Vale lot are unruly*, I thought to myself. As we were leaving I passed a paralytic Gazza Mellor sitting on the hotel steps with streams of piss running down the inside of his bare legs. His attempts to stand up and speak to me while he still peed himself were hysterical. I liked these lads, especially Gazza, who went on to be a veteran of the Rothersthorpe riot against Manchester City's firm (see *Naughty*) and Rhino, who I owed one.

That's what the days were mostly like. For the lads with money it was chilled. Football on the beach, North Stoke v South Stoke. Drinking competitions and making lists while window shopping for designer wear and perfumes. The days for skint members, like the Urchin, were spent trawling behind the others, robbing to order and ticking off the list as and when. There were some light-fingered bastards amongst us.

Several of the lads had bumped into a large party of girls who'd said they were from Derby and a couple of them claimed to know me, though I was certain they did not. *Derby? Nah.* Nevertheless, I was told that a couple of them were more than a little inquisitive about me and had told the lads to bring me out that night to meet them.

I wasn't that bothered about the women, I was already pissed off that me and Eddie, a childhood mate, had been involved in a set-to over some Irish birds he had chatted up the previous night. They were in green and white Benetton shirts and were laughing around and enjoying all the attention from my mates, who should have known better. *Yeah, go on you bastards, you all have a fucking good time together whilst our lads are over in Ulster taking shit off 'em*. Well, that was where my head was at that time, still in Armagh. I exploded and attacked both parties with tables and chairs, resulting in everyone scattering for cover and me and Ed the last men standing.

Fifteen years earlier, Ed and I had fought our first playground scrap as five-year-olds. Ed probably felt a bit guilty about hitting me in that occasion with a cricket stump and had carried it with him for years. Well, tonight we both let that memory go, shook hands and forgot it. We walked off laughing together and headed towards Stokyo Joe's. Ed commented along the way, "She was a tight cow anyway. Didn't buy a drink all fucking night."

I refused the offer of meeting the Derby birds. "Tonight I think I'm going to have a quiet one lads. You can shag them instead." No worries, they all knew I would be out and off my trolley with them later.

I was out that night, and in a worse state than I had been all holiday so far. Reports got back to some of the lads who were having another scout around the Green Parrot for Tottenham that I had just closed Stokyo Joe's by pulling the air conditioning system off the ceiling. I vaguely remember doing something like that. But hanging down off the blades of a huge rotating fan with my shorts down by my ankles and pissing over dancing women as I spun around? I'm not sure about that one, but the lads insist on it, so I suppose I'd better believe them. By all accounts the fan came crashing down from the ceiling and caused mayhem amongst the revellers. I'd single-handedly closed down the club after a week full of promises to the owner that we would start behaving. One or two of our lot decided to get me off the streets before I got arrested. It was probably a good idea.

"Oi! Ay up." The shouts came from our mates inside a softly lit roadside bar. By now I was sober enough to go in and have a drink, as we had been walking for ages. My four escorts and I decided it was time for one more for the road and have a chat about the night's capers.

It was a popular place, still busy at three in the morning, and the music was soft and welcoming. I lowered my head as I entered through an open window and greeted every one with a wry grin. I noticed the alcove they occupied had two big tables in a line and both were piled with empty glasses and packed with people. There were around fifteen of our lads and the same number of women, none of whom I'd met before. I did notice straight away, as I struck up a conversation with Quinney, that two of the girls were discreetly acknowledging my arrival.

"Jasp, how are you mate? We've been told that you've trashed the HQ."

Quinney and most of the others started laughing as they ordered up some beers for the new arrivals. I don't think I was given enough time to even start to answer my friend before one of the women was up furiously out of her seat. She flew across the table and flung a half-full glass, which passed inches from my face. Wow. Everybody stood up at once and began to argue viciously with one other. I did not need anyone to explain to me that these were clearly the women from Derby who had been asking about me so much. They squared up to me in what seemed like slow motion, their mouths going ten to the dozen, fingers pointing, heads moving backwards and forwards as they aggressively spoke their minds.

All I could think of as I watched a load of fanatical women being staved off me by a load of football casuals was that they were from a football background themselves. They had that dress sense, that aggression, that aura. The penny dropped as I homed in on the original aggressor.

"These birds aren't from Derby, they're Forest," I said.

I froze as I stared at a woman who truly looked like she wanted to kill me. She believed that I was the person responsible for cutting the throat of her boyfriend at a game against Nottingham Forest the previous season, an incident for which I was arrested – though later released – and which ultimately marked the beginning of the end of my already tarnished Army career. She bombarded me with accusations but I don't think I answered her. There was no point, as Eddie now had her round the throat. It was all getting messy and very soon the management called the Guardia Civil. The women left and then we went before any of us were arrested. I for one did not fancy getting thrown in a van with any of that lot, they were wild and would have torn us to bits.

On the way back up the hill to our hotel, the lads laughed and joked about the girls and how game they had been. I agreed, and believe me, until they left the resort three nights later, I was well on my toes. That woman was not going to give me the opportunity to explain that it was not me that had carried out the knifing. She wanted my blood, and I was expecting a glass or a blade at any minute. I went to bed that night full of thought, but not for one minute knowing that this feud would carry on for years to come. Tensions even continued in Sydney, Australia, in the late Eighties. But there you go, that's football I suppose.

The moped dealers could speak perfectly good English but chose not to because they had every intention of ripping us off one way or another when we returned the bikes. I think it was Johnson's idea for us all to get bikes. He was nuts about them and often put on shows at home by speeding past a packed pub on one wheel of his ZR, usually waving with one hand and giving us his sick grin. That day eighty of us hired yellow mopeds and marauded mostly twos-up around Magaluf looking for mischief.

Drinking and driving: not a great idea, and it wasn't a good idea either to forget to wear any protection from the sun. By late afternoon most of us were dehydrating and burnt to a crisp. It was thought by many that amphetamine sulphate crystals bought from a West African "lucky lucky" man earlier in the week would be a good cure for the burnt arms and shoulders. Not everyone indulged but sufficient did to make the final lap of the resort a memorable affair.

We mounted and set off like a posse of Texas Rangers. Psycho Johnson immediately took pole position and shouted for us all to follow him whatever happened – and anyone who didn't "was a pussy". A challenge had been laid down and we all took it up. Heading down the main drag in the centre of Magaluf was the road that we had lovingly christened the "Street of a Thousand Offs" because it had been a battlefield each night of the holiday so far. Johns scattered holidaymakers off the road and brushed them like a wave over the pavement and into bar fronts as they fled the menace on the moped. We followed on eighty-strong, filling the width of the now empty road. Everyone roared with laughter at the bemused expressions of the clubbers as we streamed past tooting our horns.

"It's that fucking Stoke lot again. Wankers."

On we headed like a herd, stopping for nothing and no-one. Johnson took a right turn and we all followed. Down the hill, gathering speed in the direction of the prom and straight towards a multitude of packed-out, brightly lit cafes and restaurants. I eased off the accelerator, as did several others. Johnson sped along like a suicide bomber on to the pavement and sent a couple of waiters sprawling as he burst through a restaurant's covered terracing. On he went, in and out of tables full of diners. Some found it hysterical while others sat utterly shocked. Johnson headed on, wheel-spinning into another restaurant and then the next before returning to the road and us. I was amazed nobody had been hurt. From where I was it looked like each family sitting outside those restaurants had been alerted by the noise and most could see that the safest thing to do was to keep still and not panic. Such was the expertise Johnson showed on that motorcycle, every obstacle was navigated and dodged and every set of steps descended perfectly. It really was a marvel of skill and people at several tables applauded their slight disruption between courses. How do you follow that?

Johnson pulled a wheelie and headed off on another mission and we all called it a day and headed back to the Don Bigote. The sun had taken its toll on a lot of us and we were knackered, so it was decided a quiet drink in the hotel disco was the best option. Besides, it would give us a chance to have a look at some Brummie birds who had arrived that morning. One of them was big like *Emmerdale*'s Lisa Dingle, just up my street.

We hadn't bothered with the hotel disco until now. A couple of the lads had kept saying it was "full of fanny" every night, but fanny to the majority of us meant later on, after we'd had a kick-off. I could never understand why lads would stand round leering at a group of women when there was fun to be had with the boys. Our rule was, "Who wants to play army? Nooo girls." I mean, when you're with the lads you're with the lads.

They were right, though, the disco was rammed with women, and the Brummies were in there too. We moved in. The girls were a party of twenty from West Bromwich and followed the Baggies. They were pretty well turned out and seemed to know about the game and our culture. I don't mind talking to girls when you can mention football and it's even more of a bonus when they like football hooligans as well. One big bird had two pinches of my arse in ten minutes. *She's fucking having it tonight mate, hooli-style.*

The club was below the hotel and to get in you had to turn right at reception and go down a steep set of stairs. The club had two mirrored bars, a large square dance floor, a seated area at the bottom and then a massive set of glass panelled doors that were pulled open. Out through them and down a small cobbled winding path through an ornamental garden was the swimming pool and patio. The pool was lit up bright blue and the gardens had solar lights dotted around, giving it a relaxed ambience. It was just right, not too hectic and no other football lads to keep your eye on. *And she keeps giving me the eye big time. Let's have another beer.*

Twenty minutes later, the atmosphere was shattered as hysterical screams drowned the music. I sat up in my seat beside the patio doors and saw a wave of people on the move, running blindly towards us. As people found cover, a huge gap opened up across the dance floor, giving me a glimpse of a yellow moped arriving at the foot of the club's staircase. It was a slightly more inebriated Johns and it looked like his bike trip was coming to a finale right here in our hotel disco.

The dance floor was now completely empty of the 200 or so previous occupants and Johns took to it, wheel-spinning the moped round and round and round, faster and faster, burning rubber and gritting his teeth like a man taking nine lashes of the cat. Amazed, we all looked on. Once more, those that were out of danger revelled at his skill and some, like us, even clapped and cheered him on.

In a flash, Johns shot from the dance floor like a glass off a Ouija board, straight past our seats, out through the doors to the patio and on towards the pool. Everyone looked in disbelief as he tore through the gardens and rode his bike straight into the deep end of the pool. SPLASH! He disappeared under a mass of bubbles and surfaced seconds later to uproar. Calmly climbing out of the pool at the other side, a sodden Johns disappeared briefly into some shrubbery and was then seen scaling a wall before vanishing from sight. God only knows what else he had got up to before he had arrived at the Don Bigote. *Show over, now where's that Brummie bitch who was pinching my arse?*

I've always had a thing about heavy women. I find them

extremely beautiful facially. They do it for me big time. As far as I'm concerned there is nothing better than lying there casually watching a voluptuous redhead dining on you. And that's exactly what I was doing thirty minutes later.

She liked him a lot I could tell. Slurping away in front of me she had a look of contentment. I decided that now was not the best time to ask her name so I grabbed a handful of her flaming red hair and yanked her head to one side. I gritted my teeth and forced my swollen bulbus deeper into her throat and started pumping slowly but forcefully. She grunted appreciatively and grabbed hold of my big shaft with her second hand. Breathing heavily, like a baited bull, I noticed the dimples on her knuckles, her cute rounded nose with little nostrils, her perfectly formed pouting lips done in cherry red, the heavy black and light green eyeliner that gave her that Color-Climax image. Argh yes, uncontrollably I blurted it out.

"Where do you want this lot, bitch?"

My grip on her hair became increasingly tighter as I began to feel that universal sensation of tension release quickly rushing further and further along my shaft.

"In my mouth. I want it in my mouth."

She sounded nasal, but fair play still managed to get her words out before I exploded in her mouth right on cue, right where she asked for it. I must have hit her with both barrels because she started to gag heavily but still refused to stop swallowing my load. I was impressed with her determination to savour every last drop. It was one of those moments of pure filth, when you are in the right place at the right time with a stranger who has the same liberal sexual morals as yourself. A time when two people can let go of their inhibitions and become a right pair of sleazy, dirty bastards with each other's bodies – and then never meet again. If only it was always like that.

Like a cat who had got the cream, she finished off and

looked me directly in my eyes. She gave her top lip a long, slow lick and with a giggle said, "Oh, I'm Sammy by the way."

"Hi Sammy, nice to meet you."

The lads dubbed her the Whale of Magaluf and joked that she was so big that I was probably shagging the rolls of fat between her legs when I did her from behind in the shower. Ha! I reckoned they just hadn't got the bollocks to be seen with a woman who isn't one of your slim, model-type lookers. No fit birds would go near them anyway, because they were always so off their heads and usually scrapping.

A commotion in the corridor tore me from Sammy's bosom right on cue. I left her room to see a hyped-up Cockney Mark running up and down the corridor screaming loudly. He and Mick Pender had been drinking heavily together for days. Mark had lost the plot and had started running over the tops of parked cars. On their return to the hotel, one or both had pulled a radiator off the wall in their room and hurled it blind off a fifth-floor balcony. The radiator had plummeted to the ground and crashed through the middle of a table tennis table, obliterating one half of it. Luckily for them it wasn't the other half, because lying flat out in a drunken stupor on the other side of the net was a now shocked and slightly miffed Eddie. Even I found that kind of behaviour extreme, as someone from outside of our party could have been an innocent victim.

As Mark was dragged screaming from the hotel by the police, I wasn't surprised when one of them turned to us and pointed to his head in a rotating motion.

"Es loco. Crazy, no?"

"Well yeah, he is, mate, that's why he knocks about with us lot."

None of us were shocked to find out the next morning from the police that Mark had been taken to a psychiatric unit at the local hospital. They were going to keep him in for a couple of days to run some tests on him to decide whether he was insane or not. On his release Mark claimed that he had spent time in a secure unit matching up patterns and putting shaped bricks through the right shaped holes.

"Fucking hell," he said. "I was only pissed up. It was that banana liqueur that Lilley kept pinching from the offy." I'd tried it too but it was minging. It was a sobering experience for our friend, who came pretty close to being sectioned into a Spanish mental hospital.

The mood around the pool that afternoon was one of excited anticipation. It was rumoured that a crew of Millwall's older Bushwackers had been sighted in several of the downtown bars the previous night. Tonight we would all get ready and go out together.

"Right, that's it then lads. Millwall are in town. We meet on the roof of the Green Parrot at nine. Agreed? Tremendous."

We spotted two of them from our rooftop stronghold. They walked along in discussion, completely oblivious to the prying menace of 100 youths above them. They were old school, you could tell, probably in their late thirties or early forties. They were thickset chunky bastards as well, and they strolled along with an ingrained confidence. I know I'm not just speaking for myself but just those two alone sent a shiver of fear up my spine. *Fuck me*, I thought, *I wonder what thirty of that lot look like together?* A huge rush of excitement flashed through our ranks. This was going to be the big one and all sorts of suggestions flew around.

"Let's try and draw them on to the beach and have it with them there in some space."

"Nah, fuck that, let's just hit them hard and unannounced. Steam the pub they're in is the best way."

Two scouts were duly appointed and the two unsuspecting

Bushwhackers were tailed from there on – or so we thought. The rest of us continued to drink and make plans for what we hoped would be the biggest result of our hoolie careers so far, the destruction and annihilation of Millwall's infamous Bushwhacker Crew. We had no idea how many of the south London mob we would be facing or how we would fare against them. All I could remember was the trepidation we had felt as kids either travelling to the Den on the supporters' coaches, or stood on a packed Boothen waiting for Harry the Dog and his F Troop to turn up and bash us with their infamous Millwall bricks, which were made from rolled-up newspaper but could do as much damage as a house brick. The general feeling among us was cold impatience as we waited for our spotters to return with the Millwall location.

"What the fuck do you mean you've lost them?"

It was a disappointing blow and also a bit worrying. How could we know whether the scouts had been sussed and we were now the ones being stalked. What if Millwall were on their way now with a bigger mob than ours, one pissed off that we'd had the audacity to even think about going there with them?

"Tool up," went the cry. We immediately went into offensive mode but kept the elevation of the rooftop as our advantage. For a brief moment I felt like Davy Crockett stood on top of the Alamo waiting for Santa Anna and his Mexican Army to arrive. Only this was different, the enemy we were expecting to appear from the burrow of hidden streets down below were a lot fucking harder than a bunch of Mexicanos. These at the time were the worst and most feared football supporters in our country, therefore the world. It's amazing what kind of scenarios your brain can play out before you at times of adrenalin intoxication.

Yeah, it's real. We live like this. What do you do for your

kicks? Play Scalextric in your loft conversion, the one with the two-seater sofa for when ALL your mates come round? That's right. You get your buzz out of watching two racing cars ripping round the same track time after time. We get our buzz out of being scared out of our minds and having to survive a precarious situation before we can cross the winning line and lift that little silver replica cup that your auntie bought you for your fourteenth birthday. That's if we haven't ended up in Casualty. We might not be liked or tolerated by society but what we do is far closer to our ancestry than people think. You've all just got carried away with your suppressive progression and left your real world discarded in the gutter. Fucking bring it on Millwall, we won't let you down. We share the same chromosomes, the little aggressive ones that for centuries generals have called upon to march that little bit further and to take that fortified hill at all costs to raise the Union Jack. And then count the dead bodies of your friends before you can have a brew. See, that's what we are. There's no need to press gang us, we're going anyway. There's the hype, let's see if the battle lives up to it.

When the scouts returned with the news that they had lost the two Bushwhackers, we should have known the night was going to be a disaster. After an hour of waiting for the Cockneys to appear, most of us had given it up as a bad job and we stood down and got pissed. "Nah, they're not going to show. They probably aren't even bothered about us lot anyway." How many of us were secretly relieved I suppose we will never know, but I for one was not and nor were Brasso and Turney.

Fifteen of us decided to take up the trail where the scouts had lost sight of them, down by Manilo's bar. It was always happy hour at Manilo's, two beers for the price of one or gargantuan measures of cheap vodka in ice-filled glasses. Happy to indulge, we spent the next three hours in self-obliteration, completely forgetting the real reason for being in this part of the resort.

It was on the way back up to Stokyo Joe's for the last hour that things took a turn for the worse. Up ahead across the street, five of our lads were being smashed all over the place by a huge Swedish fella. He was well over six feet five, in his forties, and a dead ringer for Hulk Hogan. He wore tight leather trousers and a white vest, had a head of white hair which went down his back and the same colour goatee beard. In each of his hands he held a wooden baseball bat with which he was knocking the living daylights out of our friends.

We all immediately charged, some picking up chairs and billboards to use as weapons. All fifteen of us encircled Hogan and attempted to inflict some damage but everything we threw bounced ineffectively off him and he grew even more furious at our arrival. Twenty people were now trying to get close enough to bring him down for the kill, but each was dealt a painful blow as Hogan staved off his attackers with acute accuracy. The man was an animal and none of us was getting anywhere near him. Instead, he was effectively picking each of us off. Sooner or later we would not be fit enough to fight the man. It was time for an enforced tactical retreat; either that or get done.

With the advantage of the hill he backed us down it, occasionally darting forward and catching an unsuspecting victim with another heavy blow. Every café he marched us past was relieved of a chair or a discarded bottle, which were thrown back up at the Swede, to no avail. This cunt was going to end up following us back to the hotel room and bashing us there if we couldn't get away from him. With no choice we all turned and broke into a jog, some of us laughing and others fuming that we were on our toes. "Fuck him, let's just get away from the bastard." We had been emphatically done by a mean but slightly gay-looking Hulk Hogan.

"How come the fucking police only turn up when you're getting the result and enjoying yourself?" asked someone.

Good question, but for now let's just get down this side street and away from that madman. We did and for a brief moment caught our breath and saw the funny side of things. *Sod it, it's just one of those things. The geezer was an animal, that's all. Let's get in that bar over there and have a drink.*

We headed under the canopy of the nearest bar to us and all simultaneously stopped dead in our tracks. That rearing lion, the badge and the blue shirt it was embroidered on was all it took to take our breath. Millwall! They were an ugly sight, while we must have looked like rabbits caught in headlights. We had all but succumbed by our body language alone. The Viking had knocked our confidence and left us clueless and looking gormless. Several of the Londoners were standing by the entrance and it was one of these who made the first remark about the scruffs across the street. With that they all stood up, thirty of them, half men and half women.

Turney was first in. I remember gasping as he crossed my vision and landed a flying dropkick right into the advancing Bushwhackers, fell straight on his arse and was rewarded with a boot right under his chin. It sent him skidding across the road and he remained motionless where he landed.

That's it, isn't it? When one of your mates has just been sparked out in front of you, it just happens. All the anxieties disappear and the fear ebbs, giving you that split second mass injection of adrenalin, and off you go. We clashed head-on with Millwall in a narrow back street lit only by the odd neon bar sign. It was shadowy and disguised punches' direction and weight.

These south Londoners knew their business and dished it out to us good style. When their blows connected, bones crunched and teeth flew out. We took casualties almost immediately. With tables and chairs and whatever came to hand, we tried to hold off the mob long enough for Turney to be retrieved and brought to his feet. I don't think any of us actually stood trading punches with them. We used tools, they used fists. At one point I was singled out and stood like a lion tamer, brandishing half a bar stool and swinging it about me wildly to keep them back.

BANG! A sidewinder to the temple dropped me into the gutter. Dazed, I hit the ground and looked up at a complete massacre, with all my mates and potential rescuers in pretty much the same situation as myself. I decided to crawl under a nearby parked car and curl up. I had no choice, my legs had gone.

Under the car I caught my breath and took a horizontal view of the melee. I knew who was with me because I could recognise their footwear; it just bothered me that many of them seemed lifeless. Fucking hell, we were getting battered here. It's an awful sinking feeling when you are being ragged like this. In the space of ten minutes we had been trashed all over the place, twice. Fortunately for me and the rest of us, the women called a halt to it and, like lambs, the Bushwhackers were led away from the carnage. Thank fuck they had their women with them.

This might seem absurd, but that night we all went home bruised and battered but proud as fuck. I reckon we were even prouder than if we had got the result against the Cockneys. Being done as badly as that by the top firm in the country gave us a certain kudos amongst the rest of our crew and elevated us to almost cult status. We were the ones who stood and got battered by Millwall, something that most people would fear throughout their entire football hooligan career. Not for us twenty though, our fear was now gone and one day, we told ourselves, we would overturn that result.

Hulk Hogan, in contrast, has rarely been mentioned over the years. I would like to give the man his due. I'm in my forties now and, believe me, I would not for one minute fancy taking on a gang of twenty bloodthirsty teenagers with a point to prove. So every credit to you, Mr Hogan. As for the rest of the lads that missed out on the Millwall brawl, they were all gutted; it was one not to miss.

My well-deserved break was coming to an end. Tonight was our last on the island and to celebrate we were all going to get pissed up. Stokyo Joe's was packed out. The next lot of visitors were arriving in the resort, providing fresh totty and, hopefully, another firm to play with. It had already gone off with a crew of Bristol Rovers when I arrived inside the club. By all accounts it had been a bloody affair, resulting in Bristol being driven out of the club and the owner threatening to close his venue unless we calmed down. Despite the action, I was handed another batch of free drinks tickets. Why give us free alcohol when all it does is fuel the fire? Never mind.

"Can I have a large one please, love?"

The DJ had been under pressure to find some decent punk since we had got there. "Pretty Vacant" by the Pistols was followed by the Jam's "Down in the Tube Station at Midnight" and we went berserk on the dance floor. It was whilst jumping off one of the speakers that I noticed her at the side of the dance floor. She was alone and her stare was fixed on every movement I made. With an attractive female viewer taking notice of me, I calmed a little and regained my football casual composure. I turned to look again and she was gone.

"Hello."

She startled me as she appeared from nowhere. She held two glasses of vodka and handed one to me. I liked her directness immediately. I grinned and took a sip. "Jesus, that's strong." She moved in a little closer to me and cupped my balls in the palm of her hand. She looked mischievous and told me to drink some more, as she liked her men to do exactly as they were told. I wanted to butt her, in a sexual manner; instead I slipped my hand up inside her skirt and ran my fingers across the contour of her crotch. It felt warm and padded with pussy fur. I liked it and glanced round to see if any of the lads were watching. Still pogoing to Tenpole Tudor, they were all in their own mad worlds. *This has to be worth a quick knee-trembler down on the beach*, I thought to myself.

After all my preaching to the lads, here I was, about to break the unwritten rule of sleazing off with a woman without telling the rest of them what I was up to. Bad, bad drill, but I did it all the same. Excessive vodka, punk music thrashing through your body and now a sexpot stroking my Hampton to boot, what else was I supposed to do? We left the club unnoticed by anyone except Digger. It was only when we got outside into the light that I noticed that my new friend was a lot older than I had first thought.

"What's your name?" I asked.

"Deb," she replied as she led me away by the hand. *Jesus*, I thought, *this bitch is well after it*. She was definitely in her thirties, a mature woman to me at that time. *I'm in for a right treat here*, I thought smugly. I followed on like a little schoolboy who was about to lose his cherry.

Deb did not like my idea of a quick suck and a fuck down on the beach. She insisted that she wanted me for the night and we were going back to her hotel room or nothing at all. *OK, if you insist*. I was a little bit surprised to find that Deb was only actually staying in a cheap one-star hotel, nothing more than a posh pension in a back street of the old town. I shrugged it off and followed her inside to her first floor room. I wasn't exactly Rockefeller myself, so I retrained my thoughts on to sex. Deb sat me down on the bed and told me to wait a minute while she went to the bathroom. I kicked off my boaters and relaxed back on the bed before pulling back my foreskin for a quick cheese and fluff check. *Come on then, hurry up.*

She was more than a minute getting ready so I spent the time scanning the room. It was small, probably only a single room. It had a balcony with a solitary chair that overlooked a park. Inside was a small wardrobe, a bedside table and chest of drawers at the foot of the bed. Above that was a mirror. *Nice*, I thought as I admired myself. *I will be able to watch myself do the business in that.* To the left of the mirror was the door that led into the small en-suite. Looking back I wasn't that clever, as I didn't notice that the room contained no personal effects at all. That should have set alarm bells ringing. I began to get horny again as I remembered our meeting a little over an hour ago. I knew it was going to be rough sex the minute she bit me hard on the nape of my neck. I responded by pinching the inside of her thigh even harder. She did not flinch. *Fuck, I love bitches that don't flinch.*

Just as I was about to drift off into a sexual fantasy the bathroom door opened and Deb re-entered the room. *At last.* I was immediately disappointed as she looked no different to when she first went in. *Where's the fucking sussies, love?* She said nothing as she walked slowly towards me. I braced myself for something a bit special. All she had gone on about on the walk back was how much she wanted to suck my cock. Seeing as she hadn't made the effort to dress up for me, I figured she could get on with the promised blowjob. I glanced at the mirror for one last look at my reflection when I was hit with a bolt of ice-cold fear. The light had been left on in the bathroom with the door still open. It shone behind Deb as she moved towards me, illuminating everything, including the knife she held behind her back.

She saw my expression change and lunged, bringing the

knife towards me in a swishing fashion across my neck. Panic-stricken, I moved fast, avoiding the knife on its first swipe and making a grab for her hand before it came back round and finished its job. The pain was immense as the blade cut through my three middle fingers to the bone. By mistake I had grabbed the blade. The shock of it all brought me to my senses and I jumped up off the bed and started to scream at the woman. I dodged around the bed, avoiding her almost silent attack. All I could hear was my own shouts and I could see her psychotic eyes behind the glint of the blade.

I fucking shit myself in that room. She reminded me of Evelyn Draper, Jessica Walters' psycho chick in the Clint Eastwood movie *Play Misty For Me*. On and on she came at me as I threw anything that came to hand in an attempt to stave her off and get to the door. Blood now covered everything. I was desperately attempting to avoid the knife whilst trying to get a good grip on her or get out of the room.

She started to tire and I could see it. The whole thing had gone on for less than a minute, but a lot of adrenalin had been exerted by both of us. I knew this was my chance and I made a dash for the balcony and threw myself off it blind, leaving my best pair of deck shoes behind. *Fuck it, you can have them, love. I'm out of here.* I landed badly on the grass below hurting my knee, both ankles and bit through my bottom lip, but it did not stop me from getting up and running off. I was out of there before anybody had been alerted and the Old Bill turned up.

"Jasp, Jasp. Quick mate over here."

I couldn't believe my luck. Sat in a tree nearby was Digger. He had followed us on the off chance of some tag-team action, and had climbed the tree for a better look. He had seen the whole thing through the balcony window and was in as much of a hurry to get away from there as I was. He jumped down and helped me to my feet and we both ran off back to the Don Bigote.

Now I'm not going to start throwing accusations about what happened that night, I'm going to tread a little tentatively. To this day I haven't got a clue what happened there. Either I was the victim of retribution or I just happened to meet a real fruitcake. I suppose I'll never know. I was glad to get back to Stoke the next day, though. I think we all were. What a mess we looked getting off that plane with all the scars, wounds, broken bones and bandages. Anybody would have thought we had all been involved in an horrific crash, not returning from a fortnight's well-deserved break.

Chapter Two

Dark Continent

WHEN I AGREED to go to Morocco with Akabar, I envisaged Dylan and the Stones, souks and snake charmers, psychedelic colours and beautiful dancing girls. I also pictured hashish and freedom. Lots of it. A carefree way of life. In the end it would haunt me like a legacy from the Devil himself.

In the autumn of 1984, I was running away from nothing in particular. My life had taken another turn and a gut-grown impulse sent me heading overseas with little money or direction. Several months earlier, I had received an SNLR (Services No Longer Required) from the British Army. I'd eventually got what I wanted, and in May 1984 I kissed goodbye to my country's shilling and took up a permanent role among the ranks of the Stoke hooligans, an army that gave me things in life that Her Majesty's had not: acceptance, loyalty and a sense of belonging.

That summer had been a wild one. I grew my hair in Kevin Keegan fashion with the rest of the country, fought running battles on Blackpool's promenade with the Leeds Service Crew, and our firm had its first ever holiday in Magaluf. Life was happening at an insatiable pace, and everything I tried I did to excess. Our reputation around the Potteries made regular reading in the tabloids, and my local reputation as the swashbuckling character "Jasper" was becoming synonymous with lawlessness. I provided the backdrop for a legend the people of Stoke-on-Trent wanted and created for themselves. As history depicts, every generation spawns one, and that's whether he wants it or not.

After the "Battle of the Mill", a huge fight at the Mill Country Club on the outskirts of my home town of Alsager, and the subsequent tragic suicide of its owner (see *Naughty*), the euphoria of my new-found freedom in Civvy Street ended abruptly. I decided to avoid any possible police repercussions and so, not for the first time in my life, I found myself alone; only this time I would end up in a foreign country with little money and no knowledge of the language. I bypassed Spain's Costa del Sol, and found myself back on my rock of hope, Gibraltar. It was familiar territory for me, having served on it several years earlier with the Staffordshire Regiment. Gibraltar was far enough away from the uncertainties of Stoke, but a place I was comfortable with. I was certain that for now this was the best place for me to be.

I spared no time in finding an old drinking haunt of mine. I entered as I had 1,000 times before, stooping as I passed under a low, solid oak beam. Nothing had changed. It smelt the same and was as cool and refreshing from the street outside as always. I found a stool. The bar was shaped like the stern of a ship, clustered with brass bells, yarns of rope and seafaring memorabilia. It reminded me of Nelson's mess on his flagship *Victory*. I was back in the Gibraltar Arms again.

Funds were short. I'd arrived with less than sixty quid in my pocket and a return ticket to sell. Even so, I was parched, so I eyed up the Cruzcampo pump and winked at the barmaid, who looked Spanish.

"Here yer go luvvie. That'll be forty pence, ta."

The accent was as harsh as a Tequila Slammer. Her name was Joanne, her mates called her Jo and she was from Leeds. Everyone knew Jo and she knew everyone and everything. She was a quality acquisition on the first day. Things were looking up. Within an hour, she'd stopped charging me for the ale, told me she was good mates with the Leeds Service Crew and loved hoolies. She even found me a place to live. *Another pint of Cruzcampo please, love. I'll look for a job tomorrow.*

My first night's accommodation was in the middle of Gib's "old town". Jo's flat was on the fifth floor, had two bedrooms and nine people lived in it. I was in luck, as someone had vacated their space that day. For £10 a week I was offered the balcony that led off from the main living room. It was always full of washing and people congregated on it to smoke spliffs and chat. I gave her £20 and bedded down for my first night in the open, on the leather back seat from a car.

For once it all fell into place very nicely for me. I even got £80 for my return ticket. Within two weeks I'd cemented my presence amongst the English workers on the Rock, found a job with the Ministry of Defence on the docks and moved over the border to La Linea del a Frontera, a tough Spanish town with a merciless reputation.

It had not been difficult to find unskilled work. If you were willing to graft for twenty quid a day and work alongside the North Africans, you could survive. Living in Spain on the cheap and working seven days a week, it was not long before I was starting to find my feet. I found my job the first day I went looking. Simons Construction was based on Devil's Tower Road at the foot of the Rock. They offered me a position as a scaffolder's labourer. It was an immediate start, and by lunchtime I had met the company chargehand, Big Joe. Joe Edwards looked weathered and mean. The man, like his frame, had a huge presence that carried weight. He had been residing on the Rock for many years, and few questioned him. His eyes were bright blue and quick, and he spoke with a Stoke accent. I made sure Joe heard mine at the first opportunity and we moved on from there. I got the feeling I wasn't the only one running from something.

Big Joe was chuffed there was another Stokie on the Rock. It turned out he was from the pre-fabricated Blurton estate and had been a hooligan himself in the early Seventies. He even showed me an old black and white photograph of the legendary Coddy Hughes taken in his teens; they were old pals. I knew I was keeping good company and began to feel settled. I was even managing to save some money.

Joe Edwards was good to me in many ways, as I suppose I was to him. We shared a lot of bonds and became good friends. Even so, he was still my chargehand and I never forgot that. It was only a matter of weeks before Joe gave me a break and put me with a scaffold team that worked on the docks. It was round-the-clock stuff: as one ship entered dry dock we would scaffold for the welders to make repairs to the hull, always as quickly as possible, before the ship met its deadline to sail and the next big tanker arrived.

It was during this period that I met the Moroccan everyone called Akabar. As a small boy I used to watch a television show called *The Banana Splits*, in the days when children's entertainment was purely innocent animation. On that show was a cartoon called *The Arabian Nights,* and Akabar reminded me of a princely character from it. Pushing six feet tall, he had deep-set black eyes that mesmerized all, a perfectly trimmed black beard and moustache over a chiselled jawline, and his skin was dark and unblemished. I stared hard at the man, half expecting him to raise the palms of his hands to me and below out the command "Size of an elephant!" as in the cartoon. He did not, and no magic carpet was summoned either. He was a mere scaffolder after all, and he spoke with a soft, gentle whisper in broken English. Big Joe wasn't one for formalities. Akabar was told my name was "Jasper" and I was his new labourer, then Joe's rusty silver Nissan was gone.

The big Moroccan offered me his hand and work duly commenced. Akabar climbed up on to the first stage of scaffold and pointed down towards a pile of tubes. He gestured and I passed them up to him. I was taken aback at how agile he was and even more surprised that his work shoes were a pair of size ten Adidas football boots with moulded studs. He wore a bright green, all-in-one boilersuit, and like most of the Moroccans, a little blue knitted hat at the back of his head.

Several weeks passed and little was said until one day there was an accident. A German traveller, probably about my age, twenty-one, was badly crushed when a huge piece of replacement steel hull fell from its hoist only yards from where we were working. Akabar and I stopped to look on with the rest of the dockers. We sat silently and shared a moment of sympathy for the crushed man. I think from that moment on the two continents and cultures that divided us were forgotten. Humanity sometimes needs to be forced upon us before we behave like humans. Working with Akabar changed after that day. We became friendly towards each other and he taught me bits of Spanish. I was surprised by how many languages he could speak. He would even tell me about his life and how much he missed his family back home in Tetuoan.

Most afternoons were spent suspended high above the docks. The views of the Bay of Gibraltar, the Straits and the far-off, snow-capped Atlas Mountains were breathtaking. Africa made a great backdrop for my new friend's stories. I would casually roll a big joint and smoke it whilst listening intently to him.

Life didn't get much better than this. I was happy, relaxed and felt alive.

———————

I sat in the passenger seat listening to Joe passing wind. We were due to start a new job that day and Akabar was late. It was most unlike the Moroccan and Joe showed an unusual tolerance to the delay.

"He's here now, mate," I said.

Joe wiped the tomato ketchup from around his mouth with a napkin and we both got out of the car. The Moroccan looked flushed and fervent. He was holding a letter from home. The pair spoke briefly together in confidence, then Joe bid us both adios.

A week later, Akabar chose to share his good news with me. His clan were having a celebration for the homecoming of a nephew. He was serving in the Moroccan coastguard and from what I could gather was the pride of his family. Akabar invited me to go with him to Morocco and I excitedly accepted the invitation. I suppose my persistent questioning over the next few days must have driven him insane. All of a sudden I've got a new mystical adventure ahead of me. I wanted to know everything.

"My country is the northernmost tip of Africa and the bottom lip of the Mediterranean Sea," he said. It was a geography lesson, my second favourite subject at school. Not surprisingly, Akabar, who was probably in his late thirties, was a very knowledgeable man. I was surprised to learn that his country had only a slightly bigger land mass than the state of California, a place that one day I knew I would visit. Joe wasn't surprised one bit when I told him I was going to Morocco. He told me to keep my eye on the little bastards and not to turn my back on one. They weren't all as sound as our friend. I already knew that, but I still took the advice on board.

The day we left, I drew several hundred pounds out of my post office account on Main Street. We walked over the border to Spain and caught a packed bus to the port of Algeciras. It took an hour and the sun baked us. I spent the time examining my surroundings and listening to the Flying Burrito Brothers on my headphones. Akabar sat, quiet as always, away with his secret thoughts.

The port was bustling. Spain lost its influence here and Africa filled my senses. I was becoming spellbound. Akabar's mood also changed. We stood on the top deck, where it was cold and windy. He told me to listen carefully about his people and their ways.

"I am a Berber." His voice was firm and direct, yet confiding. "I only speak with truth to you. Some people will see you as weak and an easy way of getting money. Think before you speak, my friend."

He finished speaking, though our eye contact remained steady for several seconds. He shook my shoulder. He was sure I understood his meaning. I continued my gaze out to sea.

Tangier was unnerving. The port looked like a refugee movie, with thousands of people clambering all over each other. Everybody had something to sell, everybody wanted to speak to me personally and all of a sudden I was claustro-phobic and increasingly volatile. Akabar pulled me from the dusty road and we found some space in a café. He ordered tea. We hatched our plan. We would sit a while and watch the street outside. He wanted me to see that it was just a fast pace and nothing was out of the ordinary. I couldn't believe how many donkeys had passed by, and more to the point, how many people were sitting on them. It was like looking back into medieval times.

He needed to catch a bus. It was a two-hour journey by
road to Akabar s home town, Tetuoan and he so much wanted
to see his wife and family. I wanted to score some hash and
cradle a whore. The party was planned for three days' time, a
Saturday, and I was going to do my own thing in Tangier and
catch up with him in a couple of days. We bid each other
farewell.

The room above the café was basic. My friend had secured
me two nights' lodgings before leaving. I showered off the
sweat and grime from my journey, then put on my cargo pants
and ventured out into a hectic teatime rush hour. The evening
chill was refreshing.

I knew where my destination was for that night. I'd read
about it and seen it in some of the old black and white, Sixties
movies. Tangier was renowned for having some of the best
hustlers in the world. It was a Neutral International Zone and
attracted characters from every walk of life. The Petit Socco
area was one of the sleaziest squares on the planet. I reckoned
I'd fit right in there, but I had to walk to get to it first.

Every step I took, Ahmed was a step behind me. He stank of
perspiration, his breath was rancid and I took a dislike to the
tyke the minute I stepped on to the street. He was like a leech
and I couldn't burn him off.

I had mixed feelings. I was part thrilled by my surroundings
but carried a slight mistrust and fear of the locals. Maybe I'd
better suss this Ahmed out after all. For ten dirham, he said he
would show me the way to Petit Socco. For another ten he
would show me the hotel where author William S. Burroughs
wrote his novels. I was halfway to getting what I wanted and
agreed to follow the man. He walked me around a labyrinth of
pedestrian alleyways. The smell of human urine at times became
overwhelming. Still I pressed on, stepping over strips of
cardboard and cloth, obviously some poor sod's bed for the

night. By now I was so disorientated I needed Ahmed whether I liked it or not. He kept his word, and I appeared slightly dishevelled at the edge of the small square.

That ten-minute walk had been nearly as bad as a solitary venture along Cold Blow Lane before a night fixture at Millwall. I sat in one of a multitude of small cafes and ordered a Stork beer. Ahmed gave strict orders for me to remain where I was while he fetched his friend who would sell me some kif (cannabis). *Hurry up then you little bastard.* I didn't like the man one bit.

I took his absence as an opportunity to discreetly split my cash into two. I still had all 300 on me. My musty room was so bare there was nowhere to hide it. On my return from the convenience, I was joined at my table by two characters, both European men in their fifties. They looked thoroughly acclimatised in their sweat-stained khakis and almost blended in with the rest of the film set.

"I have told Ahmed to wait out there," said one, nodding over his shoulder. "I have paid him fifteen dirham. You can pay me later. My name is Jean."

"Jasper."

I shook his hand and followed his nod out towards the Moroccan. The other man, Claude, offered me his hand too, and each of us sat back in our chairs. I assumed they were Belgian. My mind raced through our military history, trying to determine whether my companions were allies or not. *Fuck it*, I thought, *European is good enough for me around here.*

I'd decided against having a woman well over an hour ago. A couple of beers and a spliff back at my room would be enough for one night. I asked Jean how much half an ounce would cost me. They both chuckled. I think the little skunk sat perched at the café window had given these guys the wrong impression. A drawn out conversation commenced and I started to look for my exit. The two Belgians started to explain to me about how things were run around these parts and how certain traditions must be kept. I knew I would at least be parting with a percentage of my money that night. I was just a bit worried that these two were going to try and palm a couple of kilos off on me.

Three beers and three definite declines of offers later, I was beginning to lose my patience. Something was bothering me about these two. They were acting like they were heavy drug traffickers trying to sell me kilos of hash, yet they were drinking heavily and becoming loud and ostentatious. It didn't add up.

From behind a heavy brow I scrutinized them. I was a twenty-one-year-old, and didn't know then what I know now, but it suddenly dawned on me that I was in more danger than I was likely to be in over a row about a bit of hash. I concentrated on the faces of the two Belgians. Something was missing. I saw them in more detail now, their piercing blue eyes, their blond moustaches and milky white skin. My gut was yelling at me, *These are not normal men.*

With my confusion came fear. They laughed amongst themselves, slapping each other on the back. They leered at me through their laughter. *Jesus Christ, I'm on the fucking menu here.* The penny had dropped. I was definitely in way over my head and had to act fast.

I weighed up my options. My natural instinct was to slam my bottle right across the middle of Claude's forehead and make a dash for it, but that was an absurd idea and I had to repress the feeling immediately. What else? I couldn't think straight. My head began to reel. The beer, the climate, the situation. I began to sweat profusely.

He never let me down, he swore he never would and I never

really understood why Steve Bloore took his own life. He was always stronger than me and I looked up to him. As in life, in spirit my old Army pal, Steve has never left my side, though he killed himself not long before I left the Forces. To this day he guides and protects me. "He" took a seat at the table next to me. We shared a warm smile of acknowledgement invisible to the Belgians. Steve liked that.

I stopped trembling and the sweat stopped stinging my eyes. I became calm and controlled, my breathing steadied. I offered them both another shot of whisky. They drank it and I offered them some more. I was less worried about the Belgians now and more about Ahmed, who was still hovering around outside. As long as I stayed put at the table, encouraging this pair to get even drunker, the more time I had to plan an escape. I sat uncomfortably and thought deeply.

What if I told them I was going to get my friends who were after more hash than me? No, that would never work and, worse, it would give the game away that I was on to them. Could I remember my way back through the labyrinth if I made a run for it? No way, I would be seized by the Moroccans.

I decided another trip to the khazi was needed and left the table without being excused. I didn't look back as the sound of laughter was replaced with a dark mumble. The window was far too small to climb through; besides, behind it was pitch black. I cursed to myself. The toilet door opened and closed behind me and Jean appeared standing to my left. He began to pee. I watched him through the corner of my eye. He was vulnerable. *What if I slammed a heavy kick into his knee straight across the joint? That would reduce my problem by a third, but for how long? And what if he started to squeal like a bastard?* Anything I had ever done in my life that might help me resolve this problem was lost in time. I found myself opening up a conversation without choosing my words first.

"Where are we going after here?" I asked while pretending to do up my fly. Jean leaned his face into mine and licked his top lip. His moustache was wet and tar-stained on the edges.

"Somewhere a little less busy. We need to finalise our arrangement."

What fucking arrangement is that? I thought as I blurted out my next sentence. "I'd rather just go with you." I stared the man right in the eyes. His tongue appeared again briefly before he shook his head.

"We all go together," he hissed back at me.

I could feel my heart jump a beat. I really did not like my situation one bit. I sat back down at the table. More beer had been ordered. I peeled the label and nervously drank from the bottle. I noticed that Ahmed was now inside the café, perched at the bar. I got up and approached him.

"Ahmed, if I give you two hundred dirham can you get me a beautiful woman?" I spoke through frozen lips. I was banking on the lure of the money. So far Ahmed had only earned fifteen dirham and we were at least two hours into the ordeal. I was hoping he was as unscrupulous as he looked. Too fucking right he was.

I ordered another couple of shots of whisky and had it delivered to the table. Ahmed spoke in Arabic to the man serving behind the bar, who nodded his head and looked hard at me. I began to believe that I was finally finding a solution. My chances of getting away from Ahmed were greater than taking my chances with the two Belgians. Buying my way out was my only option. The man behind the bar poured my next drink into a glass and placed it in front of me on a beer mat.

His finger remained on the mat and as I looked down to

pick up my glass I saw the arrow immediately. I looked behind the bar to my right and eyed up the door. Ahmed was gone. He reappeared seconds later back outside the window. He stared at me without emotion. I waited and turned my attention to the Belgians.

Neither one of them was actually frightening by their appearance. Physically we were no mismatch and I would have fancied my chances with either or even both at the same time if I had to. It was just an accumulation of everything that was overpowering me. I was now placing my trust back in the hands of a man that a couple of hours ago I wanted to set fire to. I handed a twenty dirham note to the barman to cement our deal. Steve had been and gone. But I'd found my strength. I was alone again and it was up to me now.

Time was irrelevant. It seemed like an hour but it could have been a couple of minutes. Claude rose from his seat, which was blocking the door to the café and strode past me towards the lavatory. He made no attempt to speak. As the door closed behind Claude, Jean shuffled across into Claude's seat. His movement touched a nerve. The barman replaced the ashtray and dusted the table.

For a split second I lost sight of Jean and I made my move. Vaulting the bar, I landed hard and awkward. The bottles I kicked over made an unearthly clatter as I struggled to find my feet. The door I had been eyeing up was in touching distance. I wrenched it open and threw myself through it. At once I could taste fear.

I hurtled along the dim narrow corridor and jumped down the stairs at the end in one leap. The open street ahead of me was insanely welcome. Just an eternity away. Three huge strides and I was out.

Ahmed grabbed my arm and pulled me saying, "Money, money."

"Yes, money, I give you money. Where now, where now?"

I just wanted to get away from the place fast. The sound of music and laughter, the smell of animals and leather, everything was spinning. There was no real panic. The Belgians were so inebriated they probably hadn't noticed my flight. Yet Ahmed ushered me on at pace, away from any potential disruption of his earner.

The maze of back streets took a turn. It had been light when I made my journey into Petit Socco. The lack of street lighting at just after ten o'clock gave the area a sinister aura which was apt really because now I was away from the two paedophiles (or queers as I would have called them at the time) I was beginning to feel a bit sinister myself.

"Ahmed, you take me back to my room, yes? Then you go and get me a woman, yes? Then I give you the money."

He wasn't going to have that suggestion. I didn't think for one minute that he would. I was buying time, now I was the hustler. I'd made up my mind as soon as we got to a spot that felt right for me, I was going to smash the filthy little bastard all over the place. He repulsed me.

The opportunity arose sooner rather than later. I had found my bearings from the previous journey. My digs weren't far away. We crossed a cobbled courtyard. It was deserted. I struck without warning. Ahmed was still hanging on to the sleeve of my shirt when I smashed him in the nose with an upward swing of my elbow and dragged him down backwards on to the ground and stamped hard several times into his face, stifling any noises he made. He gurgled blood from his throat as I kicked him twice in the side of his head. I wanted to carry on and kill him. Nobody would have known or cared. Instead I fled. That was enough. I'd quenched my raw animal instinct.

I quickly collected my bag from my room and slung it over

my shoulder. I wasn't staying there tonight. I wasn't even stopping in that town. I remembered the short walk back to the docks and hailed a taxi.

"Tetuoan," I said to the driver. I didn't even ask how much. I didn't care.

The journey, in silence, seemed to take a lot longer than it probably was. I took time to reflect. My attack on Ahmed had been vicious. I wouldn't normally kick a man that many times in the head. Nevertheless, he had sold my soul without me putting it on the market. And probably for a lot less than the 200 I'd offered him to do the dirty on the Belgians. For all he cared I was going to be the sex victim of two unscrupulous nonces, then maybe even killed and my body dumped off a cliff into the sea. Fuck him. He deserved it.

The Petit Socco certainly lived up to its name. Or maybe I was just unfortunate enough to run into bad company, as usual. All the same, I learnt a lesson there that night. I had come frighteningly close to a nightmare. Tetuoan couldn't possibly be as bad as that den of iniquity, could it?

I journeyed on. I could see the spread of city lights embedded into the side of a mountain. I had arranged to meet Akabar in two days' time at the bus station. I thought it a better idea to break into my cash, find some secure accommodation and rest up for a day.

He had grown up a mountain man, the eldest son of a Berber shepherd. Akabar spoke often of the Atlas Mountains. He told me that they were their natural barrier from their tempestuous neighbours, the Algerians. He seldom spoke of his wife, Fatima, although he carried her picture with him always. I liked Akabar. I also liked the pension I was now booking into close to the main market square. Three-thirty in the morning and the city was relatively quiet. By chance, the taxi driver, who had not spoken one single word along the journey, had pulled over directly outside the small, clean-looking house with a sign written in English letters: "Pension Bernadette".

I read the piece of cardboard handed to me by the driver and gave him the 100 dirham he requested. An elderly French lady smiled as she showed me the way to a ground floor single bedroom. We both smiled and nodded as I closed the door after her. I sat down at the side of the bed, staring at my holdall and clasping my head with sweaty palms. I was starving, had no fresh water with me and was too tired and disorientated to venture out to search for any. Instead, I collapsed, fully clothed, and buried my head deep into the solitary pillow. I was wiped out.

I slept undisturbed for more than twelve hours. The sun hammered through the shuttered window. I woke up drenched in sweat, with a blistering headache. Completely drained of energy, I pulled myself on to the floor and stood up to make my way to the sink in the corner of my room. I staggered twice, then shocked myself when I released a stream of diarrhoea down the inside of each of my legs. It turned cold within seconds and became excruciating. I sank into despair when I looked at the bed and saw it was covered in wet excrement. I'd been lying in my own liquidised body waste for hours.

I summoned the strength to pull the sheets from the bed and throw them in the corner of the room. They were sodden, as was I. I peeled my clothes from my shit-stinking body and replaced them with clean ones from my bag. With no hot water or shower at hand, they were pulled over the mess I'd made. I didn't care, I just needed to get warm. I was starting to shiver uncontrollably and my teeth began to hammer against themselves. The small, claustrophobic room began to spin. I lost consciousness. I must have just dropped to the floor where I stood.

When I came round, the sun had moved on and the room

was full of late afternoon shadows. Lord knows how long I had lain on the floor. I pulled myself up on to the bed and lay in the foetal position, rocking myself gently, and began to slowly peel my sponge-like tongue from the roof of my mouth. I was parched. My head was painful and leaden. I felt completely lost and close to panic. I could not move to help myself.

I remained delirious for most of the day and evening, desperately dehydrated and suffering from a mild form of AMS (acute mountain sickness). At times I thought that maybe this was going to be my final resting place: a cheap pension in a far-off mountain city in north Africa. It wasn't really what I had planned; I was far too young to die and besides, I still had not seen Stoke City lift a trophy at Wembley. For most of the day I could hear the soft sound of a French radio station playing in reception but my crippling stomach cramps prevented me from hailing any of the people who came and went. The only thing between me and salvation was a closed door. It was soul destroying.

I heard the turning of the handle. I barely opened my eyes. The vile stench of my excrement had reached beyond the room to save my life. It was well into the early hours and I remember little, other than the sound of two soft female voices, one French, the other Arab.

Later, I decided that being able to sit up in bed without being bent over double in pain was the best feeling in the world. They fed me broth and fruit, mopped my brow with cool aloe vera and tended to me for hours. I was extremely grateful and mightily humbled by the experience.

I left to meet Akabar light-headed and weak, but feeling 1,000 times better than I had a couple of days previously. He moved graciously towards me through the bustling market. I stood firm, leaning against the post he had told me to find and not move away from. His huge smile lifted my spirits. Akabar told me I looked frail and that we should go to his home immediately. He was concerned, which kind of worried me.

I remember little if anything of his family get-together, although each member of his family was introduced. I rested up for a couple of days in a makeshift shelter Akabar had erected for me on the roof of his house. It consisted of a large one-piece flysheet thrown over a line and secured, and was the size of a garden shed. Laid out on the floor were reed mats and several huge, comfortable pillows. If I had not felt so shitty I would have likened it to a harem, but for the moment it was just a welcome bed.

Akabar and Fatima had four sons, the eldest being Yousef. It was he who took over the role of head of family while his father was working in Gibraltar. He was fourteen. Akabar's visit home was short. He needed to get back and earn money. He encouraged me to stay, however, and get better, during which time Yousef would show me their culture. I agreed to stay. I was beginning to get my strength back and I wanted to get on with my journey of life.

I began to enjoy the Moroccan lifestyle. Several weeks passed and I familiarised myself with my surroundings. Tetuoan was a flat city with few buildings above five storeys. The skyline was mostly dominated by mosques and at night I would lie inside my tent, smoking kif, looking up at the stars and listening at what the city threw at me. It could be quite haunting.

During the days I would sit on my haunches smoking kif through a hookah pipe and drinking mint tea with Akabar's extended family. It was whilst doing this that I met Simmi, Akabar's youngest brother. At first I wasn't sure whether I liked Simmi. He was far more westernised than anyone else I had met, quite trendy with his fashion: he had slicked-back hair, wore Lois jeans with leather loafers, tee-shirts and a black leather bomber jacket. I did like the jacket. Again, I wasn't sure whether the man liked me either. I decided to treat him with much more caution than the rest. You need to be wary of anyone with that many scars on his face.

A month went by. I had given Yousef the equivalent of £100 to give to his mother towards my board. Every time I asked if they wanted some more money they refused and smiled saying, "Enough, enough." It was an easy existence and I was loving it. And more to the point, nobody in the world knew where the hell I was.

I got to know Simmi better quite out of the blue. I had noticed him trying to read my tattooed arms on a number of occasions. Eventually I lifted my arm for him to see. His English was better than I had first given him credit for, unless he had just chosen his moment when to use it. He asked me about the British Bulldog and the inscription above it.

"Stoke, Stoke City," I read slowly as I ran my finger along it. "English football team, very good in England. Me English football hooligan, yeah? You know hooligans?"

Simmi laughed in acknowledgement, nodding his head with a huge smile. We both laughed, him more than me. We had touched base. Simmi told me he was a football supporter but not a hooligan. His local team was Moghreb de Tetuoan. He said that they were playing their rivals Itihad Tangier soon and we should go and watch. I was chuffed at the suggestion and toked hard on the hookah pipe.

That night Simmi showed me how he earned his living. Tetuoan was a vibrant place in its own right, though less geared up for tourism than Tangier. Nevertheless, when the odd unsuspecting Westerner showed up in search of their own elusive grail, they fell victim to Simmi's thieving ways.

Over the next week I ventured out at night with him and hung with his crew. I christened them the Hawks. Their favourite victims were very similar to how I had been in Tangier, mostly male travellers looking for some dope or a brothel. They would befriend them and promise to take them away from all the street-hustling and barging about, take them to a backstreet café and tell them to wait on the promise of some of the finest hashish in Morocco. They would always leave someone to watch and protect their quarry from other sharp eyes. After some time, Simmi would return to the café on the back of a moped. He would always look perturbed, like he had gone so far out of his way to accommodate their request. Each time he tried to push the amount of dope wanted even higher.

In my naivety, the first time I saw them do it I actually thought it was a straight bit of business. I sat with a couple of the Hawks in a café opposite, our eyes trained on four teenage Israelis. They looked relaxed and drank tea whilst awaiting their hashish. In time, the moped clattered to a stop on the dusty, rock-strewn road and Simmi coolly stepped off the back and swaggered inside the café, sat down and ordered tea. He kept the Israelis waiting, spinning his spiel and exaggerating his concerns about the street outside. The travellers eventually conceded to his persistence and accepted two nine-bars (cannabis resin is often sold in nine-ounce bars) of hash wrapped in gold and green silk scarves. Simmi shoved the cash inside his jacket pocket, jumped back on the waiting moped and left.

The two Hawks I was with remained seated and composed as they watched. I did the same. The Israelis began to gather their belongings for their exit. Almost immediately, one then the other sharply took to their seats again. They looked ruffled. I stared on. Four police officers entered the open-fronted café, each taking off his hat and placing it on a vacant table. They sat down. The Israeli teenagers looked perturbed, their discomfort blatantly apparent. They reached for empty teacups and pretended to drink. None spoke a word. I still hadn't fully switched on with what was unfolding in front of me, but shared the teenagers' dismay. When one of the soiled-looking police officers left his table and approached them, the Hawks next to me fidgeted excitedly in their seats.

"Passports, s'il vous plait."

The officer gesticulated for each to show their ID. Each of the four handed their blue passports to the man, who then sat back down with his colleagues and began to examine them thoroughly. The four friends sat nervously awaiting their fate. Four sets of chair legs scuffed the worn wooden floor as the police all stood up together. Their approach was slow and their search of the Israelis' bags methodical. The silk scarves were placed on the table in front of the ashen-faced friends. Each had frozen and three were now crying.

They were collectively stood up and marched away from the café, led along the packed avenue and disappeared amongst a throng of jostling bystanders. One policeman remained seated at his table, one foot on the floor the other stretched across a chair. He looked smug. The sound of a moped brought movement from the Hawks. I stood too. Again Simmi stepped off his pillion and entered the café. He sat down at the table and spoke with the bent copper. In the blink of an eye their dealings were done. Simmi left the scene. We followed on foot.

Back at their barber shop HQ, the door shutters were pulled to. The rewards were then split amongst the six-strong gang. In effect they had come out of the scam with the two bars of hash they had started with, plus half of the money taken from the Israelis. I sat and said nothing. All of a sudden I didn't like the gang I was in anymore. Still, I found it amazing to watch as they celebrated their triumph with a Berber throat cry. I got a gut feeling that Simmi in some kind of a way was taunting me. I skinned up a joint and smoked it.

I watched the Hawks for over a fortnight and even picked up a bit of their language. They were all excellent pickpockets and drew no line whatsoever on who their next target would be. When I attended the much-awaited Tetuoan v Tangier game, they pilfered at least a dozen wallets. The game itself was the first real reminder of home since I left Europe. Any preconceptions I had before the game were dispelled on entering the ramshackle stadium. It was open at all ends, with grass growing through cracks on most of the parched terrace steps, a far cry from Stoke City and its Boothen End packed to the rafters with 15,000 expectant fans. *Then again*, I thought, *where else in the world would you find that kind of passion other than in Stoke?*

I rested my case and continued to examine the sparse crowd. There were maybe 3,000 people in there, with probably 200 from Tangier. All were male so there was still a little chance of a little bit of crowd disorder. The first fifteen minutes of the game were dominated by the away side but the Hawks paid little attention to either the game or me. One of them had spotted an unsuspecting and lucrative-looking target.

The English couple away to our left stuck out like sore thumbs. The fella even had a big camera hanging around his neck. They looked in their late twenties, the arty type. She looked decidedly nervous as she watched her partner become embroiled in a one-way conversation from the gutter. I could tell from their attire and the way they held themselves that the pair were clean-living people and had no understanding of the streets and its perils. I'm from the street and I had been suckered twice already. They might be worried for their purses and passports but would have no idea at all that they would soon be on their way to a Moroccan jail. It was too much for my conscience. I got it in my head right away that no way would I let my own countrymen fall prey to the Hawks.

Rather than alarm them straight away, I spoke to Simmi and played on the fact that one of them was a woman. Simmi's English was suddenly minimal again. I did not even bother to say they were from my homeland. As if they cared. This was going to be a good earner for the Hawks. They had just robbed their own people blind during the match. They certainly didn't care about two Westerners, and that camera would fetch a fortune. At the final whistle I made my move.

"Hello, how did you find the game?" I imposed my handshake on the Brit.

"Oh, fascinating. A bit different to back home." At once I detected a West Country accent. The woman looked pleased I had appeared.

"Where are you from back home?" I carried on my chat as I walked alongside Simmi's sidekick, Mustapha. It was his scam. He tried to move me to one side and pick up his spiel on the couple.

"Look if you're wanting some hash I've got about five grams in my pocket. You're welcome to it. Or I will just bite you a chunk off if you like." I desperately wanted them to say yes because failing that I was just going to have to tell them out loud that they were being set up for a scam. I was hoping I wouldn't have to do that, as it could cause us all to be the victims of a brutal street mugging there and then. After that, I would have to face the consequences of Simmi and his cronies.

Disappointingly, he refused my offer and went on to tell me that Sandra, his fiancée and old school friend, wanted to take some slippers home for her mother. *Fuck me, this is getting worse*, I thought to myself as we breached the stadium wall and approached the bustling streets outside.

Mustapha began to hail taxis to speed away his victims to

his "uncle's slipper shop". He was well on to me as were the rest of the Hawks. They commandeered bicycles and pedalled out of sight.

"Hey, thanks for the offer. Nice chatting to you." The gawky looking Englishman bumped his head on the roof of the car as he sat down on the back seat next to Mustapha, who had strategically placed himself in the middle. They shared a laugh. I saw him leave with a smug smile on his face, content that he had now finally snared his victims. I saw him as a sly, stinking bastard, and I wanted to kick his fucking head in. I was coming to the end of my time in Morocco, I could feel it.

The taxi pulled away in a swirl of dust, leaving me standing in a busy North African street. Sandra stared back out of the window whilst Mustapha placed his arm around her fiancé's shoulder. I caught her lost stare and gave her the thumbs down signal. Whether she ever responded to it, I will never know.

The night sky over Tetuoan was as bright as I had seen during my two-month stay in North Africa. I lay back on my pillows and searched for guidance under a multitude of spangled stars. I was stoned again. It had been more than a week without any sign of Simmi after the football run-in. I could only assume that they had pulled off a successful scam on the English couple, or else they might have paid me a visit. I'd drunk about as much mint tea as I could take by now, had scores of cooking lessons from Fatima and played in goals for Yousef and his Back Alley Select 100 times. In the morning I was going to pay my thanks and wish them all farewell. Final decision.

I decided to smoke myself into oblivion that last night on the roof. I had more than half an ounce of kif and thought better of attempting to take it back into Europe. I decided to make use of my new clay chalice and smoke it as neat as I could get it. It was not long before I was in a sense of deep anxiety at the sounds inside my head.

For two months I had slept out in the open above the majestic city. It had thrown many strange sounds up at me whilst emptying its bowels in the dead of the night. None so strange though as the ones that had me straining my senses the way I did that night. Demonic forces were at work and I was about to be thrown into the pit of hell amongst them.

A rampant tomcat, I first thought. Then, no, it began to sound like a child sobbing. I crushed out my spliff and crawled out of my shelter. I stood up slowly hardly daring to make any sound. The night had an unearthly feeling to it. I felt frightened and uneasy. I walked around the rooftop slowly, stopping every few yards to strain my hearing. There it was again, a child's cry. It was hauntingly familiar.

The layout of Akabar's house was unlike anything we had at home. Covering three floors, most of the living space was below street level, with the cooking and washing area taking most of the first floor. In the two rooms above lived his other family members, and above them, his four children. The rooms were sparse, the corridors narrow and tiled. The doorways were arches with heavy curtains for doors. There was no electricity. All the lighting was either natural or candle. At night the house was spooky. I much preferred being in the open, up on the roof.

I leaned on the door handle and took my time to lift it off its latch. I was going to go inside and see if one of the boys was having a nightmare or a fever. I trod carefully down a set of moonlit stairs and walked at a snail's pace along the confined corridor to where the children slept. If one of the boys was having a bad dream or a fever, why was I treading so lightly? My senses were telling me that something didn't add up. I froze. There it was again. I held my breath and cursed my heart for beating so loudly. I was sure I heard something else this time. I remained still, inches from the doorway, wanting to pull the curtain to one side and walk in. But not having the courage.

The sound of shuffling. A boy's whimper. A man's grunt of sexual satisfaction. I gulped hard and remained frozen to the icy stone wall. I began to tremble uncontrollably. *Oh my God. Funny isn't it? You don't bother going to see Him. But He's the first person you call for when you need serious help.* On reflection, I was utterly confused. I certainly wasn't prepared for what I might see. My guts told me it would be bad. My heart told me not to turn away. I reached slowly for the curtain and held it for some time before I pulled it slowly to one side. It was like going over the top at the Somme. Once I had made my move I was going in.

The room was moonlit, full of hazy shadows and stank of alcohol and sweat. The three youngest boys all sat tightly together in the corner of the room, their backs up against the walls, their knees pulled tightly up into their chests, their heads and faces buried deeply behind their legs. None of them made sound or twitched. Movement tore my stare away from them and into the centre of the room.

Mortified, paralysed, I cringed at the scene taking place ahead of me on the floor of the room. Yousef, Akabar's eldest son, looked small and limp, his face harrowed and tortured. He made no expression as I stared into the face of his uncle behind him. Simmi's face hung clear over the boy's shoulder. He was naked. His body glistened with sweat. His mouth hung open. His evil eyes burnt me up. I screamed without making a sound. I couldn't speak, no word could leave my lips. My limbs felt like lead. I cried but no tears fell. I'm ashamed to say, I stood and watched.

Simmi could see my distress. He knew from then on that I

was going to do nothing. He continued to abuse the boy in front of me. Pumping hard, then slowing his strokes. He gyrated behind Yousef, his face contorted with evil pleasure. The sweat continued to roll down his brow. I could not remove my stare from the man's eyes. I was transfixed, denying myself the torture of seeing Yousef's desperate face once again.

Simmi grunted with pleasure, a sick smile covering his face as he began to speak to me in Arabic. His voice had a demonic undertone to it. He climaxed inside his nephew and immediately stood up and faced me. Yousef lay motionless at his feet. I said nothing, turned and left the room. Back in my tent I packed my chalice with kif. My hands shook as I lit it. My mind was full of sick panic and began to race away from me. *Oh my God! What had I just seen?* It was beyond my comprehension. Several times over the months I had heard noises in the dead of night but had no idea what may have been taking place only a matter of yards away from me. I started to fill up with emotion.

What on earth was the solution? What could be done to help these poor children? Anger started to build up inside of me. All of a sudden I wanted to kill the bastard. What else could I do? So many questions, so few answers. A multitude of scenarios flashed through my mind, all with the same ending; bloodshed and a lifetime of incarceration inside a Moroccan gaol.

I fingered the bone handle of my lock knife. I had carried it with me ever since my first night in Spain, when I witnessed the brutal killing of a Spanish contraband smuggler. Until now I had no cause to use it. At that moment I wanted to cut Simmi's bollocks off with it and put them in his mouth. I purposely cut my finger, placed it in my mouth and drank the blood. On reflection, I suppose, I just felt the need to draw blood in one way or another.

Reality sank in, thankfully. I now hated Simmi more than I hated anything else in the entire world. And that included the person that by rights should have been my world: my own bloodline. I felt an immense sadness for Yousef and his brothers. I can only assume that the other three boys would be subjected to the same abuse soon, if not already.

If I killed Simmi I would never get out of the country. I would be a murderer. I might even face execution. If I left without word, I would be condemning the children to a lifetime of sexual depravity. Either way it was a no-win situation. I was still a condemned man, guilty of doing nothing, sentenced to carry a tombstone weighted with guilt with me for the rest of my life. Believe me, at times it has weighed heavily.

I left Tetouan that very night, on foot. I walked for some time, just walked. At first light I, along with several others, jumped on to the back of a truck heading for the port of Ceuta. I said nothing, just stared. Occasionally, I picked dust particles from the corners of my eyes.

For three nights I slept on a deserted beach before I finally mustered the strength to make the ferry journey back over to Algeciras. Still I said nothing, not one word to a single soul. I walked from Algeciras to La Linea. It took me over eight hours. So what? I wasn't in any rush to get anywhere. I slept heavily that night and the next day crossed the border into Gibraltar and emptied my Post Office account. I was going to hit the road for a while and I had no room for any passengers.

My Moroccan nightmare. They say it helps to put things down in words sometimes and I would have to agree with that to a point. I exorcised several ghosts from my life in the writing of *Naughty*. Some might say I've now put them all to bed forever. Reliving this story, however, I feel has made me feel worse. I'm an older man now. I'm as hardened to life as we all are. We've got to be. Child abuse is a worldwide disease. It's more than probable that it takes place under your very own noses, as it did mine. What are you going to do about it? Run out and attack your neighbour, or turn a blind eye, thankful that it's happening to someone else and not you. Ask yourself the question.

I turned my back and walked away from what I felt would end up a life sentence in a Moroccan gaol, despite the fact that by that action I may have been sentencing those boys to years of sexual abuse at the hands of their own uncle. For that I am deeply sorry. The incident has affected me deeply ever since. And, for the record, I feel no better for writing about it. How could I?

Chapter Three

Two Pints of Benskins

I RETURNED HOME from North Africa a humbled man. Morocco had taken a small part of my soul, a part I needed back. I slipped into a depression, and decided that after living at such an impoverished level over there, I now needed to go as far down into the pit of my own society as I could. Before I could ever look another man in the eye again and say that I knew better than him, I needed to learn about some things few people ever do.

I decided my next adventure in life was to become a homeless down-and-out, surviving in squalor, in places few in their right minds would want to go, with nothing but my wits. I hooked up with some druggies and found a squat in Stoke. Life was different, very different.

Fast Freddie was the name of my favourite hookah pipe. It was a demon hitter and provided me with some of my best ever tokes, and there have been many. I used to smoke the hash through a two-foot length of rubber tubing attached to a glass bowl containing a large measure of Remy Martin brandy. I'd feel warm all over before sliding peacefully into unconsciousness. Milly, an old biker mate from school, had made Freddie for me as a coming home present. In late autumn, daylight was rationed and the nights were painfully long and cruel with boredom. We only had the comfort of a two-bar electric fire to keep the whole of the upstairs of our end terraced squat warm. Nevertheless it was good to be back home in Stoke.

I knew I was going to try the mushrooms, no matter what. I had seen the state of Cliff and Eedy at their squat in Crewe the previous day and I had been in stitches watching the pair of them tripping out together like two old hippies, even though they were only in their early twenties. It looked like a lot of fun, but the idea of actually eating what was gathered on the newspaper in front of me was a bit stomach churning. They were little brown nipples on the end of long white stalks. They looked disgusting and smelt worse.

"We can always boil them and make a brew if you want, works just as good."

Big Wayne raised his left eyebrow at me and chuckled deeply with a goliath undertone. His huge hands fluffed up the mushrooms and with a crane-like motion he raised fifty or so up towards his mouth and dropped them inside. Still chuckling, he began to chew slowly in a circular motion, and then, like a feeding stork, he swallowed them down his long neck and smiled at me. Jesus. I couldn't believe he had just done that.

"Go on then, fifty's enough for your first time. Just swallow them and have a swig of beer afterwards."

I did, and spent the next twenty minutes grilling my giant friend about what to expect next. All the time I was wondering what the hell was going on inside my stomach as I listened to gurgling noises and felt strange bowel movements. After twenty minutes I began to feel warm all over and started to stretch out my arms and legs. Ooh! I began to giggle and so did Wayne. *This is alright*, I thought to myself. All of a sudden I felt clean and fresh and, do you know, I had never noticed before how lovely those net blinds were in the kitchen. *Wonderful. Shall I skin up, mate?*

It can go either way whether you have a good trip or a bad trip. Wayne knew this. Several years older than me and coming from the biker fraternity, he was a veteran on the drug scene. He knew that by keeping me in the relatively safe environment of our squat, my trip should be a relaxed one as long as I didn't allow myself to lose my head. This can happen no matter how much of a vet you are. He told me just as I was about to come up on the hallucinogenic drug that people who lost it badly on their first time were normally in an environment where outside interferences could upset the apple cart, and after that anything could happen. It was known as overloading, he said.

I don't know why, but I found his last remark highly amusing and from there on in I had one of the funniest experiences of my life, belly rolling in uncontrollable laughter for hours and hours at things that would normally pass me by without registering. It was like entering a transparent world in a different parallel. It was something I liked, and there was a good chance that I would end up taking this stuff every day until it stopped growing at the end of October, plus stash as many mushrooms as I could. Tomorrow we were going to get up at dawn and stock up before any of the other druggies who lived around the Butt Lane area could get their hands on the "shrooms".

It was the same routine every day for a week. Up bleary-eyed at the crack of dawn, we would walk straight into the fields around Kidsgrove and Bathpool. Each morning I'd swallow the first twenty or so mushrooms I picked. From there on I marvelled at how green the fields were and how the jackdaw's cry carried on forever in the mid-autumn morning mist. Life began to take on a new, peaceful meaning.

Maybe I should have just become a biker in the first place, I thought, *and gone to gigs and bike rallies instead of rampaging lawlessly across terraces*. It was a fleeting thought of what might have been, enhanced by the drug and the company I was keeping. But I was never going to be a peaceful person; I was too committed. It was only four seasons down the line that I would be with the lads, stamping our authority on the leagues while tripping out on Purple Hommes and microdot acid trips. Jesus, brawling on that stuff was an experience.

We returned to our squat at midday, chuffed with our large haul of shrooms. We had thousands of them drying under the bed, enough to last the whole winter. Milly even suggested we take a load across to Switzerland to sell them to the Swiss dopeheads who paid over the odds for English mushrooms. Yeah, good idea, I was up for that. Wayne paused sharply as he put the key in the lock. To our dismay the door swung open. Without a word we both reached for our tools and made our way silently up the stairs to our first floor flat.

Greeting us at the top of the landing, pinned on the wall in front of us, was a search warrant. Above the fireplace in the lounge was another piece of paper telling us what items had been removed from the premises by the police. It made gut-churning reading: one telescopic cosh, one bowie knife (used), one high-powered air rifle with scope, a kilo of grade A cannabis resin, one hookah pipe (Fast Freddie) and an untold amount of hallucinogenic mushrooms. Also on the list was one passport in the name of Mark David Chester. The warrants were made out in my name, and said just one thing to me: immediate prison.

Cliff came ambling up the stairs, stoned. He had only just moved into the flat downstairs that week and was present when the police had arrived, literally minutes after we had left that morning. Apparently they had busted our place looking for the previous tenant, a burglar who specialised in Doulton figurines. The thieving bastard, he had just brought it right on top for us lot, especially me. Now I was a wanted man and the trip was turning sour.

With little time to think what to do next, our drug-induced decision was to fuck off to London and hide out down there for a while. Milly had some contacts who would help us out if they could. So we grabbed a few holdalls, packed them with the mushrooms we had just picked and whatever else was salvageable from our personal belongings. Within seconds we were ready. Outlaws on the run! We knew the old Skoda we were driving around would probably only get us as far as Birmingham before it blew up, so it was scrapped at McGuinness's for forty quid and we headed on foot to Sandbach service station to begin our journey by thumbing a lift off a lorry driver. Milly and Wayne grabbed their lifts well before me, promising to wait around Kings Cross station until we were reunited.

Alone, I had time to mull things over. *Fuck it. Let them come. Catch me if you can. I'd been on the run before and they hadn't caught me then, and London was a big place to get lost in.* I was sure I had made totally the right decision. Thankfully, just as the boredom of waiting for a lift was becoming unbearable, I climbed up into a warm and slightly sweat-odoured cab at four-thirty in the morning. The driver was a Scouser in his forties, wore a *Never Mind the Bollocks* tee-shirt and seemed well chuffed when I asked him if I could light the rest of my half-smoked spliff. He had the first couple of drags then passed it back.

"Get your head down when you've had that mate, if you want. I'll wake you when I stop at Watford Gap for a slash and a brew."

Nice one, mate. I would have stayed awake and chatted, just out of politeness for his favour, but exhaustion had me crushing out my roach, curling up, and trying to find a comfy spot for an hour or so. As I drifted off I thought back to the warrant above the fireplace. *Fucking hell, they've taken Freddie with them. Gutted.* After that I can't remember a thing except the glare of oncoming traffic and an endless stream of white lines.

I had slept on the streets of London before. While in the fourth year at school, me and Leaky, an orphaned friend of mine from Leigh in Lancashire, had run away together: the same thing, hitching a lift down to London from Sandbach, only we were going down to watch Prince Charles marry Lady Diana Spencer. After splashing about in the fountains in a sun-drenched Trafalgar Square and pulling moonies to some CNN reporters, we spoke briefly to a man who was reading that day's paper. He told us that Toxteth in Liverpool was due its second night of rioting and that there were rumours in the press that Moss Side in Manchester was about to blow as well. That was more tantalising than the wedding celebrations to me and my friend, and facing our second shivery night in a doorway huddled under my Union Jack/Stoke City flag, we decided to head back up north to Manchester as soon as it got light. If there was going to be some looting, I wanted one of those new Walkmans with little sponge speakers that disappeared inside your earhole. Neither of us slept a wink that night. We didn't dare. London was a frightening place for two fourteen-year-olds and the propositions we received from faceless strangers who whispered with whisky-stained breath from the shadows were highly disconcerting.

That was the unpleasant memory I had of London as I arrived again in the capital that morning. I was mightily relieved to see Milly and Wayne sat in the window of a café, sharing a coffee between them and arguing about the number of lumps of sugar Milly had forced into the small white cup and overflowing saucer. I smiled and they smiled straight back. We had made it, and all we had to do now was find a place to live. *That shouldn't be too much of a problem, should it?*

For the first couple of nights we crashed with some other kids from our school in Alsager. They had been down there several years, trying to make it in the music business. Happily for them they had just secured the contract for the theme tune for that year's America's Cup. It was party time and for now the arrest warrant was blotted from my consciousness.

"Squats are hard to come by these days, Jasp," said one of the kids. "We were well lucky dropping on this pad. We've had it two years, but time's run out on us and we've now received a final eviction order. I think we are heading south of the river to have a look over there."

That wasn't comforting news, and to be honest I hadn't given a thought to how hard it might get down here. Wayne, to his credit, had managed to get a job as a dispatch rider almost immediately. That tied him to the Acton area of north-west London. Milly headed south with the others to Camberwell, as he had interests over there and was not in the slightest bit perturbed that he would be living in Millwall country.

"Bushwhackers, who are they then?"

"Nothing Mill, forget it."

With one holdall between us, two sleeping bags and a bag of tools for breaking and entering, Big Wayne and I set out on to the cold, harsh streets in search of a place to live. And there were many.

I felt safe with Wayne. Nobody in their right mind would attempt to upset him, he looked what he was, a big brawler. But the real Wayne was the archetypal Big Soft Giant; his sting in the tail was his whiplash sense of humour. If you shared it you had a pisser, if you didn't you didn't stay around longer than necessary. I shared it, and being a down-and-out in his company was one of the funniest periods of my life. I also saw some of the saddest, lonely moments.

For the first three nights, we slept rough. Time was not on

our side as winter was drawing closer, and an element of desperation began to creep in although neither of us showed it. During the day we hung around the back streets, trawling for a possible squat that we could return to at night and break into. There was a slight danger in this, mostly from being arrested for loitering with intent, or possibly even getting inside somewhere to find that it already had a set of disgruntled squatters in occupation.

The result we were hoping so badly for arrived on the third night. We had walked for hours in the dead of a crisp moonlit night, softly singing Paul Simon's classic song "Homeless" and giggling to ourselves about nearing our wit's end when we came across a Georgian downstairs flat, partly boarded up and in desperate need of repair. It did not matter; we were having it there and then, regardless of its state. We got in and immediately changed the locks. We both breathed a sigh of relief and fumbled about in the dark, using our cigarette lighters to see. It looked as though the previous tenants had only just vacated the place and we couldn't blame them. If we hadn't been so desperate we would have given it a knockback straight away. Scattered about the lived-out place was the odd packet of soup, a couple of candles, a piss-stained blanket, a mountain of unopened mail and, strangely, loads of cardboard tubes that looked like the ones you would find inside rolls of tin foil. It smelt of damp and wood rot, and there was no electricity. But there was running water and the front room, big and empty, was half liveable.

We threw our sleeping bags down in the corners of the room and skinned up to celebrate with some black oil we had got from the Alsager lads. The search for an abode was for now over. Tomorrow, when it was light and Wayne went to start work, I planned to give the gaff a brush up and a clean, get a bit of discipline about the place.

"Night, Wayne." I crushed out my reefer, blew out my candle and tucked up into the foetal position inside my old Army gonk bag and then cosily zipped it up over my head.

"Night Jasp."

My stay in London as a down-and-out would last for about three months. Many things happened that were either funny enough or shocking enough to include in a book, but three in particular demand mention, as they had a lasting effect on me as a person and on the way I chose to live the rest of my life.

The first involved Hannah. She insisted her name was Hannah even though the rest of the tramps called her Gerty. I didn't need telling that Hannah had originally come from very good stock. I'd go as far as to say that she went to finishing school and possibly held a title, such was her manner. She looked so out of place, yet fitted in so well as a kind of mother figure. After she befriended me, I started to really understand how fickle and often frightening life could be on the street.

OK, fair enough, everyone who was sitting on the steps of that rundown church, drinking spirits and beers from brown paper bags on that damp Thursday afternoon, had their own terrible stories of life to live off. But what was her sad story? She intrigued me. How could an obviously once beautiful woman have fallen so far from grace. I was utterly intrigued and made a subtle effort to get to know her more. If I could and if she would let me, I wanted to help her. If there was such a thing called help.

As Wayne left in the mornings, I told him that I was going out each day looking for employment, but instead I walked from Acton to Ealing to the old boarded-up Presbyterian Church along Uxbridge Road where Hannah lived. I had picked her up out of the gutter after she had been knocked over by a taxi in the rain. It seemed to me he could have swerved to avoid her but didn't, maybe because she was an old tramp and she didn't matter. But I saw it and I decided to help her up and escorted her back to Ealing by bus, to where she told me she stayed with some friends. She said they would worry if she did not get back.

Hannah's command of the Queen's English was impressive. Her posture was upright and somewhat gentrified. Her clothes, though worn and threadbare, were co-ordinated and well thought out. She had bright red hair, slightly silvering, which she tied back from her brow with a piece of suede. Her face was weathered and heavily wrinkled, but still attractive. Although her teeth were no doubt once pearls, they now looked like broken tombstones gathering moss. Her hazel eyes carried a lost look of sadness, yet were still caring. I never asked her how old she was, as you don't ask ladies that question, but I guess she was in her late fifties, and had definitely been a looker in her day. She did tell me that she was actually from London, but I never found out which part. A blowing piece of rubbish or a stray animal would always take her attention and distract her from further conversation.

She for me blew the myth of lost and lonely people from up north heading for the streets of London to either disappear or search out their destiny. She was a local woman and there was a good chance that Hannah would have had family somewhere not far away. Yet sadly, she had obviously been left out to rot with the rest of London's lost souls. It was a shame, but there you go, it's nothing new. Hannah, for whatever reason, had hit rock bottom and her plight was beginning to touch me immensely.

Most days were rain-sodden but I still felt the need to go and see her. I would normally arrive in Ealing around ten-thirty in the morning after a brisk walk. The tramps would be around the set of twelve worn concrete steps that led up to the boarded church entrance. "NO ENTRY. CONDEMNED

BUILDING," read the dilapidated sign on the huge oak door. Little attention to that or any other sign was paid by these unseen people. Most of them were already on their second bottle of booze by the time of my mid morning arrival.

The gathering would normally consist of a dozen or so men and women, and all characters in their own right. The friendlier ones tended to sit around on two worn-out and discarded Sixties-style settees that lacked cushions and smelt disgusting. I took a seat here with Hannah and a quiet man called Aaron, who had been badly mauled at some stage by a dog that had bitten off a piece of his nose. Some of the unfortunates I liked, others I kept an eye on. The majority suffered mental health problems. Joseph was one. Here was a bully who blamed all his woes on the relentless beatings he received as a child from his father. He was not worth another mention other than that I was chuffed to bits when he caught pneumonia after collapsing drunk on the street during a heavy frost. Shame he didn't fucking die. I hate bullies. Why bully others when all you go on about is how bad you were bullied yourself? You would think that most people who have suffered like that would make an effort to treat people the way they wish they had been treated, not the opposite. Joseph was a cunt and most of the others detested him and wished he would find some other place to hang out.

They gave me a once over and I think I was dismissed as a runaway trying to cadge a fag or a quick warm by their small wastepaper-bin fire. No one offered me a swig of their drinks or a puff on their rolled up wafer-thin smokes. Thankfully! For five or six hours each day I would sit with them, hidden from sight, and watch the world pass by. The most interesting part of this experience was the people themselves. Not the tramps, but everyone else, those with a destination, somewhere to head for. You know the ones. Off for a cooked dinner with all the trimmings and a blowjob off the missus for pudding, or even a quick round of squash before settling down to watch that night's live TV coverage of an important European football fixture that you've placed a £50 bet on earlier that day. It's fucking amazing what people choose to see and what not to see.

Yeah, that's right, lady. You turn and look in some shop window that sells something you don't even want. And you mate, why don't you just put your head down and keep on walking, you won't even notice we are here, that is unless you can smell the caked-on layers of dried piss that stains everyone's crotch.

I was starting to dislike what I was seeing and people in general. Out of a thousand passers by, the tramps would probably get five looks of acknowledgment and the same number of looks of sympathy. It's amazing how cold people can be. It was such a lonely world inside such a busy and uncaring place, like a huddle of condemned people. All they had was each other and there was little or no chance of any of them ever leaving those church steps alive.

It was so grim I was actually relieved to get back to the comfort of our squalid, smelly squat each night and chill out with Wayne with a couple of spliffs and a warm beer, taxing our brains with trivia such as who starred alongside Robert Mitchum in the Fifites classic *Heaven Knows, Mr Allison*? It took us four hours, but we got there in the end. Deborah Kerr. Jesus. That oil we were smoking was strong, it cabbaged your memory completely.

"Find a job today, Jasp?"

"Nah. And I tried everywhere as well."

Wayne got paid cash in hand at the end of every month. So after four weeks of eating bread and packet soups, and being rationed to six cans of ale apiece each night, we did a shop and stocked up with beans and tuna, making sure we had plenty of money left to go on a bender south of the river to see how Milly was getting on.

It was a Saturday morning in late November and the plan was to get on the train at Ealing Broadway and travel on the tube network while completely tripping our heads off with the 100 or so magic mushrooms we had salvaged from the squat back in Stoke. After a hearty breakfast of bread and cold beans, we had two large blasts of Liquid Gold amyl nitrate each, then halved the mushies and dropped them with a guzzle of warm beer. We chuckled at the prospect of the day ahead, but decided to make it a working adventure as well. Our place, as much as it served its purpose, was dire and fucking freezing at night. If we saw anything suitable while in south London, we were going to break in, squat it immediately and then go back for our kit later.

We strolled, chatting together for half an hour or so, and arrived bang on opening time. The Broadway pub on the main street in Ealing was empty, but the orange table lamps and old world ambience were cosily inviting. We walked in and stood together at the empty bar. We waited silently in anticipation, eyeing up the bar pumps for the cheapest pint of bitter.

"Ahem." The cough was slightly exaggerated but still within the bounds of politeness and got the attention of the barman, who was cleaning glasses on a shelf below the bar. He popped up in front of us like a camp Jack in the Box.

"Yes please," he lisped ever so pleasantly, with a trolley-dolly smile.

"Erm." I glanced at Wayne and then back to the barman. "Erm, I think we will try two pints of your Benskins bitter, please."

"Ooh!" He sounded over the moon for us. "Two pints of Benskins," and off he fruitily trotted, glass in hand, to the bitter pumps.

Wayne and I must have come up on those mushrooms bang at the same split second, the barman obviously being the trigger. We looked at each other and simultaneously raised our eyebrows, and then together in a high pitched camp voice, both repeated, "Two pintsss of Benskinsss" with slight lisps. We fell about uncontrollably, oblivious to any feelings we may have hurt. From that moment on the day became more and more hysterical until at the end of it I finally found out what Wayne meant by overloading.

The journey south was merrily berserk. Furry boots, multi-coloured puffer coats, all the things on a tube train that caught our eyes in our drug induced state seemed to be funny. And then came the paranoia that goes with it. *Fucking hell, how long have I been staring at that woman? Has she just got off at that last stop because I was leching at her? Jesus Christ, that fella's got a blonde wig on and it's moving.*

The train was becoming stifling when we saw our destination, Brixton. We stepped on to the cold, tiled platform and followed the exit sign. Surprisingly, no one else got off, and as the train disappeared into the black tunnel, the place felt a little eerie. We walked on. I strained my ears and listened. Someone somewhere was busking. It lifted me a little, as it was a Dylan number that I liked, "I Shall Be Released". We quickened our step. The music stopped and we heard a growl.

"Fuck me, Wayne, what was that?"

"What?"

"That fucking big growling noise that came from where the busker was."

All of a sudden I went into *American Werewolf in London* mode, thinking that something deadly was stalking us below ground. Wayne was adamant that I was hearing things but we jogged on anyway, round and round the tiled corridors, counting countless billboards, and finally up the never-ending sets of escalators, still thinking that the sound of our own hurried footsteps belonged to something else, until eventually we reached the street and comparative safety.

The drug had obviously got the better of me for a while in the tube system. Now we were out of it with fresh cans in our hands and headed towards a Rumbelows electrical store in the hope of catching the Stoke result on the multitude of television screens in the window. This was something I did often and it brought me round a bit. I started to relax a little too, especially as Stoke were winning 3–0 away with six minutes to play.

Stoke got the result and we happily turned away from the shop window intending to walk to Camberwell. Wayne took a last swig out of his can and dropped it into a large street bin. We walked together. Several paces later we both heard a dull thud as the can hit the bottom of the bin. We both stopped dead in our tracks and looked at each other. *Fucking hell mate, how deep is that bin?* I looked at the can I still had in my hand. We nodded and walked back towards the bin. Drinking my last drop down, I held the empty can in front of me and let it go. Wayne and I watched it as it disappeared out of sight into the blackness. Nothing. We waited. Nothing. Dismissing the first incident we turned and walked off. Several yards on we heard it again, a distant "bummff" as the can again reached the bottom of the bin. We shook our heads and took to the back streets of Brixton.

It was quite a long walk to Mill's place, and soon we were lost in the dark and hopelessly disorientated inside the warren that south London is. All the streets and houses looked the same, Victorian and once grand. We went into squat-hunting mode, and tried to make the best of a bad situation. On and on we walked along the dimly lit terraced streets. Then Wayne stopped. He crossed the road hurriedly and headed towards a terraced place with three steps leading from the front door down to the pavement. I followed him. It had a cast iron railing protecting the front window from prying eyes. We both quietly climbed over it and attempted to peer through the ancient net curtains to get a better look inside. The windows were.dusty and cobwebbed. It was in a dilapidated state, neglected and definitely vacant. That was just what we wanted. It was about time we had a change of luck.

"I can't see fuck all, mate, can you?"

"Nah, let's try and get round the back of the place, so no one can see us." We both turned to step away from the window and went down an alleyway leading us to the back of the property.

"Fuck. What was that?"

"What?"

"That flickering."

"What flickering?"

"I've just seen some flickering in the hallway inside the house."

Wayne was adamant, and I had no reason not to believe him. We both stepped back over the railing and began to peer sheepishly back inside. I shivered. It was cold, but up until now I hadn't noticed how cold. My breath covered the glass and I rubbed it away with the sleeve of my jacket, half wishing I wasn't there.

"There Jasp. It's there again."

Man, I did not need telling. This time I could see it for myself. I wanted to leg it, but my big friend was steadfast, so I remained by his side, gulping. It was obviously only a candle but in my drugged condition I couldn't understand why someone would be walking about in the dark carrying one. Instead of considering that maybe the meter had run out and the person was fettling around in the dark, I immediately thought it was something more sinister.

"Argh, shit!" Now I was frightened. Wayne grabbed the

sleeve of my jacket and whispered, "They've seen us, Jasp. Look, the light is coming towards the window." Seeing Wayne alarmed had me wanting to leg it, but my feet felt like lead weights and I couldn't move them. I braced myself in a cold grip of fear for what was about to appear from behind the nets. Our flash new Victorian pad was no longer looking inviting.

It would be a massive help for me to explain what we saw next if you have seen the film *Chitty Chitty Bang Bang*. In it, inventor Caractacus Potts's father, Grandpa Potts, is kidnapped by a couple of spies sent by Baron Bomburst of Vulgaria, who is desperate to recreate the magical flying car produced by Potts Jnr. On his arrival at the Baron's magnificent castle, he is flung into a dungeon deep within the building. Inside the dungeon is a laboratory housing a host of other elderly inventors who too have been kidnapped to work on the flying car. They had been there for decades, and it showed. They wore shiny black winkle pickers, black drainpipe trousers and black fish-tail evening jackets, and each had bald crowns with straggly grey hair falling down their backs, long shaggy beards and Kitchener-style sideburns. I watched it on Christmas Day as a kid and they freaked me out.

Twenty years on and the man standing before me, staring right back at me, was freaking me out more. I was spooked speechless. He looked just like one of the inventors.

"Oh my God, Wayne. Look at him."

Just as I thought it could not get any worse, more lights appeared behind him, moving slowly towards the window. Amazed, we watched as more and more people, all looking the same, manifested from the blackness and appeared, motionless and scarily expressionless, before us. Mostly they were old men but there were several women among them, which only added to my anxiety. We were both pinned there with fear and said little for what must have been twenty seconds, though it seemed like twenty minutes. Now, either that was the original cast from the film on a reunion, or we had just stumbled on something frighteningly bizarre, a sect or a coven or something similar. The way they stood there, examining us as an alien would his first human specimen, had me wondering who the hell they were and why did they live and look in such a way.

"Fuck it, Wayne, I'm off. Are you coming or what?"

We had seen enough and got on our toes sharpish. *Sod it, we'll see Mill another day.* I was more prepared to get back on the tube and take my chances with the werewolf than hang around the back streets of Brixton looking at the ghosts of Christmas past. That place wasn't for us; it was miles from the nearest tube and shops anyway. Time to get back across the river. London sucked. I had had enough of the place. Wayne and Mill loved it down there and made it their home. I was ready for the next step of my life. Somewhere hot and sunny, maybe the south of France.

Christmas was only three weeks away, so I decided to see that through first and head off somewhere in the New Year. I thought it best to gain some quick employment in the weeks ahead so I could go home to Stoke with a couple of quid in my pocket. Boxing Day and its football fixture was the one time of the year that you would see all your football family together in one place. Home or away, the lads were there; they even travelled home from abroad for that fixture. To those of us with no real family to speak of, it was our Christmas Day and I was not about to miss it. I thumbed through a day-old *Evening Standard*, found the employment section and read the relevant page: low paid, unskilled and no references required. The advert read, "Building labourers wanted, west London area, good rates of pay." It was a London-based Irish construction company and the next morning I caught a bus from Acton to Southall and was on site at 7:30am, freezing my bollocks off, along with a host of other shady-looking bastards, and wishing I wasn't there.

I spent the first couple of weeks doing groundwork on a building site. Most of the other workers were Irish and kept it tight between themselves, which suited me. I actually began to enjoy getting up in the morning and feeling tired at the end of the day, instead of sitting up until four in the morning, smoking huge joints of oil out of a sugar bowl.

In the third week, a couple of days before Christmas Eve, a foreman from another job shouted over and asked if I could drive a forklift.

"Yes, I can."

What the fucking hell have I just said that for? I had never driven a car, let alone a forklift truck. The man told me I was to go to a bank they were working on near Uxbridge. Their driver had been injured and could not operate the machinery. He could not stress too highly how important it was that the lorry loads of breeze blocks due to arrive shortly were stacked up for the brickies so that they could complete the inside of the bank and get it shut up and secure for the festive season.

It seemed like he was in a bit of a pickle and needed a favour. *Loading pallets of blocks on a forklift shouldn't be too difficult*, I guessed. *The wheels on those things are tiny. How hard can it be?* I decided to say nothing and help the man out. It was the least I could do, being Christmas and all.

I was driven to Uxbridge and shown the job. Just move things from A to B, as simple as that. I climbed up on to the forklift and took to it like a natural, loading up for the bricklayers who were all on different levels of scaffolding. One or two of them even started saying, "Cheers, mate," such was their admiration of my efficiency. I went back to the squat that night feeling chuffed with my day's work and looking forward to doing it again the following morning. Maybe I had found my vocation in life at last.

Wayne returned home later that evening looking well chuffed. He threw his helmet down and took off his leather jacket, reached inside his jeans pocket and pulled out some Cellophane. Inside was something I had never seen or heard of before, a grass called Thai stick. It was Wayne's Christmas present to himself. The oil we had been smoking was rare enough but to have an ounce of this stuff in the 1980s was more than a little special.

Two joints later we had both collapsed and I awoke for work the next morning shivering and still wearing the previous day's clothes. I arrived for work fifteen minutes late. Two wagons had already arrived and were parked on the main street waiting to be unloaded. There were more than a couple of disgruntled expressions around the site as I climbed into the cab of the forklift and pushed the start button. I thought that going for a quick brew would push them over the edge so opted to make an attempt at catching up with the unloading. Even at elevenses, when everyone else retired to the brew hut, I plodded on with it in an attempt to pacify the brickies.

It could have been the monotony of the job coupled with the heavy head from the previous night's Thai stick, but I began to lose concentration. Forks up. Lower. Slide under pallet. Forks up again. Lift loaded pallet. Reverse slowly. Lower load again. Turn vehicle round and then drive slowly and safely in through the bank entrance, making sure not to collide with anything or anybody.

While everyone else sat reading the paper or chatting over a hot cup of tea, another wagon arrived. I pointed the driver towards the tea hut and said I would be as quick as I could with the unloading. He said cheers and disappeared.

I had one pallet left on the truck. The forks slid perfectly underneath and I raised them, taking the heavy pallet high up into the air. I did as I had done all morning, turning the vehicle round to re-enter the bank. *Yeah, this is easy*, I thought. Unfortunately that momentary lapse in concentration cost me dearly. As I was thinking about how easy I was finding my new skilled job, I forgot to lower the pallet back down before going back inside the bank.

Crash! Bang! Wallop! The entire gable end of the bank came down on top of me as the pallet smashed through the wall, with me in the forklift below it. The noise and the dust made it sound and look bad enough, but the sight of that bank frontage coming down around me had me mortified as I sat inside the metal safety cage. The look on the bricklayers' faces as they ran out of the brew hut at pace led me to believe that it would not keep me safe for much longer.

Genuinely sorry for what I had done, I weighed up the situation. The damage was irreparable, or at least couldn't be fixed overnight. Everybody present could see that and that's why I decided to jump down off my seat before I got my head kicked in. Stumbling across broken masonry and debris that was strewn across the pavement and street, I legged it.

Forklift driving was alright, but it will end up calamitous if you mix it with Thai stick. Another lesson learned. I made a real mess of that bank, and possibly ruined some people's Christmas holiday. For that I feel ashamed and sorry. I probably did deserve a kicking off those builders, but I could not wait around for the police to come and arrest me for criminal damage and driving machinery without the appropriate licence, especially when I already had an outstanding warrant hanging over me. I legged it, not just back to the squat but back home, regardless of the danger of arrest up there. If I was going to be roughing it, I might as well be roughing it in Stoke. At least I could have oatcakes for my breakfast back there.

Wayne's response was several minutes of hysterics while I replayed the day's escapades over a spliff. He understood, though, that I had to go home to be with my football family over Christmas. I was straight with him and said I would not be back in the New Year. We said our farewells and parted company. But before I made my way to the Edgware Road to start my journey back north, there was somewhere I had to go and someone to whom I had to say goodbye.

I had not seen Hannah for several weeks, and I could not bring myself to leave London without speaking to her. I don't know what was in my head, maybe I was kidding myself that she would come with me and find a life away from the street. That was rich coming from someone who did not even know where he was sleeping that night. But if she did come, perhaps I could get her into some kind of sheltered accommodation. After all, our country is generous at giving help to homeless people with a problem, especially people from overseas. Surely with Hannah being a national she would be entitled to help. Or maybe I wanted to ease my own guilt of leaving someone to rot, knowing full well she would refuse my offer and stay with what she knew best. At least I would have tried. It's so bloody easy to ease your conscience when you want to, I'm all right Jack and all that. But it wasn't like that. I did care, a lot. Enough to spend twelve quid of my Christmas beer money on a taxi to get to her as quickly as I could.

I arrived at the church early in the evening in a torrential downpour. I was carrying everything I owned, and it was saturated and weighed heavy from my ten-minute wait for a taxi. The gathering on the church steps was smaller than usual, with several new faces, plus that sad bastard Joseph, who ignored me as I approached the settee he was commanding.

"Joseph, where are Hannah and the others?"

There was no sign of Aaron, Alice the Cornish lady who

spoke with a cleft palate, or Samuel, the old Jamaican who swore that one day he would return to Kingston to marry his childhood sweetheart and bring her back to live at the church with them. I liked Samuel a lot, he was a gentleman, and it began to concern me why all the nice, quieter tramps seemed to have disappeared, to be replaced by a rough bunch of misfits, mostly from Scotland. I challenged Joseph openly and caught the attention of the rest.

"Oi. I've just asked you a question. Don't cunt me off, you sad bastard. Where's Hannah?"

A gravelly voice replied. "Ay Jimmy, you talking about the old bint?" He moved up the steps towards me. His friend joined in too. "Ay, she liked it that one."

I did not like that Jock's tone one bit and immediately lined him up for the butt as he drew closer. I was outnumbered in a world where consequences mattered nothing. Young and hot-headed, I lost my cool and grabbed Joseph by the neck, grabbed his Adam's apple firmly in my palm and squeezed hard, like my old Regimental Sergeant Major used to do to me every morning on his cell inspection. The stinking tramp lost what little colour he had as he tried to fathom out whether I was going to kill him or not. I knew I wasn't, but in his harsh world it was a clear possibility.

Bang! The blow had me reeling in pain and confusion, but if that was the Jock's attempt at getting me to free Joseph, he was wasting his time. My attackers moved slowly towards me, hissing through their teeth as they tried to decide whether their opponent was dangerous or not. Two beads of warm blood trickled down the side of my forehead and my cheek to the corner of my mouth. I could taste the iron and moved into an even more aggressive stance over Joseph.

As I shuffled position, my foot scuffed a bottle beside me. Quickly, I picked it up. It was an Irn Bru bottle, thick and heavy. Inside was what looked like a full measure of urine. It might have been a bit smelly but it was an ideal weapon. Holding the bottle tightly by the neck, I smashed it on the wall beside me, and in a swift sweeping movement brought the jagged neck end around and under Joseph's chin. The situation was firmly back in my hands again.

"Yeah, you fucking want some do you, you sad Jock cunt?" I pushed the bottle firmly into Joseph's neck without breaking the skin.

If I thought that old chestnut was going to get me out of this situation, I was badly wrong. Two of the closest Scottish tramps hit me at once, throwing their bottles and charging with little concern for Joseph's safety. I raised my arm, half in defence and half in an attempt to slice Joseph. In the melee he managed to bolt away, leaving me brawling with the two Jocks. Joseph legged it with three others and all my belongings, which I had dropped on the steps.

The other two, obviously enraged by my interference, continued to kick and punch at me, whilst all the time staving off my frantic lunges with the jagged broken bottle. The fight continued down the steps and on to the pavement. Crazed, the Jocks began to overwhelm me and I lost my footing and stumbled, giving one of them enough time to slam me again over the head. Disorientated, I tried desperately to force my feet in the direction of my belongings, which were now being fought over and torn apart fifty yards away. Here I was, fighting for my life while those bastards are fighting over my dirty laundry.

Crack! *Now that fucker did hurt.* I fell against the frame of a bus shelter, which kept me on my feet, but only just. I was getting done and I knew it. I swung another desperate blow with the bottle and then threw it at my attackers as they began to run off. My immediate thought was that the others had stumbled on my Walkman and tapes, and these two were after them for themselves. But then two Indian kids came speeding past me, aiming kicks and punches. They chased the tramps off while their mother, a Sikh, kindly attended to my wounds. I was very grateful to them all, though bitterly disappointed that my belongings were irretrievable.

I'm going to be honest; I was fucking frightened during that fight. That brawl was like no other. Kicking the fuck out of each other at the football match was dangerous enough, and although weapons were sometimes brandished they were mostly used only to scar, to remind people who they had come up against and what the outcome was. Football hoolies rarely kick to kill, even though it says so on their calling cards. Here I had found myself in a much different set of circumstances. Not only were my attackers from Scotland, whose violent population was renowned for carrying weapons and using them with intent, but they were obviously mentally ill and living in the bleakest and most dangerous world imaginable.

To them I would have been another laughable statistic, the punter that tried it on who got battered and robbed blind for his troubles. Like they gave a fuck about anyone or anything. Would they have stopped their attack if those two kids had not helped me out?" I was struggling, there is no denying that.

Grateful to be going, I left London sad to the pit of my stomach that I never got the opportunity to say goodbye to my friend, which hurt all the more not knowing what happened to her. I take solace in the fact that the others had disappeared too. Maybe they had all found another, safer place, away from bullies, a place to live happily together, if happy is what you can call it.

I was never really a down-and-out. It was an adventure, a game, a test, something that I was in control of at all times. I could go home at any given moment, I always knew it. That was my cushion, my luxury, the fuel that kept my fire burning. Hannah is probably dead now, sadly. Life expectancy on the street speaks for itself. Tonight as we settle down, there are many desperate lost souls trawling the streets of our country, looking for a place to lay their heads. They don't have the luxury that I did, of knowing that in the morning you could say goodbye to it all and go home. Think about that the next time you turn to look the other way.

By the mid-Eighties, foreign travel and its pleasures and opportunities were beckoning many Stoke lads. At home it was a time of mass unemployment. Money was tight, jobs were scarce and opportunities were few. It was only natural, then, that enterprising lads with red blood in their veins would look for excitement further afield. One of them was Podge, who was typical of certain members of our football firm in that period. This is his story:

"A lad from Liverpool settled in the Trent Vale area of Stoke and set up home with the sister of one of our main lads. 'H' became a massive influence on us young lads from Trent Vale. I had met him at a few Liverpool games and knew him to be one of their main faces. I had strayed from Stoke City because they were going through a poor patch on and off the field. Lowest ever points in the First Division and general apathy with the firm meant that hardly anyone was going to away games.

"I was sixteen and eager for the hooligan scene, so I started going to Liverpool games with a lad who supported them. It was a different world, massive firms clashing at Chelsea, West Ham and Spurs, and it really opened my eyes. That was where

I first met H and so when he moved to Stoke I was already a familiar face.

"He soon started coming out with us and proved what a game lad he was in various scraps in local pubs, clubs and even the odd Stoke game when we could persuade him to come with us. He would tell us about his many trips abroad and how easy it was to rob gear across Europe, especially Switzerland. My half-scally mate Rich's ears pricked up at this and he soon came up with a plan: Inter-rail cards to Switzerland for a few days, then up to Stockholm for England v Sweden. The Inter-rail pass was £101 and you had unlimited travel across Europe for a month. Rich got hold of a book of European train timetables and H told us where to head. We were to stay at a youth hostel in Interlaken and hit the nearby towns of Brigg and Thun.

"So that's why one Friday night in September 1986, myself, Rich, Brasso, Spiv, Cockney Darren and Keejo caught the midnight train down to Euston. We had a few pints in London on the Saturday and headed down to Dover, straight on the ferry and into duty free, where we each bought a case of Stella, except for Spiv who set the tone for the trip by stealing his. We went up onto the top deck and started drinking.

"All we had was the clothes on our backs, a change of underwear and Head bags that were empty, ready to be filled with casual gear and whatever else we could get that was worth selling. We got to Calais a bit worse for wear after sinking back half a case of Stella each and put the remainder in our Head bags, clunking about as we left the ferry to catch the train to Basel on the Swiss border. The journey took nine hours and by then we were all pissed and in high spirits. The train had old-fashioned carriages that sat eight people with a pull-out bed under the seat, so I got my head down and fell asleep.

"I was woken in the middle of the night by a boot in my

side. Standing over me was a big copper, who ordered me out. Confused, I looked out of the window and realised we had arrived in Basel. The copper was getting more agitated and started to drag me by the arm. *What the fuck is up with him?* I thought, getting more confused by the minute.

"Once off the train, I met the others and found that they had been dragged off too. Some of them had gone nuts, writing graffiti and smashing up a toilet. Spiv had also nicked a leather jacket from somewhere but luckily this hadn't been reported yet. The police lined us up in an office, searched us, and after finding that all we had in our bags were bottles of beer, demanded to know how much money we had. Thankfully, everyone had around £100. There was no way they would have let us in if we'd had less, as they rightly suspected that we would just rob our way around the country. After a bit of abuse and a few kicks up the arse, they let us into Switzerland.

"What a country. Stunning doesn't describe it. We caught a train through the Alps, eyes like saucers as we looked out at the mountains and lakes. I had never been abroad before. We arrived in beautiful Interlaken and followed H's directions to the youth hostel, where we booked in. Fuck me, how out of place did we look? We were six scruffy twats with empty holdalls, stinking of stale ale, surrounded by backpackers from the USA, Canada, Australia and New Zealand. It was a great place, though. We had our first decent meal, shower and a proper kip.

"The next day we split into three teams and went our separate ways on the rob. I was with Rich, Darren was with Spiv, and Brasso with Keejo. Spiv, Darren and Rich were all natural thieves. I used to flap a bit. Brasso and Keejo weren't that bothered and had come for the crack.

"The idea was you would go in a shop and distract the assistant by taking him away from what you wanted, while your partner did the business. We were after leather jackets, Lacoste stuff, expensive aftershave, anything that we could flog back home. Rich and I did pretty well, though I think Rich would have got a lot more if he'd had someone with a bit more front with him. Darren and Spiv excelled themselves, their bags were crammed full and they had to steal two more holdalls to carry their booty. Spiv went through some changing rooms and into a staff room to nick a wallet, though when Darren found this out, he punched him and made him put it back. Rightly so, as the police would have been all over us.

"Back in Interlaken that evening, Darren and Spiv kindly shared out some of the stuff and the next morning we happily trooped off to the train station to make the long journey up to Stockholm. I don't know how Rich made head or tail of that timetable brochure, but he did. Interlaken to Basel, Basel to Cologne, Cologne to Copenhagen and Copenhagen to Stockholm. A long, long journey with only a few hours off here and there, with more and more England fans getting on board in dribs and drabs.

"We arrived in Stockholm on the morning of the match and though there were about 100 England on the train, everyone went their own way. This suited us because we were off on the rob again. Darren and Spiv were insatiable. Unfortunately for us, the Swedes were a lot more switched on, so we were regarded with suspicion as soon as we walked into any clothes shops. It's not impossible that the empty holdalls on our backs brought us to the attention of security.

"We spent the day tramping the streets and thought we'd try one last shop. The woman in charge was on her own and didn't seem at all fazed when we all traipsed in and started to look around. Darren started chatting to her, asking where the football ground was and how to get there? To our utter amazement, she offered to show him which way to go and walked out of the shop and up the street. We looked at each other for a second and then started tearing round the shop, cramming anything and everything into our bags. Five minutes later they were back and we were innocently browsing again, leaving her oblivious when we headed back to Stockholm Central.

"At the station we dumped our heavy bags in the lockups and switched to football mode. It was now six o'clock and we'd seen no England fans all day. Though we were hoping for some trouble it did not seem very likely, so we were delighted when, as we approached the underground escalators, we heard the familiar roar. We flew down the escalators and at the bottom could see about twenty England lads who beckoned us to hurry up. Together, we steamed around the corner and came face to face with about forty skinheads.

"In the middle were three coppers with batons drawn, and though there were a few surges to get at the skinheads on the narrow platform, we were easily beaten back. The skins just wanted to sing at us. From their 'herdy-gerdy' chants, I gathered they were from Gothenburg. More police arrived and pushed us well apart, then shoved the skinheads on to a train. We caught the next one and were about five minutes behind them.

"When we arrived at the station near the ground there were no police at all and we followed a trail of punched England fans up to the ground. We went straight round their end, where they were still singing their ludicrous songs. This time we got straight into them and a look of complete shock on their faces had me wondering if they really did just sing to each other. The police finally arrived and shoved us around to our end. The match was typical England at that time, garbage and we lost 1–0. Nothing much happened after that. We were escorted back to the tube station and we were back at Stockholm Central in less than an hour.

"By midnight there were about eighty England fans lying

about on the station floor, on their bags, having a kip or whatever, waiting for the train to Copenhagen. Luckily we, apart from Rich, were all standing in an open air café which had metal poles roped together as a barrier. It was lucky because just then came a tremendous roar as 200 skinheads and Bon Jovi lookalikes came piling in from three different directions. It would have done the Bushwhackers justice and the entire England firm were on their toes up the station. We picked up the metal poles and none of the Swedes dared to come near us. After England's initial embarrassment, we came storming back and took the offensive, running into them, brandishing our poles. They were run out of the doors just as police arrived in force with batons flying, but fuck me, what a shock.

"We were buzzing because nobody had budged us, but Rich had been talking to a Chelsea lad he knew and was caught in the initial stampede. He was gutted. It took us another two days to get back to England, stopping at various European cities. There was a constant supply of buffet carts and kiosks left unattended so there was never a problem getting food. It was a mad eye-opener of a trip.

"Within a week of getting back to Stoke, Rich rang me. 'I've got next year's train timetable. How about February?'

"*Fuck me*, I thought. *Here we go again*."

Chapter Four

Ask The Stoke Lads

"ASK THE STOKE lads, they'll have some." You would hear that remark whispered dozens of times on any of the packed, sun-drenched side streets of Benidorm during the summer seasons of 1987 and 1988. We were not gangsters. We never pretended or wanted to be. We were football hoolies doing what football hoolies do while living abroad. We were living on the edge and using our wits and instinct to survive and prosper, chancing along with selling a few recreational drugs. The twenty-strong crew that arrived unannounced early in the summer season of 1987 certainly fit those criteria.

After my spell as a down-and-out, I returned to terrace action and was there at the formal birth of the Naughty Forty on a riotous trip to Portsmouth in 1985, events which are covered fully in *Naughty*. On Christmas Eve 1986, however, I was involved in a large-scale disturbance during over-exuberant festive celebrations in Hanley, and ended up with a conviction for assaulting two police officers. I subsequently hit the road to Spain again.

Ever since I had first arrived in Gibraltar as a lonely young rookie soldier in 1982, not only did Gib become my very own rock of hope, it also became a quick getaway base for many of the Stoke firm who were on the run. By early 1986, our number out in southern Spain was pushing the thirty mark, some coming and going, others settled permanently. Mostly living in southern Andalucian towns and villages like La Linea, San Roque, Campamento and Puente de la Majorca, the Stokie misfits cemented their reputation amongst the English ex-pats and Spanish alike as a likeable bunch of lads who occasionally, if given cause, could be a stiff test of anyone's nerves. Apart from that, the Stoke lads did their own thing and got on with it quietly.

It was no different there than to the UK when you live in a "firm" environment with a structure such as ours. Some of the lads, mostly the older heads, tended to work for a living over on Gibraltar's busy docks. They earned a steady income and most acquired Spanish girlfriends to help them idle away the winter months. The younger members preferred to scally for a living; there was no getting up at seven in the morning for them. They were nighthawks cashing in on the lucrative drug trade in and around La Linea's unpredictable town centre. Kiting was also another way of supporting themselves – using stolen credit cards and travellers cheques to gain street cred and boost their already snappy wardrobes. But the most lucrative earner, if you had the bottle for it, was smuggling.

Hash runs from Morocco to Spain and then by land and air to the UK were by far the most exciting way to earn a crust. And in those days a kilo of hashish could sell for £2,800 and above on the British market, but could be bought for as little as £2-300 in Spain – or cheaper still in Morocco. The profit margin made the risk worthwhile for many, and several of our number, still in their early twenties, took to this illicit lifestyle like ducks to water, gaining respect both here and back home for their daring and their bottle.

Throughout the winter months, mules from home would

regularly arrive at Malaga International, usually two or three at a time, sometimes a couple with a child, sometimes golfers heading for the fairway. They would be treated to a long weekend on the lash, all expenses paid, and then travel back to the UK strapped up with as much cannabis resin as humanly possible, usually about four or five kilos per person.

They would then be followed home by several of the lads who had funded the trip, usually to coincide with an important Stoke City fixture. Each of the funders of the operation would also travel home with a bonus one-and-a-half kilo each, always swallowed in what we called "caramellos" – bullet-shaped packs carried through Customs inside the intestines. To open up your stomach to accommodate the caramellos, people would swallow "testers" – shelled Brazil nuts, which are about the same size and accustom your stomach to taking the quantities of drugs. I only ever managed to swallow just under a kilo of those testers, and even that had me gipping badly. Steptoe managed to neck two kilo and two ounces of drugs, carrying the remaining thirty-four ounces inside his cowboy boots. Blatant, yes, but when you put it into perspective and take into consideration the inefficiency of HM Customs in the Eighties, it was well worth a try.

Once the hash had all safely arrived in the UK, it was stashed on a barge in Cheshire until the rest of the stuff had safely passed through the body system and been shat out like torpedoes into buckets. This was then always washed thoroughly and re-sealed. The haul would be taken by train to the Glasgow area and sold to elements linked to Loyalist paramilitaries for a better price than you would get anywhere else in the country. But it was done more for the buzz of getting away with it than profiting from large-scale drug importing. Sod that lark, far too stressful according to the lads. They said stick with the mischief.

This kind of trade went on for several years, earning my friends a considerable income and comfortable lifestyles, not to mention some quality contacts. Eventually, as they say, all good things must come to an end. On certain routes in to the UK in the late Eighties, Customs began to use sniffer dogs. They were let loose on planes as their passengers disembarked and queued up unknowingly to collect their baggage. If any residue was found by the dog, the seat number was matched with a name and that person was pulled and searched. Thoroughly.

In 1989, Billy Burton was arrested at Manchester airport concealing five kilos of Grade A pollen on his body. He was sentenced to four years in prison. After Billy the runs ceased. Well, at least the UK runs did. Sweden, Italy and Germany were also visited by the traffickers from the football crew.

Back in La Linea in 1985-86, more than all those earners mentioned, the most lucrative was right under our noses and the Stoke crew were in on it first: Marlboro cigarettes, smuggled from duty free Gibraltar into Spain and sold in massive amounts to bars and shops as far west as Algeciras and as far up the Costa del Sol as the city of Malaga itself. The cigarettes pretty much sold themselves. No need to cut them open or burn them to test their authenticity, just a quick flash from inside a holdall and the customer would gladly buy as many sleeves as you could carry for them. For cash. In those days the money just kept on rolling in for our little crew, and in those days life was happy and carefree.

We all carried blades in La Linea, mostly for protection, as fights with the locals were commonplace. They were mainly over turf and jealousy, but occasionally just for the hell of it. At home, if you were going to have a straightener with an English youth maybe one out of ten would pull a blade and use it. With the Spanish youths, the ratio was the opposite. It was a case of us English having to adapt to their way of warring. Just as many of them got cut as we did. It doesn't take you long to adapt when you have to.

Nobody can really remember whose idea it was to make that long journey up to Benidorm on the north-east coast of Spain. Torremolinos was just over an hour's drive up the coast and would have been far better for us logistically, but the northern resort was the one that was calling heavy in the Mediterranean midnight winds. Stoke had been to the resort once before. Our second ever firm holiday was there, exactly twelve months on from Magaluf. Mainland Spain had been chosen that time simply because being on an island the previous year made it virtually impossible to get out of the country if mischief had been replaced by madness. On our departure from Majorca, several of the lads had been arrested and jailed for things they had done more than a week previously. The mainland this time made sense.

Discussions were held over how much hash should be taken up there, who was to take what, and what means of transport they should use. Ten kilos was considered sufficient to get us started. The idea was not to sell it in large amounts but in two mil (£10) deals, that way you could get far more for your money plus keep the punters dependent and always coming back for more. There was no point in spoiling them, if they'd got a problem with it they should have brought their own gear.

The bulk of the hash was taken up the coast inside the spare-wheel arches of two Vespas brought over from England. They were white with British bulldogs roaring in front of a Union Jack painted on the tanks; I think somewhere along the line The Jam's musical influence had crept in amongst some of us. While some argued that The Jam were punks and not Mods, you could not dispute the fact that most football hoolies were influenced by them in some way or another during the early

Eighties. "You've got to walk and talk in football times." Too right Paul, great lyrics. Apart from the football lads, no fucker else was flying the flag in those days. We felt privileged to be what we were and be acknowledged in music the way we were. The other members brought the rest of the stuff by coach from the port of Algeciras. Within five days we had all reached our destination and secured long term accommodation in the rundown Aquarius apartment blocks on the north side of town, a place popular with skint ex-pats working out there and living on a shoestring.

There was no point in just turning up and bullying people by pushing our wares on them. First of all we had a look around to see who was who and what was what, and find out where, if anywhere, there was competition. Each night for a week, after playing rounds and rounds of insane drinking games and listening to the Housemartins, we would leave Aquarius around midnight and stroll casually, firm-handed, down the rolling hill and on to the main drag of the heaving resort. It hits you suddenly and brings you round sharpish from your gormless drunken state. Madness, music, flashing lights, screeching mopeds, incessant laughter, girls screaming, boys cheering, the smell of hot dogs, the waft of drink-laced vomit and the thrill of not knowing what will happen next or when. Alive!

We went to work and spent no time at all in getting to know the workers, known as "props", who we allowed to pull us off the street into the clubs they were working for so tirelessly. The ones that we liked and thought we could trust, mostly girls, were considered by the drug pushers amongst us as potential employees. Within weeks, after several honesty tests they were directing hordes of expectant punters towards the square in which the dealers had set up as discreetly as possible. The girls were also well chuffed, because each punter brought them some commission. Some of the girls made more money in a month doing this, especially in Glasgow Fortnight, than they would have earned all season under the exploitation of the Spanish bar owners who only paid them a measly £10 a night. It was a cozy arrangement between the props and the lads and kept both parties very happy. Money is the incentive with anything. If you are working in a job that pays little, you are always looking for a little sideline, everyone wants to be involved. Nobody wants to be a vegetable watching a desk clock five days a week. *Pass the skins, I'll roll another. Live the life, don't think about it.* Unless, that is, you were grassed on or seen by the Guardia Civil.

The Spanish police were real tough bastards and totally ruthless. They all looked upon the English workers with disdain and took any opportunity to beat and lock them up and then fined them ridiculous amounts they couldn't afford. The workers would rely on money from home to pay the fines and nine times out of ten went back there after their ordeal was over, swearing never to return to Espanola. It was a quick way of cleaning up the streets of illegal workers. After several harsh warnings, we decided to keep a close eye on the coppers patrolling slowly by in their brown uniforms, with their gun holsters and cigarettes that hung loosely from the corners of their tight, cursing lips, and stares hidden behind their mirror shades. *Jesus*, we thought, *if they lock people up for just trying to earn a crust, God help any of the lads who get caught dealing hash.*

We didn't all sell the gear, although most of the crew profited from it. Benidorm was rammed full of bars and clubs all vying for custom. To keep trade brisk, entertainment was brought in on certain evenings, acts such as Sticky Vicky, a peroxide Spaniard well into her fifties and still in extremely good nick for her age. Wherever Sticky Vicky was performing there was always a full house of goggle-eyed Brits amazed at the way she could open a bottle of San Miguel with her fanny muscles, and groaning in disgust as the chosen nineteen-year-old embarrassingly gulped it down on her command. "Goo on yer dirty bastard!" Everyone wanted to do it really; we bet she was a dynamite shag.

Apart from Vicky and the odd live band and bingo night, there was little if anything laid on for the ladies. Eddie and Maggot had an idea. Maybe there was an opening here to earn some dough? They put the tongue-in-cheek idea to the rest of the lads at our apartment one night.

"Well, if you two have got the bottle to strip off in front of a load of screaming women, that's up to you," I replied. Most of the rest also declined but Choppsy and Animal were game for anything. The four of them put their ideas to a couple of the less busy clubs along the main strip. The idea was liked by the English owners and Eddie, Maggot, Choppsy and Animal became the Balloon Boys two nights a week, and the Shaving Foam Men on Saturdays and Sundays, depending on demand.

An opening appeared here for me too. As sharp as ever, I hatched a plan with the Balloon Boys to tell the owner they were concerned about how crazy the women were going to get and they needed some kind of security. Amazingly, he agreed. The Balloon Boys were taking off big time, and the women were behaving worse than the lads, thankfully, providing me with a security job that paid exceptionally well too.

Lazy sun-drenched days spent on the beach, or cruising the prom on a Vespa looking for lulus to whistle at. No rush, no major agenda, we were self-sufficient, needed no-one and everybody was starting to love us. Happy days.

Still only twenty-three and now enjoying being away from England, my outlook on life was, to my surprise, relaxing a bit. I was no longer fuming. Though still bitter about the death of my close Army friend, Steve Bloore, I was beginning to put life into perspective for once, although looking back now, it was totally the wrong one; I had a terrible attitude. The way I looked at it was that as long as I was left alone and nobody from outside the football world I was embroiled in bothered me, I was happy and non-violent. Prone to the odd tantrum, OK, but essentially non-violent. The only time I would fight was if it was actually brought to me, or at the match with a legitimate target. People who know me might laugh at that statement, but most of my fighting took place on the doors of seedy backstreet pubs and clubs. Isn't that legitimate??

While the lads were out peddling their wares, my efficiency as a bouncer for the Balloon Boys had not gone unnoticed and pretty soon I was working the doors of one Benidorm's liveliest clubs, Champions. The lads began to use Champions too, partly because I was there and also because it was a favourite with the Swedish.

The Swedes were a funny bunch. All the women were stunning lookers and all the men were big and ugly, and I mean big and ugly. Drink in Sweden was very expensive, so all the Swedes did when they arrived in cheap old Spain was drink excessively and then pass out on the street. They were not really a problem other than it was difficult to pick up a seventeen stone man in an inebriated state and throw him out of a club for pissing up the side of the bar instead of going to the toilets. That was what "Garth" the Swede was doing when the management called me over to complain about the giant in the white vest and multi-coloured Bermuda shorts. *Oh shit, now he is throwing up all over the place.*

"Jasp, get him out of here quickly mate, he is turning customers away."

I swallowed hard at the thought of the task ahead. Garth was not his real name; I never got round to asking him that. He just reminded me of a huge character from a cartoon strip in the *Daily Express*. Like his cartoon image, the big man in front of me had muscles on muscles and a jaw line like Desperate Dan. My immediate thought was to hit him over the head with a bar stool to save any embarrassment, but I couldn't do that, not with job protocol and all. I looked round the club sharpish for some back-up from the lads but it was still only early doors and there were none, not from Stoke anyway.

A couple of twenty-year-olds sat casually at the bar enjoying the happy hour and the view of the barmaids' tits. I had clocked them on the way inside. Pleasant enough, they both acknowledged me. I winked and that was that. They were football, that was obvious to me, and not northern football either. They were definitely southern but did not have that Cockney swagger. One was tall, the other short and stubby, both were skinheads and both were extremely well turned out.

As the Swede I was asking politely to leave the premises grew increasingly more aggressive, both stood up slowly from their stools and flanked me side-on, letting me know that if I wanted help, it was there. *Fucking nice one, lads*. I positioned myself between the Swede and the bar and gently walked him backwards towards the street. He was compliant enough, happy to walk but insistent on asking why he had to leave.

On the busy road outside, Garth made his last stand, more for his dignity in front of a load of his queuing countrymen than because he wanted trouble, but nevertheless pushing me into a position where, if he didn't give over, I would shortly have to defend my own dignity.

"Why? Why do I have to leave, why?"

Garth's bony finger came closer to my face each time he shouted and pointed simultaneously in a huge Nordic roar. The gathering crowd drew in closer and much excitement and anticipation blew up like a sandstorm around me and the big horrible motherfucker of a Viking.

It's that trip switch, the split-second tsunami of hate, fear and aggression. Get it in quick and get it in hard. SMASH! Two vicious, lightning head butts connected so sweetly. He wobbled. He was bleeding heavily from a deep facial cut. I wanted him down now. Two slammers from the right holster straight on the jaw. *Shit!* I swear that second blow actually kept him on his feet. I was in again quickly as he looked like he was coming round, grabbed the long, blond hair firmly, and slammed him down, straight into the bonnet of the parked car behind him. This was a massive rush. This cunt was going down. I held on to his locks and pulled him down off the bonnet. One, two. My kicks slammed up into his already shocked and bloated face. Job done.

Right, got to dispose of the body because he's going nowhere by himself. I dragged Garth by his blood-sodden hair several yards along the pavement and dumped him in the middle of some prickly bushes, which wasn't very nice, I know, but they were all that was available at short notice. My back-up arrived with some venom, not bang on time but near as damn it. Eddie and Animal jumped off their Vespa as Garth's trainers were disappearing out of sight.

"You alright, J?"

"Yeah. He isn't though."

The three of us went back inside to the applause of the management and props. What a bloody fluke that was. I'd been absolutely shitting myself before I got stuck into that giant. He had more or less pushed me into a corner and left me no option. With the growing crowd, I'd felt like a gladiator in an arena, fighting for my freedom. Almost from nowhere the growing adrenalin pumping though my veins became like a bolt of electricity that shot through my body and out into

Garth, almost leaving me watching the whole incident from behind the camera, so to speak. But I wouldn't have liked to have fought the man if he had not been so drunk.

As I chatted with Animal and Ed about the incident, I told them about the two English lads that had stood with me. They both said that they had seen them around for several weeks with a tidy little firm of others, and didn't think they were just over for a holiday. They both agreed that they were football as well. Out of respect I approached them and offered them both a beer. They asked who we were before we could ask them who they were. Both parties knew the score.

"We're Stoke."

"We're Pompey."

Nice one. "How you doing? What you having?"

Milly and Fudger were younger members of an already established and well respected firm in England, Portsmouth's 6.57 Crew. Unlike us younger Stoke lads, they came from a firm with structure and respect for the older members of the crew. They were accepted by their hierarchy and nurtured in the way of life they had chosen, unlike us, who were viewed by the older Stoke as a nuisance and cocksure trendies. We were doing it our own way and learning as we went. The Pompey lads were schooled, and the reason they looked so dapper was that they were caning the plastic. They also liked a row.

After the fight with Garth, word began to spread around Benidorm, obviously exaggerated, that the Stoke lads were a right bunch of hard nuts. This brought some attention from certain corners, not least the police, but also a local gang of hoodlums who supplied drugs to the Spanish and held the doors of the locals' night spots.

The night they came to have a look at us, we were under strength by a dozen or so, although bolstered by a couple of the

6.57. They initiated a confrontation by pretending to buy hash from one of our younger lads, the Urchin, then robbing him and giving him a slap. His cries for help were heard and we gave chase in the direction he was pointing.

One of the Vespas was kicked into life, the Urchin was pulled on to the seat, and he and his driver sped off in search of the Spanish. They didn't have time to get into third gear before the Urchin pointed at a number of men running down the steps of a seedy-looking basement club with a narrow stairway leading down inside. The Vespa stopped and we quickly caught up. We stood in the silent street, which was slightly away from the usual nightly mayhem in a more residential quarter. There were nine of us, young but not stupid. We decided that steaming straight in through the doors would result in injury or even loss of life. Just by looking at the dimly lit place, we could tell it wouldn't be full of youngsters and we were probably up against some formidable opposition for a change.

"Right is everybody tooled?" My voice was calm and carried authority. Everybody was. And our arrival had not gone unnoticed either. A dozen or so hunched men appeared through the door and began to file calmly up the stairs in pairs. They were not shouting or behaving in a threatening way at all, but we all knew why. At that moment, we had all the advantages, psychologically and physically. We each knew that they were aware that unless they all managed to get up those stairs and into some space on the street, they did not stand a chance.

Maggot reacted on instinct. He was in charge of the Vespa, so he had our biggest gun. He shot across the road and up on to the pavement just as the first couple of Spaniards were reaching the last couple of steps. Literally feet away, he jumped from the speeding machine, aiming it directly down the steps and into the Spanish heavies – and annihilated them in seconds. *Fucking come on then!* They had brought it to us; they fucking wanted it. And that makes you all the worse. We tore into them like a spiteful swarm of African killer bees. Even though they outnumbered us, we were all over them like a bad dose of impetigo, smashing, slashing and booting them, and all the while Maggot was trying to retrieve the firm transport and trying to stamp on the odd head as well.

Our deeply satisfying "result" cemented a friendship between two different sets of lads, the icing on the cake of what we both already knew. We didn't all come out of it completely unscathed, as the Spanish did have a good go back. A couple of us were cut, me included. I didn't mind taking a wound, but when you get stabbed with a skewer it's a bit blunter than a knife and leaves a big puncture hole in your stomach that's sore to touch and oozes blood for days.

Surprisingly enough, we never received any retribution from that Spanish gang, not even the following year. However, it was something we never forgot, and none of us ever went anywhere on our own if it could be helped, not even when we were shagging birds. Benidorm had an icy edge after that, which was fine by us as it didn't half get humid at night.

All the old faces were still there; the props, the 6.57 with a few new faces, and Dave Fartuncle and his madcap musical comedy. All the groundwork had been done the previous year. The mood was set, everyone was happy and ready to party again. We had about the same numbers as 1987 with a couple of new faces. The Urchin was also there again, the thieving little bastard. "If he doesn't start cleaning his teeth he's going to get a regimental bath, I'm telling you," was one comment. He was a proper Urchin.

Two other new members were right up the Urchin's street. He rubbed his hands slyly when he saw Max and Lucy, her partner in deceit, arrive on the same floor as us at Aquarius 2. These pair of minxes were only in their late teens but full of it. A little crew of them used to follow us around at the match. They would conceal weapons and if any of the lads got nicked after a brawl, one would go crying to the police officers and convince them that he was her boyfriend and he'd been attacked while defending her. In those days, more often than not it worked. I was glad to see them, they made me laugh at their antics and in-your-face cheek. They could also fight, and after one drawn-out brawl, again with northern Europeans in the early hours of another heavy night, Max saved my bacon. I owe her on that one; myself, Maggot and Max got through a real bruiser together that morning.

"Does she keep looking over at me?"

"Who?"

"Her sat by the window."

"What, the old piece?"

"Yeah, I like her."

"You're fucking horrible you are, Jasp. Here get this down your neck."

Choppsy handed me a large one and went off to shower before his performance that night as a Shaving Foam Man. I watched him go and side-glanced ever so slightly to see what the well-dressed woman sat in the window was doing. She was bang on it. Playing the game. Telepathic seduction. *Well don't try too hard darling, I'm on the door at Champions in an hour.*

I knew who Debbie was, I had seen her talking to Dave Fartuncle. I had passed comment on how tidy she looked for her age, but he told me she had been out here for years and only mixed with money. Maybe so, but what I saw was a sexually frustrated middle-aged woman looking for a bit of rough, and I wasn't about to turn it down. I flirted with Debbie until I left for work. For now I was happy to play along; after all, she was the frustrated one.

After work that night, I headed to the Club Penelope. It was a flash place, had the Pacia logo outside and was normally impenetrable unless you were a local or known by the management, which we now were. Debbie was in there, looking seductive. If I could liken her to anyone it would be Kathleen Turner, only sterner and with heavy make-up, *Dynasty*-style. She was sat having attention lavished on her by a small group of Frank Lopez (from *Scarface*) lookalikes. I chuckled at the sight of them all drooling in hope and found a spot with the lads.

It was cleverly done, but so predictable. Her card had her apartment number on it and a quick note: "Follow me, I want you." *Really? Well I'll just neck this large short and I'll be with you lady.* I casually bid farewell to my smiling friends and headed off with a strut into a sexual fantasy land.

Debbie was Canadian. She came from Edmonton, Alberta, a tough steel and oil town in the arse-end of nowhere. She liked men. That became apparent the moment I stepped inside her plush apartment in the old town area of the resort. I think I had rather underestimated her. Far from frustrated, Debbie was a full-on insatiable nymphomaniac. The first real one I had ever met.

She put on some soft music and placed a fine bottle of vintage rioja in front of me. The glasses chinked as she sat smoothly down beside me on the deep sunken suede sofa. *Bloody hell, this is alright*, I thought as I adjusted my position to allow her more access to my crotch. She leaned in close, reaching past me to extinguish the lamp behind me. From the moment the light went out I was all hers. And man it was intense.

I sit and talk to my Hampton everyday, most of us do. They

don't answer us back but there you go, it's a comfort thing. If you've got one you will know what I'm on about. Debbie slowly released my already throbbing cock from inside my Levis. He was glad to get out, and by the look on Debbie's face she was glad to see him. He was looking good that night, pumped up and glowing. She grabbed a handful and pulled him towards her as she knelt down purposefully in front of me.

"Oooh look at you, aren't you a handsome boy."

She engaged me filthily in the eye, then blew softly over the end of my bulbus sending me rigid. *Bloody Hell, she was talking to him.* I lowered my posture once again giving her access to my balls.

Debbie continued to talk seductively to him. No touching, just talk, and then a slow soft blow up the entire length of my twitching shaft. I tried to run my fingers through her hair. She resisted and pushed my hand back down.

"Ah ah. No touching, just talking."

Her accent blew me away now she was cooing all these evocative innuendos at me. I succumbed to her completely and after what seemed like an hour of pure priming she took my whole length right in her mouth, just when I wasn't expecting it. It was soft, moist greedy and red hot.

From the moment she tasted some of the premature secretion that layered the whole of my eye and chicken string, she exploded. What clothes we had left on were torn and ripped apart, which, for a very brief moment, bothered me because that Chevignon top I had on was the bollocks and everyone said so. The deadly attractive woman in front of me began to groan and gyrate with pleasure as she licked my full length, then sucked hungrily at my tender scrotum. I will give her this: when your bollocks are in a woman's mouth you do lose concentration for a short time. If you've been seeing her for a while you pick up on flashes of past arguments and wonder to yourself had she forgotten about it or if she's going to bite the bastards out of spite. Either way, putting your goolies in someone else's trust can be painful if not done properly. Tonight, though, my bursting bollocks were being sucked like they had never been sucked before.

"WE ARE THE FAMOUS FOOTBALL HOOLIGANS!"

She was good, she could read my body and a minute or so before I reached the vinegar stroke she stopped and looked up at me again, keeping a firm grip and still pulling my shaft in long, slow strokes.

"Jaasperr." Oh there was that sexy North American drawl again. "Jaasperr, where do you want to cum?" She raised herself up and cupped me with her fully bronzed breasts. She used them to carry on with the slow, tantalising masturbation.

I was out of breath. She was taking me to the limit here. She knew full well where I wanted to shoot that load. She didn't need telling. So instead I lunged forward and grabbed her hair and thrust the bitch back down on me. She liked that, I could tell. Off she goes again. Sucking, slurping, wanking, moving him up and down faster and faster, grip getting firmer, cum getting closer. Head spinning, teeth gritting, arse cheeks pumping. *Here it fucking cums!*

One, two, three convulsions. Four, five hot jets of thick rich creamy primetime explodes inside her mouth. "Yeeearghhh!" Get in there.

Debbie continued to swallow on. I was now at that tender part where all you really fancy doing is rolling a nice spliff and having a stiff drink. Well, if I thought I was going to have a quick breather I was wrong, because the only stiffy Debbie was interested in was the one that she was blowing off again. *Who've Stoke got tomorrow?* Usually that's exactly what I think about after I have climaxed as heavy as that. Well that and I also wonder if they will bring any boys as well.

116

Experienced, Debbie also knew that this stage was crucial to her night and by keeping me hard through that redundant ten minutes she would soon have me wanting some deep penetration with little chance of premature ejaculation. And she was right. We moved to her bedroom via the bathroom. And still she wanted more.

I flung her forcefully across her bedroom. She was bringing the beast out in me. She landed on her bed, naked, laughing uncontrollably and taunting me with sex jibes. *I think she wants me to knock her about a bit here.* I landed hard on top of her, pinning her arms behind her head and sinking my teeth deep into her succulent neck flesh. I bit hard. She bit me back. I bit harder. Wrapping her legs around my waist she pulled me towards her, seeking penetration. I obliged, thankful that she was not expecting head. Now I pride myself on my cunnilingus. In my mind when I am performing this age-old stimulation, not only do I do it for my own personal pride but for my club and country as well. But tonight, as much as the old girl was getting me off, there was no way any of that was on my menu. No chance. The Canadian had the biggest pair of droopy danglers I had ever seen in my life. You know, the ones that are that long and far away from the honey pot that they get all wet and cold. Even worse than those, Debbie also had the hairiest welcome mat imaginable, thicker than the Ardennes Forest. There were no Brazilian waxes in our day. I don't think the young 'uns realize how good they've got it today.

I gave her my full length in one heavy thrust. She bucked on it receptively and the duel commenced. We locked horns like two stags, foreheads pressed hard together, neither giving an inch. Eye contact deep, intense and almost hate-filled. Pumping hard fucking fast, sweating profusely, groaning loudly, I shoved my fingers in her mouth. She bit down on them hard, drawing blood, I flinched. I wanted to kill her. Instead I bit back, crucifying her swollen nipple. I tasted blood too. It drove me wild.

"Oh yes, yes, I'm going to cum, give it to me harder."

Anything you say, lady. I arched my back and gave her my last inch. Fingers inside her arse, fingers inside mine, why fucking not? Bollocks to it, anything goes, neither cares, why should they? This is as good as it gets. This is pure filth at its sordid best.

Argghh, fuck! She gripped me tight and started screaming hysterically as she lost control and gushed jets of steaming hot urine all over the place, soaking us both and everything else. Now I'm quite simply struck aghast at her bodily reactions. *Jesus Christ, I have never seen that happen before. What's that all about?* Bemused at what I had just seen, I took her near-exhaustion as a chance to grab a quick spliff break. I had earned it, and disappeared briskly back to the lounge.

I eventually crawled exhausted out of Debbie's apartment more than forty-eight sex-filled hours later, straight into the burning heat of the afternoon sun. Blinded, I went by cab wearily back to Aquarius 2 and knocked up the lads. I was feeling a bit guilty about not letting any of them know that I was OK, something that I enforced daily. A dishevelled-looking Gaggioli appeared at the door, holding his semi in one hand and rubbing his bleary eyes with the other.

"Sorry to get you up, Gag."

"No problem my mate."

"Heh, I've had a mental time with that Canadian piece."

He chuckled and we went inside for a joint. My bed was vacant and I stripped off and fell into it. Placed neatly on my pillow was a note. It was in Debbie's handwriting. It simply read: "DO NOT EXPECT TO SEE HIM FOR TWO DAYS." She was slick with that one. I hadn't seen her pass it to the lads who were in the Penelope with me. So there you go, they knew where I was all the time.

As for Debbie, the mature Canadian nymph from Edmonton, Alberta, she was obviously a woman who knew what she wanted, and fair play to her, she got it as well. Experienced women. Don't you just love 'em?

With all this free love and promiscuity going on, did any of us care about our health? No. None of us did at that time. Sex was a conquest test to us all and we had a score chart for who had shagged the most women. The Stoke lads had a lot of charm, and that air of danger they also carried was a magnet to the girls, who were getting nailed by the score. Jesus, even Miss Gibraltar was on the 1987 list. Any one of us unlucky enough to contract a dose or the mind-destroying crabs was sent on the next hash run back to La Linea. They could then use the clap clinic for free on Gibraltar's National Health Service and bring back some penicillin as well the hash. Two birds with one stone. Result!

"Have you seen how thick that German fella's wallet is?"

The Urchin nodded through the packed dance floor towards the staggering man with the protruding back pocket. The paralytic German was about to become a victim of the darker side of the Stoke firm – the third that night. Max and Lucy danced their way over towards him and dropped their handbags on the floor beside his feet.

"Got a light mate?"

He fumbled hopelessly in his pocket for his lighter. Staggering backwards and then forwards, his hand became stuck inside his pocket. He was in a mess.

"Here you are love, I'll get it for you."

Chuffed to bits that he had a woman ruffling around inside his trousers, he failed to notice just how many hands were in which pockets. The cigarette lit, the girls danced away.

"Cheers mate."

The wallet was delivered to the waiting Urchin, where it was vigorously inspected, and the girls were subtly handed a roll of notes. The Urchin was like an ugly little Fagin, sneering grotesquely in delight at another easy earner with little risk to himself, and then only paying the girls a quarter of the haul. I used to laugh when I saw it. As long as they did not tax any of the English lads, I couldn't give a damn. The girls would have done a lot better for themselves had they decided to turn freelance but I suppose they were just happy to be a part of the firm.

This they did every night of the week, until by chance I found out that they had duped some English youths into taking them back to their apartment for a party. While the girls occupied their intended victims, the Urchin slipped in un-noticed and robbed them of their cash and passports. Now that really did fucking annoy me. Robbing them was bad enough, but taking their passports knowing it would cause them real distress and ruin a hard-saved-for holiday was too much. If they're going to rob the English they might as well rob us as well. Double standards, I know, but I still called the lads together.

I did not ask anybody's opinion of this piss-poor performance; everyone agreed with mine. We were all hacked off with it. The girls were simply told that this was not our way, and not to do anything like it ever again. And the Urchin, as far as I was concerned, was out of the firm for life. Without receiving the kicking he deserved, the condemned Urchin left Benidorm immediately and has never been seen down the match since. He was the only person we turned our backs on for being a sly, thieving cunt in all the years of the firm. And he's not missed one bit. (2005 author's update: Evo, Stoke Under-Fives, another thieving snide. Gone!)

The debauchery continued every day. Life in Spain for us young twenty-somethings was decadent and immoral. At that time we were peaking with confidence and enjoying every minute of life. We were young and full of ourselves, our bodies were still supple and minds relatively unscathed. Up until the closing weeks of the 1988 summer season, if we weren't drunk we were probably stoned. Occasionally we would take speed, and myself and one other didn't mind the odd cheeky gram of cocaine. Bad enough, but not as bad as what was about to arrive on the scene with a small crew of Blackpool hooligans en route to a party in Ibiza. The world was on the brink of a pill invasion that was about to devour every social class.

Champions had been closed down early for the night after it had kicked off badly between English and German gangs for the third time that week. Sod it, I had had enough. Maybe I was on a better wage doing the door than most of the other workers, but they weren't going home with bust lips and broken knuckles. I decided to go to Top of the Pops and get drunk like the rest for a change. It was probably the most popular club in Benidorm with the British holidaymakers. The doormen were Spanish and big and horrible, but effective, and there was little trouble in the underground venue. That's why I decided to go in there that night. It was to prove a fateful decision.

The place was heaving and damp with sweat. Salt-N-Pepa cried, "Ooh, baby baby," and I fancied the blonde piece sat on top of the speaker over by the DJ. I bought a shot and sleazed casually over. She wanted me, I could tell, and she was already on the board. This was going to be the fifth one of this week so far, and the second today. I played my smile right on time. But as I approached the speaker my attention was drawn to the strange sight of a man with his head inside it. His eyes were closed tight and he was bouncing with the vibrations and pulling an awfully strange face that reminded me of Les Dawson.

The geezer jumped up in front of me and started dancing almost like a shadow boxer. Dropping my chin just in case, I stared at him carefully. He opened his eyes and looked at me. Immediately the penny dropped with both of us. We were a long way from home, but we knew each other. Ginger Bertie was one of the unruly "Bisons" gang that used to plague the Coral Island amusement arcade and Shades, the nightclub where I had worked in Blackpool before I came to Spain. The Bisons were a nasty little bunch. Even so, I could see through that and in every bunch there is the odd likeable rogue. Bertie and Scotty were two I liked – from a distance anyway.

He hugged me, which I thought was strange. I put it down to him being caught up in the moment and all that. Then I noticed how big his eyes were and that Les Dawson impression was hounding me again.

"Yeah good to see you, Bertie."

He forced a small white tablet into my hand. And I think he said, though it was a bit slurred, "Take this man it's Ecstasy. It's fucking brilliant."

Really? Well I don't mind feeling brilliant mate, but if it means I'm going to be pulling faces like you, I'll stick to the weed, I thought as I inspected the pill. *Fuck it.* It was in my mouth and being swilled down. *Hey, I know how strong I am with the gear, it won't make me pull hideous faces like Bertie is doing.*

Within an hour we were both sitting on top of the speaker, gurning happily at each other and having the best night of our lives. Ecstasy had well and truly arrived, and as the Blackpool crew headed down to Valencia to catch their ferry, we sent

Animal up to Amsterdam to fetch us back some of this love drug.

Looking back, I wonder if at that very moment, all the music and film industry trendsetters had any idea that now the football hooligans had discovered E they would soon be turning up at the exclusive parties where it was already secretly being taken. Were we about to bring it all down around them, once the masses followed us?

Chapter Five

Fancy Another One?

"FANCY ANOTHER ONE?"

"What?" I said.

"Do you want another pill?"

"Oh go on then." I can't remember ever saying no.

I was surprised that I had managed to string a coherent sentence together and even more surprised that Gary could undo the tight sweated knot he had put in his bag of Ecstasy tablets.

"Cheers Gag, nice one." I swallowed it down without looking at it with a bottle of tepid beer, slightly gipping as it frothed up in the back of my throat. I burped out my observation.

"Fucking hell, these New Yorkers are berserk mate."

"I know, I've had five of the fuckers and can't feel me feet."

"What?"

"My feet. I said I can't feel my fuckin' feet."

"Oh right, nice one. Have you seen Turney in here?"

It was difficult to hear what anyone was saying. That may be why all the hugging started in the first place, because the music was so loud everybody turned primeval in their attempts to communicate. A huge cheer went up through the dry ice and the warehouse began to pump to the beat of Joe Smooth and "Promised Land".

Another Friday night in London had seen four carloads of us head for Kings Cross to a disused warehouse. The night was called Ibiza-2000AD and for the several months it ran it was not far behind Manchester's Hacienda as the best night out on the pills. The year was 1989.

The Ibiza at Kings Cross could have been moody but it wasn't. It was filled with the right calibre of people. It was the uncharted early days in the warehouse scene and the nights were magical to all those that can remember them. I must admit, I was not really into the music as much as some of the lads. I would recognise the odd favourite tune, but could not tell you who had sung it. I liked the crack, the bonding on a new front and the travelling to other parts of the country, still as a crew but on a different agenda. Even so, standards were always to be kept up, even if your jaw had gone across your face. You were still Stoke City N40 and you were still on show. We always remained cool and kept that aura about us. That never changed.

It was the same across the country: mostly it was the football firms who were organising the parties in their own areas. They were the ones setting the standards and they were the ones who were making all the money. West Ham and Pompey were very lively during the party era and always at the bashes. You would hear the Portsmouth crew through the smoke as they danced and sang, "Mental mental, mental mental mental" in their unmistakable Pompey accents. West Ham usually just observed. Like me, the ICF were not dancers.

One thing that I found difficult throughout that rave period was the occasional introduction to a member of another firm who was off his face and pretending to be your old mate's new best friend.

"Jasp, Jasp, this is Danny. Danny, Jasper. Danny's Millwall, mate."

"Yeah, so why the fuck have you brought the fella over to speak to me then? You know I fuckin' hate Millwall . . . All right, Danny, how are yer?"

I always made an effort, mostly because I didn't want to embarrass someone I loved. But it would normally be my cue to go and administer some first aid to one of our lot who had started to hyperventilate or something. I just could not see where all this new-found friendship was coming from or going to. It galled me. Most of the football lads fell as casualties to the happy pills but I was not one of them. Stoke had got Bradford away tomorrow, and I was in the van regardless of how fucked I was feeling. I was going travelling to another part of the country once again. Only this time we were back to the main agenda, football violence.

Out of the entire late-Eighties firm of hundreds of lads, there were only really fifteen of us who got heavily involved in the drug and dance scene. The rest were on their way, but not for a couple of years yet. We, the druggies of the firm, were mostly from Alsager and had all grown up together. Those hedonistic and mind-threatening years were ones of sheer over-indulgence and lack of self-control.

If you looked at the dance scene through the spectacles of a pill-popping hoolie, one of the main fixtures of the calendar year would definitely be the closing night at the club Amnesia on Ibiza. Word had it that all the main party heads from all over the country were flying over to the island to be at this event. Boy George was even using it to celebrate his birthday. Tickets were like gold dust and for us dozen Stoke lads at least, it would be like getting to Wembley and not being able to see the match if we couldn't get in. Undeterred, we headed to the island a week before the event, all determined that one way or another we would be at that gig.

Twelve of us were ferried in Gwilty's furniture van to

Manchester Airport. En route we took a couple of pills each to celebrate and stashed the rest inside our persons. Two weeks to go, twelve of us partying, that's about five pills a night each, plus some spares to use as currency. The lads had about 1,000 pills with them, several ounces of high-grade pollen and a mountain of cocaine. You know, better be prepared in case you can't find a drug dealer nearby. In these circumstances you've got to learn from your past experiences to prevent disappointments.

We arrived in Ibiza on schedule and checked into our five-star apartments in Playa d'en Bossa. The accommodation was tasteful and we immediately paired off for our rooms. I was with my old mate and attention-seeking partner Bamf, alias Nobby Oatcake. He was one of the stronger personalities in the group and perhaps as I was renowned for Army tricks, like shitting in people's beds, the only one brave enough to share with me. Neither of us knew on that first night that in fourteen days' time Bamf would be instrumental in preventing me from slipping into a drug-induced coma. I still think to this day that I owe him my life.

Royston had been right about the difference between Ibiza Town and the resort of San Antonio. It was a stark contrast in people and atmosphere: Ibiza Town was old and rustic, San Antonio full of lager louts. Most of the lads I was with were quite cultured and enjoyed restaurants and the ambience of Spanish street life. Ibiza town was where we headed most nights before hitting a designated club somewhere on the island. It was authentic, the people relaxed and the cocaine we had was dynamite. We settled in nicely over the next several days, making Passia our HQ in case of emergency and Space if it was after five in the morning. All the logistics were in place, which was essential considering the states we were about to get ourselves in.

Each day was as sweltering as the last and
through them at speed, drinking a little water but
and locally produced spirits. Several of us would g
late afternoon and head over to the other side of th
watch the sunset and the beautiful women viewing
del Mar. The potheads amongst us enjoyed del Mar, w
would have a cheeky pill, usually on the strength of the
and how good it was to be alive. *Peace, man*. The others
just be getting ready at about nine o'clock when we arr
back in our hired black Seats. We'd congregate in one roc
usually Gag's, where we would have a couple of hours
listening to tunes, drinking, snorting and smoking dope. A
midnight we all popped our first pills in unison and headed out
to the bars. The night would probably take in two or three
clubs, usually finishing off at Space at around about 10am. If
you had pulled, then bully for you. If you hadn't, it was back to
Gag's to smoke a couple of bongs and neck some temazecs
(temazepam) before climbing into your own chariot for a quick
pull over the girl with the dancing eyes that you were sure
fancied you until that flash Italian cunt pulled up in his Porsche
and whisked her away. *Hope she's there again tonight. I won't
get in such a mess this time. And that cunt can have it as well if
he wants it*.

Every night we tried and failed to score some tickets for
Amnesia. They were proving hard to find. Finally it was just a
night away and still eight of us were ticketless. The lucky ones
had either paid several hundred pounds or risked life and limb
in daring snatch-and-grab raids on the street touts. I was one of
those without a ticket so I decided it would be a good idea to go
and have a recce at the club to see if there were any weaknesses
in their security that could be exploited. There was one. It
looked a bit precarious but it was definitely worth a go. Gag
and I were going to attempt to get into Amnesia by climbing a

rby tree with branches that spanned over a courtyard inside
club. As long as they could hold our weight I reckoned we
re in. The ever-hopeful Gag agreed.

This was the event of the year and all present that night
dded to an immense atmosphere of anticipation. Even people
with tickets who queued outside in large numbers looked
nervous until actually breaching the security at the main doors.
The security guys were big Spanish weightlifters, they were
tooled up and looked horrible, dressed in tight black tee-shirts
and tight black pants. They were in charge and you could tell
they enjoyed it. Speaking little to anyone, male or female, they
mostly used hand gestures. You were in or you weren't. There
was no discussion.

Beautiful girls pulled sad faces, others chose seduction, but
all to no avail. Friends and relatives of the DJs were told that
with no passes they stayed outside on the street to wait in hope
that their message reached its destination. It was strict and
people were becoming anxious. With anxious people on drugs,
an atmosphere can change in seconds. Gag and I chose our
moment to push through the queue and start our ascent of the
tree. I just hoped and prayed that the people below us let us get
on with it without kicking up a stink and getting us caught.

It was weird trying to climb a tree while rushing from a pill.
I chose a fine time to suffer from vertigo but all of a sudden I
began to get clammy and my head started to spin. I could do
nothing but cling on to the branch that I was halfway along.
What a prat I must have looked.

The sight that brought me to my senses had to be a football
one. Just when I needed some sanity, it appeared right below
me on the road outside the club. Five open-topped Suzuki
jeeps pulled up in a line. Their heavy engines remained
running. I knew straight away, so did Gag; anyone who came
from our background would have known immediately that

the firm of men and women exiting the vehicles and heading straight to the front of that desperate queue were the unmistakeable ICF. Few people in the queue questioned the gatecrashers. The security, though, spoke in frantic Spanish into their mouthpieces and hurriedly put a chain across the entrance.

I was halfway across my branch by now, almost directly above the club's reception. A few more yards and I'd be on to the roof and in. I heard every word of what was said next and have recited it 1,000 times. As the West Ham firm crowded into the reception, one of them took control of the situation while one of his Spanish counterparts took control of theirs. They got a massive "No chance" from the head doorman. He was adamant and almost looked as if he was going to pull his pistol at one stage. I thought from my perch above that I was about to see a mental row. That was until the tall, curly-haired Cockney leaned towards the Spaniard and said bluntly, "Listen to me, you cunt. If you don't invite us to your party, you ain't fackin' havin' one. Alright?" They didn't wait for an answer; a crowd of twenty or so Cockneys breezed straight in. What a fucking entrance. You've got to give it to them.

That was my cue. Amid the confusion, I slipped over the roof and into the courtyard in the middle of Amnesia. *What a blinding result. Let's have another pill.* It was an immense rush getting in. My immediate thought was to get my bearings and find any of the lads who might already have made it in. I strolled casually around a sizeable, stylish courtyard which had the feel of a Mexican hacienda, like the one on the *High Chaparral*. The people who stood or sat around it were mostly Continental and all attractive. It was proper, and that was probably the reason why people like me, undesirable scallies, had to find their own way of getting into it.

I ordered myself a drink and sat model-like at the side of an ornamental fountain. I was looking good, I could tell. People, mostly women, were acknowledging me. "Hello," I'd smile. It was a clear night just coming dark. I could see the Plough followed by the North Star. I raised my glass and winked towards the north and Stoke and all who lived there. Something I often do, no matter where I am in the world.

I'd chosen a good place to sit and wait. Within an hour most of us were together, laughing at each story of how we'd managed to blag it into one of the top nights in the world. We drank Champagne and sniffed cocaine, we popped pills and rocked with the rest of the place. It was amazing. I opened my eyes after a mad moment of pure inner body rushes and saw all my friends laughing and smiling like I had never seen before, interacting with total strangers and not mentioning football violence and the off. Everything was over-enhanced, at other times slightly muted and robotic. Strobe lights, sweating people asking unanswerable questions, waiters swaying in and out with trays of fluorescent liquids, carrying bundles of rolled up pesetas and never forgetting to come back and serve you. And the beat gets stronger. And you get hotter and she looks hornier than she did ten minutes before. *Fuck, I'd give her one.*

"Jasper mate, can I have a word a min?" Wheaty was off his crust. He'd turned a worrying shade of grey and stood sweating profusely next to me in his best Nike trainers, holding a glass of Jack Daniels in one hand and a coke spliff in the other. He looked determined to string out his words, so I thought I'd better listen.

"Jasp, that bird that you keep staring at over there is a bit dodgy mate."

This was one of those E moments where two intense heads get embroiled in a fast-moving conversation about fuck all – other than the girl that I apparently keep staring at is with the ICF!

"Oh, right Mick. I'm with yer mate, cheers."

Most other hooligans in my situation right now would make an excuse and move away. I understood the threat but decided to stay where I was. Besides, it was she who kept staring at me, and she was just how I like 'em, stern and filthy looking.

I was well chuffed with Wheaty's bit of vital information and I did take heed. Around fifteen ICF were to my right only about twenty people away, sat around the fountains. Circled around them was a two-people wide gap. You did not have to come from the hooligan world to appreciate serious danger when it was near you. They looked mean, they looked affluent and they gave off an aura that said "Listen, forget it. We are here to relax, party and enjoy ourselves. Just don't involve yourself with us and everything will be right. If we unnerve you, tough. If we don't, fine. That's up to you."

I had a little chuckle, as I recognised a couple of them, in particular D, as the lads off a documentary called *Knockers* that had been screened in the mid Eighties, a fly-on-the-wall investigation which showed them door-to-door selling around the housing estates of east London. They used their flash charm on housewives and then travelled to the match in the van with the lads at weekends, showing off all the dosh they had made. It looked to me that they had done alright for themselves. I took another swig of vodka and cupped my hands for Warley to skin up in. Observation over, I peered over my friend's shoulder to the other side of the fountains and winked at the dancing redhead with the stern, seductive look who kept dangerous friends.

A woman's cry in the distance hailed a new and soulful beat. The crowd were receptive and excited appreciation greeted Voodoo Ray's self-named track. It was still dark in the skies above the club, a cool breeze lifted my senses and I closed my eyes and went with it. The atmosphere was now reaching fever pitch, this was when every person at that venue was on the same massive rush of love and excitement all at once. It was pumping mad. Everyone looked about ready to explode into a frenzy of lust and happiness.

She had planned her move precisely and executed it with pinpoint accuracy. My eyes were still closed when I felt her hands cup my face and my lips being pulled slowly and seductively down on to hers. I opened my eyes and looked into the face of the redhead. She smiled at me and said, "Hello, you're a cute northerner, ain't ya." She was Maria, and Wheaty was right, she was with the ICF. She was also spellbindingly gorgeous and I had no qualms at all when she invited me over to her group for a drink.

West Ham may well have had that presence about them but so did we, and as always our lads were networking the top tables where all of the most stunning women congregated around the obvious wealth and fame. Before long Royston was serving a quartet of Boy George's entourage with pills. They were completely off it already but still cleaned Roy out of his last thirty New Yorkers, and that was in the days when each E was more than a score. Roy declined the offer of a relaxed drink back on George's boat. He liked the song "Karma Chameleon" because he could change the lyrics and sing to the away fans, "Come a, come a, come a, come on in the Boothen End," as he gesticulated to them, but he'd rather run the gauntlet with me and the ICF than be stranded on a boat with George and his swashbuckling crew off their heads on the love drug. *Gulp. No thanks, I've got to be up in the morning because we are going to Aqua World for the day*.

Every football firm, I'm sure, has an eccentric or nutty bird that hangs around with them. Stoke have had several over the years, and Maria was, I presume, West Ham's. I could tell they all quietly kept an eye on her and she was more than comfortable in conversation with them. I reviewed my situation. Here I am on the best night of the year in the hippest club on Ibiza. I've bunked in for nothing. I'm off my chunk on Ecstasy and cocaine mixed with numerous beers and spirits, my mates are serving up the celebrities and I'm stood with a hell of a tasty woman who put me right in the middle of some of West Ham's top boys. *Terrific.*

Whoa, is that Duggie and Maggot talking to Phil Collins or am I in a bad way? It was Phil Collins and he looked to be enjoying his huddled conversation with several members of a hooligan firm. There really were no boundaries in those ecstatic liberal mindsets of the E pioneers. Everybody wanted to listen to each other and spread the word. *Can you feel it?*

As the first tiny rays of the sun appeared over the shadowed mountains, the club turned briefly sombre. A new re-mix was being played. I'd heard it once before at Kings Cross, but this morning it had a new meaning as we were actually in his company. It was Phil Collins' "In the Air Tonight" and Amnesia went absolutely ballistic. I was pulled into the fountains by dozens of loved-up ladies. Had it been a bloke that had pulled me into knee-deep water for a jig, especially as I don't dance, I would have thrown a punch, but it was mostly sex-crazed scantily dressed model-type women, so I decided to become a part of dance history instead of making it with an unsightly punch-up.

I did not speak to Phil Collins but apparently he was a really nice fella. When questioned about how he felt about having his song played in such a way and the reception it had received, he seemed pleased and took that opportunity to talk about the song and the meaning of the lyrics. I was intrigued to find out that it had a hint of revenge to it, and a deeper meaning than I first thought. According to my friend who sat most of the night with the music heads, Phil had written this song when he was at university, pre-Genesis. One particular winter, the River Thames froze over. Phil and several close friends, all fellow students, headed on to the ice to lark around. Unfortunately, in one area the ice was unable to hold the weight of one of his friends. It broke and he crashed through into the bitterly cold water. The rest of them managed to scramble their way to the bank and safety but the victim couldn't swim and neither could all bar one of the others. It was down to one man to go into the Thames and save his drowning friend. He froze in a different way, and they all had to endure the agony of watching a loved friend die. It was obviously a pain which he had carried around with him ever since. By all accounts, he carried the memory for many years until at a Wembley concert in 1981 he revealed his new song live and shamed his old friend in the meantime. I pondered a while on hearing that story. It moved me.

Maria said goodbye and headed off with the rest of her crew. It was seven in the morning and all the beautiful people looked haggard and pale now. She told me that tonight was her last night on the island, and that I along with my friends were invited to their villa for a last mad party before home. I said I would be there even if I was on my own.

Most of the lads were of the same opinion that afternoon: "Fuck it, Jasp. I wouldn't bother going there, mate." Gag was up for it though. He could see I was after a bit of romance but agreed with the lads that it could get precarious when away from the public domain, and was not about to let me go alone. I thought quietly, *Fucking hell, how often do you get the chance to go to some big tidy villa for a back-stage party with the Inter City Firm?* I surmised that from all the glimpses I'd had of West Ham over the years, be it with England or on the domestic front, they were always alright with Stoke. Always.

It was on that basis that later that night Gag and I got a cab to the other side of the island and attended the party. I was more excited to be at this party than I was at Amnesia the night before. It was held in the secluded grounds of a villa some way from the coast, set in the foothills of a mountain. Electronic gates, winding drive, a huge open-fronted place with tennis courts and a floodlit pool. It was around the pool where the music was set up. The smell of food floated from the house. It was civilised enough and our first thoughts were cool. We were told by an older fella wearing a Billy Bunter-style cricket cap, who was chilling with a beer on a swing chair, that Maria was in the kitchen. I liked that, as obviously she had discussed our being there beforehand. We went in. She was made up to see us and immediately opened a bottle of bubbly. Gag lit a spliff and passed it around. Any worries we may have had were so far unfounded. I mingled and chatted. We were both made to feel extremely welcome.

The party was spot-on, with just the right amount and mix of people. It went on into the early hours until abruptly the serenity was smashed by a piercing scream from one of the bedrooms. Immediately the music went off and the lights came on. The ICF were not the friendly hosts any more. The temperature plummeted to nine below zero and other guests started to look nervous.

Gag and I moved closer together and stood and listened intently as the accusations flew. A couple of black kids who both Gag and I thought were Arsenal Gooners seemed to be the focal point of a woman's accusations. She announced that the two of them had been inside her room and had emptied it of a large sum of cash and some jewellery. That did not sound good at all. The party had come to an abrupt end. It was one of those icy moments that had got fuck-all to do with you but you were stuck in the middle of anyway.

Maria appeared by my side and gave me a note with her phone number. She told us that the party was over. We thanked her for the invite and left the premises. As we turned at the edge of the drive I could hear raised voices, mostly the black kids pleading their innocence. They may well have let us go because they did not want us to witness something that had nothing to do with us. It was painfully obvious that it was going to turn very ugly. The ICF allowed Gag and me to leave that crime scene without even a mention of a search, although we had both been inside the villa several times. I saw that as a massive mark of respect towards us. When we met up with the lads later that night in Space and told them what had gone on, they agreed.

I actually did see Maria again quite soon afterwards. We were at a rave in Kings Cross when quite surprisingly it kicked off between a group of black girls and a group of white girls. It ended with a big black girl brawling in a vicious one-on-one with who else but Maria. After that night, I think Ibiza-2000AD closed down. It was starting to get moody at the raves now. Lots of money was being made by people who were vulnerable and easy to lean on. Street life was finding the new drug life and bringing some old habits with it. I wasn't bothered though. The seedier it got the more I loved it.

Es Paradis, a venue in San Antonio that filled up with water and bubbles at the end of the evening, was the club we chose to get in our last mess together. We started on it early, straight after the sunset at nearby del Mar. We parked our three Seats and became boozy Brits abroad for several hours until the clubs got going. The last dance was always going to be messy. We each knew that, and with no intention of taking any pills back to England, we were all going to be on five or six numbers each. It doesn't sound a lot, but on top of everything else we had used to poison our bodies, it might just be enough to push one of us over the edge.

The night was rocking and Es Paradis was rammed to the rafters with Scandinavian women and mad clubbers. West Ham were also in there, just the lads, and they had a few new arrivals with them. They looked moodier tonight but still kept to themselves. We had a new arrival with us too. Animal had arrived from Amsterdam on his motorbike with a friend of ours from Leeds. They had ridden a couple of racing bikes over which had both been packed with Es, just like Hopper and Fonda in *Easy Rider*.

Animal surprised none of us when he also proclaimed that he had 1,000 acid tabs on him. "Smiley Faces," he said. Turney chuckled to me devilishly. "Are we having one, J?" I declined. I was already wishing the night was over. It had been a gruelling session and it was starting to weigh heavy with me.

Half an hour later was the turning point in the evening for me. Turney and Warley were in raptures as they pulled me along. "J, come and have a look at Gary." Gag was stood in the mist like a centurion, alone between two Roman pillars. He wore red Kickers with faded baggy jeans, his long sleeve tee-shirt was in bright green and had "Chippy" embroided across it. He was motionless, his hands clasped before him. His eyes remained tightly closed yet he looked up to the heavens with the biggest smiley face any of us had ever seen. Gag looked like he was in heaven. *Fuck it. Where's Animal?* Like fools, we all had to indulge.

Taking acid and then driving was not a good idea at all but we had no choice, the cars had to be handed back to the rental company before nine that morning, plus we had to vacate the apartments by eleven. We set off back to Playa d'en Bossa in a three-car convoy. I was in the lead vehicle, being driven by a tripped-out Turney. It was 5:30am and already the sun was up and at us. Like vampires, we craved the darkened sanctuary of Gag's apartment. We had well over an ounce of pollen to polish off yet. Turney put his foot down and blasted up the music. Like we needed that.

I could see the onion seller on his pushbike. Even Bamf and Warley could see him from in the back. I saw him from more than 500 yards away, clear as day. Turney later said I should have told him at the time. I just saw the bike rider's petrified expression as he pedalled like a man possessed to avoid his deliverance to evil. All three panic-stricken passengers screamed at the driver at once. It was too late CRACK! The cyclist was fortunately shunted up in the air instead of being crushed below the wheels, which kind of softened the shocked stomach blow I felt immediately. He let go of his handlebars in mid-flight and was a good three feet in the air as he watched his departing bicycle land in a ditch several yards away. We all turned and looked at the shocked expressions on our friends' faces in the cars behind us, all mortified, except for Gag, who still had a huge smile on his face and his eyes tightly closed. The lads in the rear car said the bloke was definitely alright because he was on his feet again in seconds, gesticulating as they passed. His bike was a mess though.

I looked at Turney, who was driving on, oblivious of all the fuss. "What?" he asked. His huge smile was innocently evil. I was tempted to suggest that he had really seen the cyclist and had driven over him in a moment of madness, but thought better of it. Instead I offered to drive but he refused to let go of the wheel. We were all more than a little relieved to be back in Gag's apartment, watching him putting the finishing touches to his bucket bong. We still had five hours before we had to vacate the rooms.

When we had arrived back, Roy and Duggie were asleep in bed. They had failed to make it out the previous night so were relatively fresh and obviously had not participated in the acid trip. I sat at the bottom of Roy's bed watching Gag at the table in front of me lovingly loading his bong, his face still creased with laughter lines. Gag had always been known as the Bong

Master General of our firm. He packed them with tons of weed and always had it so the hit was through a nice matured brandy, which gave it that warmth. Now, while in familiar surroundings, the acid overwhelmingly started to kick in.

Everyone found a comfy spot in the apartment and the party started. All left-over drugs, mostly cannabis and cocaine, were declared and thrown on the table in front of Gag, who threw it all into the mix and rubbed his hands as he smiled appreciatively. He toked hard, filling his lungs to capacity. He turned blue before he exhaled, coughed and gipped before reloading. I gipped watching him and I was next up for the bong. After a quick preliminary line of coke, I took a huge cannabis hit through brandy, which I held in to ingest before exhaling. It blew my head off. I softly sat back down on the foot of Roy's bed, then observed the debauchery at close quarters. Everyone was off his head, including Roy and Duggie, who had now started to participate in the mischief.

After my second hit on Gag's bucket bong I began to feel clammy. My conversation ceased. I felt out of it. Everyone else seemed to be OK and partied on at pace. That began to unnerve me a little. I had never lost it before, although I had seen plenty who had, including people present. My confusion levels were rising and I was sure I was about to lose the plot completely. I swallowed hard at the thought of the third hit of cocaine and weed. It was my turn again.

I smiled assuredly at Bamf as I reached forward to take my turn on the big hitter. Gag lit it and I toked hard until I was about to burst. I felt strange but I wasn't about to start acting strange in front of my friends. I was involved with an inner struggle to remain steadfast and composed, then, "Boom." My head exploded again and this time I fell back down into my spot on Roy's bed. Click, the snap of a camera. Warley had been taking pictures of our expressions as we came up from a bong explosion. My expression on that particular shot was lost and vacant, combined with illness and starvation. I looked a fucking mess, but no picture could portray the harrowing experience I was about to endure.

I could feel Roy's legs moving on the bed behind me and I could see Bamf and Gary chuckling between themselves at the table in front of me. All the lads were still sat round doing their thing, only I could not hear them. My head was filled with a dull hollow tone, similar to one you might hear in a hearing test. Only this tone was a little bit different; it sounded sinister and strangely human. I clasped my hands together on my knees and gulped for air. It was at this point that not only could I not hear anyone, I could no longer see anyone. Gone. Blank. All of a sudden it was just me and my nightmares. My vision, for some reason, became focused on my hands down in front of me. They were cupped together and the hollow gap between my entwined thumbs and forefingers looked like a dark, Toblerone-shaped tunnel that disappeared somewhere inside my hands.

Aware of nothing except the tunnel in front of me, my mind pursued its intense train of thought deep into the particles of my epidermis. Everything was magnified to the point that I could actually see the pores of my skin breathing. The dark humming sound in my brain built in momentum as my fascination with the tunnel grew stronger. Now, inside the dark triangular mass, a yellow and black moving chessboard effect appeared. It grabbed my train of thought and pulled me in harder as the noise built again in intensity.

Just as I stepped towards the chessboard that was heading down into the narrowness of the endless tunnel, I was showered in light from flames that burst into life all around the triangular entrance. I noticed hieroglyphics beneath the fire, which unnerved me even more. *What is this tunnel? Where does it go to?* I was starting to fall inside it and I didn't like it.

Bump. According to Bamf, my head just nodded forwards as if I was dozing in the car. He wasn't overly concerned but he knew it wasn't like me and kept his eye on me for a minute. Meanwhile, I sat motionless, fighting the hardest battle of my entire life. Every last morsel of my energy from my stomach up was fighting to stop myself from going down that tunnel. It must have been the moment that Bamf saw my head drop, because against everything my mind was telling me about holding on, I fell over the edge.

Plummeting at a great speed, the chessboard shapes were endless and went on and on, becoming thinner and thinner into the darkness. I was still fighting inside myself to stop and climb back out but it was too late, I had no strength and that dark humming was freaking me out, man. *Who is it? What is it? How will I ever get back from this? Please, no! I don't want to die in here.*

Slap! "Charlie, are you OK?"

My closest mates often called me Charlie after Charlie Chester, the old-time comedian. Bamf had hit me hard across my leg. The interaction catapulted me from deep within myself. I came out of that tunnel in a bolt-action standing movement. Up off the bed and screaming at the top of my voice in sheer terror and relief to be alive and out of that hell. Then I went into convulsions and started gasping for breath. Bamf in one movement slid open the patio door and pulled me through it into the daylight. Everyone in the room sat tight; it was left entirely to Bamf, there was no need to crowd and fuss. Another bong was lit and another camera flash lit the room.

"You're OK man, you've just had too much gear. Take it easy and drink some orange juice." How many times had I said that to some other poor sod. Bamf was easy and relaxed and for a brief moment I could acknowledge to myself that at least I was with someone who knew the score and I could trust. Assessment over, I became confused again, mostly as to where the hell my mind had gone inside that tunnel. The frightening thing was that Bamf had not been there with me so the experience was not shared and therefore could not be resolved jointly. I was on my own and beginning to think that my mind was still inside the tunnel and had not come back out with me.

I turned to Bamf once again in an attempt to explain my anxiety, when his face shattered in front of me. It cracked into a mosaic. From then on, everything I looked at, including buildings, cars, people, the sky, myself, all had a tiled effect. Now I was starting to hate it.

He decided that a brisk walk along the promenade would be the best idea. It would surely bring me round a bit. Nine thirty in the morning and it was already getting hot. People were about. Traffic rushed past as did dogs and a cat, or was that a rat? It moved so quickly. I was feeling alright now, my legs were moving and blood was pumping.

"Good. Keep walking, mate, it will sort you right out. This is just what we needed."

Bamf was doing his best and it was working until, ping, my mind flew across to the other side of the road and I stood there in silence, watching myself and Bamf as he walked alongside me, giving me reassurance. I looked fucking pathetic and I'm not ashamed to admit it. I must have looked a proper cunt to those people with their families trying to cross the road next to me to get to the beach. Babbling like a kid with another grown man next to me trying to coax me along.

Whoosh! I was back staring at Bamf's shattered complexion. "Bamf, I went over there. I went over there. Why did I go over there?" I was now frantic, firm in my belief that I had lost a part of my mind due to the tunnel incident. I wanted it back. I was not prepared to go on in life without it. I was hopelessly trying to explain all this to Bamf as I hyperventilated and had a series of fits. Then I started to run up and down the street in blind panic, looking for what I thought I was missing. It was a comically insane but deadly serious situation. Bamf started to hit me hard with questions that he knew were relevant to me in an attempt to occupy my mind and try to get me back a bit.

"Jasp, Jasp, listen to me, listen to me." He held my shoulders firmly. "Who won the cup in '72 mate? Who won the cup in '72?"

"We did."

"And which player broke your heart by signing for Manchester United?"

"Jimmy Greenhoff."

"Correct. And if you could live anywhere in the world you wanted to, where would it be?"

"Corpus Christi." The Gulf Coast of Texas was my dream destination.

He'd got me back. Quickfire questions worked, but only for as long as Bamf could keep it up. If he stopped asking me the questions my mind pinged into another scenario of me looking on at myself in heartfelt despair. It was soul-destroying for me. Each time I went over there, Bamf yelled, "You're losing it," and my mind immediately returned home and continued to stare into his face once again.

It was taking too long. He decided to take me back to the lads in the hope they would be able to give him a hand. We arrived back at the apartments expecting to find everyone still sat round, casually smoking dope. On the contrary, it was like a scene from *One Flew Over the Cuckoo's Nest* and our arrival was about to make it all the more insane.

I'm sure none of us, including Bamf, had any conception of the time of day it was, but it had gone eleven and on our return the first thing we saw was a rather perturbed maid trying to converse in broken English with Warley. He was standing rooted to the spot in the corridor of one of the apartments wearing only a pair of yellow Bermuda shorts. His lips were blue, he was shaking uncontrollably and cradled an air horn to his chest as would a mother with a child. He looked at the pair of us with a blank, open expression as if he had never seen either of us before in his life.

As I approached him he hugged his air horn tighter as if I were about to take it away from him. It might sound cruel but seeing Warley in such a pathetic state made me feel a whole lot better than I had five minutes earlier. In our absence, Gag had completely demolished the rest of the lads with his bongs. The place stank of hash and Duggie's panic was that any minute the manager, who had already been called by the impatient cleaners, would turn up with the police and we would all be carted off. He had a point. A handful of crumpled and sweaty currency bought us an extra hour to pack our things and clear off. In disgust the management and maids left us to it, or should I say, to Duggie and Roy.

All of us who had participated in Animal's acid were totally smashed out of our brains. Roy and Dugg sat us down in one room and then led two at a time to a pile of clothes and a selection of holdalls. Each item of clothing was then held up and shown and on the strength of a nod it would be packed away as luggage. This was a prolonged affair, as every item that was packed was then removed unseen by Gag and placed on another pile. Roy and Dugg both said that if they had their time again they would have thrown everything in together and sorted it out when we got back home. You live and learn.

I sat alone on a chair in the long corridor between the bedrooms and the lounge, where everyone else was congregated in silence. I could see them all from where I was. Each dribbled childishly and rocked in motion, and some even took to inspecting at length the patterns on the furniture. If I looked the other way I could see Warley still standing silently, cradling his air horn as he stared inside the bedroom at whatever his trip was showing him. He looked terrified.

Without Bamf to coax me along, my mind started to go again. I asked Warley if he knew why it was that I went down that tunnel and why I kept going over there. His tiled expression was vacant and he made no attempt at speech. *Oh my God, what has happened to us?* This was a bunch of lads that partied hard every week all over the country, got in some real messes together and enjoyed every minute of it. This was the first ever time that we had all fed off each other in such a way that it had gone badly for us.

I was falling hard down that tunnel. No strength. There seemed no turning back from that blackness. Then my mind was yanked back out by Bamf's slap on my leg. He got me out of there. I was now positively convinced that I had been dying and going to hell for all my sins. It was my time. I remember conceding to the situation. I really had gone, I know that for a fact. I mean, what was at the end of that fucking tunnel? Coma? Death? I don't know to this day, but that was where all the confusion of my trip was coming from. *Was I in this awful state because Bamf had pulled me back prematurely from death and in doing so left a piece of my mind behind, causing me to be in this nightmare world of tiled confusion? Fuck, I'm hot.*

I was mentally overloading again. Feeling hot and uncomfortable, I chose to slide down off my seat and lie face down on the cold corridor floor. *Oh no, not again. It was back.* "No, please, it's coming to take me away." I started to slither face down along the corridor, almost like an evolving sea creature reaching terra firma for the first time. Neither I nor Warley paid any attention to each other as I passed by his feet and slithered out of sight into the bathroom. I could not feel or use my legs, so reached up with my arm and grabbed hold of the basin. Still convinced I was going to die, I also knew I needed water.

With what strength I could muster, it took me several minutes to finally pull myself level with the taps. Using one hand to steady myself and the other to splash my face, I began talking out loud in an incoherent panic. "It's not working is it? The water's not working. I really am fucked aren't I? Oh my God." Devastated, I mulled over my reflection in the mirror before me. Never had I seen such a face of death, my own dead face. I looked shattered, my eyes lifeless and set deeply in the back of my head. Beat up and forlorn, I slid back down on to the floor and proceeded to stare resignedly at my feet. It was over for me, I'd gone.

I took no part in the packing of my belongings, that was done for me and I spent the rest of that day lying on a sunbed in the shade with everyone else. Wheaty had eventually managed to get me to drink some orange juice and I started to come round a bit. There was still nine hours to wait before our flight so we hung around the pool. Funnily enough, no one else did. It was a scorching day and not one other person would come anywhere near us. We must have looked a right state.

We got home. And Gwilty kept his promise to bring us all a pill for our journey back to Stoke in his furniture van.

"Jasp. Are you having this pill or what mate?"

"What sort is it?"

"I don't know but it's in a capsule. Looks alright."

"All right then. Chuck us one over. Cheers. I don't mind a pill, especially if it's a clean one, but I'm not having fucking acid ever again."

I never have. I did take Es for another three or four years though, probably up until the point when we'd sit around at Brunty's flat from Friday until Monday with four or five others, demolish about twenty pills a day and then complain in the taxi later on about having heart convulsions and not being able to see past your nose. I think it was at that point I gave up the Es and just made my tipple the odd reefer and my old advocate, Sir Charles himself.

Most us got through it, sadly some did not. But the E culture and its deadly accompaniments tore us away from the mundane and choking society we came from. When we few lads from Stoke started going to the dance parties, the scene was in its infancy. Everybody who attended those bashes was in the know. It started with the London clique and spread through a creative grapevine, attracting the country's most flamboyant people. It must be our fault then, the way it turned out. It was all fine and dandy when the first few football heads found that new platform to perform on. Perhaps we brought what is seedy about our culture with us. Perhaps we dragged it down.

When I finally cleaned myself up in 1994, the drug culture I was rid of had finally turned sour. Es were a quid apiece and normally manufactured locally. You were literally risking your life on a pill and too many people around me were losing theirs. It didn't make sense.

As for my thoughts on my experience in the tunnel, I owe Bamf for that one. I wasn't coming back and I'm glad he got me. I do think still that a part of my mind was lost somewhere that morning. I have suffered from black mood swings ever since, regularly have open conversations with myself, and find it very difficult to play chess. You've gotta have a laugh though, haven't you?

Chapter Six

Crazy Danny

"TELL HIM TO open the bag so I can look at them properly."

I didn't like the way he just shoved the one nine-bar at me to have a look at. Yeah, it burnt right and it smelt the bollocks but I wasn't handing over a penny until I'd tested what was in the bag as well.

The ageing Spanish gypsy was taking us for a bunch of mugs. We could tell he was reluctant to hand over the bag with the other five kilos in, and that's never a good sign in this business, especially when you've got several grand with you, you're miles away from the nearest road, the Finca you're in is full of cutthroats, and roaming about outside are some of the meanest looking dogs you've ever set eyes on.

As usual, it was me doing the negotiating. I thought to myself, *How the fuck have I allowed Wilson to drag me over to Spain, several years after I had left it behind. Just because he's now divorced and is determined to be able to say he's been and done it too.* I unconsciously rubbed my elbow across the carving knife I had hidden inside my shirt. I was thinking about our conversation on the way up in the motor.

"Right it's simple. If it comes on top we just start stabbing and get the fuck out of the place, OK?"

151

I knew that both Wilson and Tommy were carrying weaponry and neither would hesitate to use it. I'd thought we would be searched before we entered the remote, ramshackle building. When we weren't, I'd thought, *Great, this is going to be straight business*, but now I wasn't sure. La Linea de la Frontera had changed on my return. All the old contacts from the early Eighties were either dead or serving stiff jail sentences in Algeciras nick. After much thought and against my better judgement I ventured inside the ruthless high-rise Coneco estate in the west end of the town. I remembered it well: I'd been coshed, robbed and left for dead in the gutter after taking a drunken wrong turn one night and getting lost in the maze of identical apartment blocks. I was only twenty-two at the time and I was that pissed I can't remember what happened. Apparently I was found by some street sweepers early the next morning and was taken to hospital, where I was treated for concussion and two broken fingers on my right hand.

It was a place that I would normally avoid at all costs, but with Wilson wanting to fulfil his dream of being in a Spanish adventure that he could tell everyone about back home, I reluctantly went inside the estate, found someone who looked like a hash dealer, and struck up a conversation in my pidgin Spanish. A rushed deal was set up and that very night we ended up here, in this fucking hole with this lot, fifteen miles inland from the coast, up a dirt track and over a mile away from where we had parked our car. *Nice one, Wilson, I hope you're happy now because that last bar of soap I just tasted was fucking pudding and this cunt knows that we are on to them.*

I'm gonna stab this bastard in front of me first, then the one by the doors, I thought, although I was praying it wouldn't come to that.

The argument started and we stood up immediately. The

gypsies in the room all became agitated and started talking in fast Andalucian slang, which was good because it was the slang that I understood and not the proper Spanish language. Two of the five were obviously against the scam and began telling the man with the bag that we knew the score. The Spanish argued with each other until I abruptly interrupted them.

"Hey, que pasa?"

I grabbed the bag he was carrying and pulled out two of the bars I had tried and waved them at him.

"No bueno. No fucking bueno."

Only two of the kilos they'd brought were real, the other three were formula and not worth a dime. I reckoned the only way to get out of there without conflict was to strike up a deal for the two good ones and then fuck off sharpish. The Spanish calmed down when I pulled the money belt from around my waist. Now was the time, if it was coming, that they would attempt to rob us. A glance to the left and then to the right told me that Tommy and Wilson were both ready and had their fingers on the trigger.

The exchange took place simultaneously, then the gypsy began to laugh, followed by the rest of them. He shook the bag containing the formula and continued laughing.

"This no good, eh, no good."

"No it fucking isn't, mate. It's shit. Merde."

Confidently, the three of us made our way towards the door of the Finca and left one at a time. I turned and spied the gypsies thumbing through the bundle of peseta notes. They looked like a pack of hungry hyenas around fallen prey, sad bastards. It's a good job I know the score with the hash or we would have been had right over there.

Maybe I should have seen the warning signs and heeded them straight away. Things had changed since I had last been over there. Old haunts closed down, friends in jail and robbing bastards with dodgy gear. I wondered if Benidorm was still the same?

Like we had a couple of years before, Tommy, Wilson and I took the overnight coach from Algeciras up to northern Spain, which for those with the back seat to themselves was a breeze. Being clever, I grabbed a seat to myself and ended up being crushed against the window from the mountain city of Granada onward by the smelliest Spanish Fatty Arbuckle imaginable. He turned me blue in the face every time we went round a corner as he suffocated me without even noticing. Two stops down the line, Arbuckle chose to relocate to another part of the coach when another seat became vacant. Although they pretended to be asleep, I could still hear that pair of bastards laughing at my first real tantrum of the trip.

I couldn't sleep, my veins were pumping adrenalin. With my mind racing I sat looking out into the blackness, half admiring myself in my reflection, half counting the endless stream of telegraph poles. I found coach journeys monotonous when they were not heading to a football ground. I analysed my situation once again to see if I could make some sense of my best mate's request to take him on a mad adventure somewhere abroad.

I love Tommy to bits. He's been there from the start and is one of our biggest, roughest-looking bruisers. But he should never have come with us on that trip. Like Wilson, he was coming out of a broken marriage. Unlike Wilson, he was not devoid of emotion and, as big and horrible as he looked, was a deeply sensitive and caring man at heart. His separation was made all the more worse because he had children.

I rested my head back against my seat. Here I was on a coach travelling through the night in a foreign country, carrying an amount of cannabis resin in a sports bag and also carrying the weight of two newly divorced men, one emotionally imbalanced, the other a complete lunatic, a former pro boxer who had just found speed and cannabis to go with new-found freedom from an Italian wife who was just as bad as him. Nothing was ever straight with Wilson, it was high tension all the way. *God knows what he will be like when I get him to Benidorm and introduce him to acid and Ecstasy.*

It was an unbalanced ship with an impetuous loony on one side, a sad deflated hulk on the other, and me in the middle. Wilson mad for it, Tommy lost, and me wishing I had never opened the bloody door that hazy Sunday morning and agreed to go with him even though I was quite happy and the bird I was screwing at the time was a belter. What I decided to do was, as always, enjoy myself; shag as many women as I could, get Wilson completely off his head and keep a close eye on Tommy. Next stop Benidorm. I never say no to a friend.

I did not fancy staying in the scummy, rundown Aquarius apartment block one bit, but no, Wilson had to do it, just like Eddie and the lads had when they'd been over here. *Can't have anyone doing something you haven't done as well, can you mate?* We paid for a month up front, I wouldn't let Wilson pay for any longer. For some reason I could not see us being there that long.

I led the two of them down the hill into the heart of the teeming resort, reminiscing along the way. I was not going to be a selfish bastard and tell them that it was crap and not as good as it used to be, and it was still full of fanny anyway, so I took them straight into Top of the Pops, where we proceeded to get stinking drunk. We staggered home at gone seven in the morning. None of us had pulled.

There was no getting away from it. Benidorm had changed, and significantly. I noticed a sinister air to the place, unlike my memory of sun-baked frolics and casual sex. What I saw now was suspicion and nervousness dand no casual sex. Don't get me wrong, the sleaze was still there, it always will be. It's just that when I'm in an environment that is icy and unpredictable, I very rarely look at a woman as anything other than a potential problem. I become stern and unapproachable. Couple that with the fact that my two travelling companions were in a different queue to me when the good looks were given out, at any club we went in we stood out like three spare pricks at a wedding.

We needed some drugs to liven things up. With none of the old props there to point us in the right direction, we had to weed out the dealers for ourselves and decide whether they looked kosher or not. Eventually we met a kid from Coventry who had acid and pills. He said he was football but we doubted it. Nevertheless, his gear looked bang on so we bought it. He noticed my spliff and asked if he could buy a joint from me, as he'd not had a smoke for more than a week. This seemed strange for someone with a pocketful of drugs and I inquired why.

"Can't get it at the moment mate, we're waiting for Danny to get us some."

I left the conversation there. Danny was the supplier, and obviously, at the moment had none of his own. Tommy, Wilson and I might decide to help out this Danny, whoever he was. I bit off a lump of my dope and gave it to the youth.

"Right, we're off. Cheers for the pills, mate."

"Yeah, no problem lads, you'll fucking love them."

Actually, I was sick of them and it had been well over a year since I had contaminated my body with the stuff. What I was going to enjoy, though, was watching the state of Wilson after I gave him his first ever acid trip and E at the same time. This I could not wait to see, I just wished some of the others back home could witness it as well, especially the ones who had endured his selfish lack of understanding of how sensitive people can be whilst under the influence of such things. The list of people who have not received a heavy-handed bollocking from Wilson round our way is very limited indeed. I'm not knocking him, he's my best mate, although I haven't always understood why we have ended up in the particular warring factions we did at certain times, largely through his actions. Despite our own venomous arguments, I have stuck by him and always will. At the end of the day I think we just love to differ, and I suppose that is something that will never change. It's the way we are with each other, and one reason why people in Stoke see us as so unpredictable whenever we are out together.

I knew that the next twenty or so hours was going to be a scream, well, at least for me and Tommy. What Wilson would be like throughout would be down to how he handled his trip and how much I decided to freak him out.

"How you feeling, Ode?" – Ode being a Stoke expression of friendship. Wilson was at the dining table, thumbing through a deck of cards and staring vacantly at a frameless Spanish fishing village scene that hung askew on the living room wall, and moved only his bulging eyes in reply. His mouth began to open and shut but nothing audible came out. I looked at my watch and winked at Tommy. It had been more than half an hour since he had dropped a red windowpane (acid tab) and a white dove (Ecstasy) simultaneously and he was approaching a bomb-blast reaction in his head.

"Jasp, turn the music up."

"Why?"

"It's fucking brilliant."

"It's Spanish radio, mate."

"I know. I love it."

Wilson drew back his chair and started to perform what looked like a skinhead moonstomp combined with the cha-cha. He was coming up and me and Tommy were hysterical watching it. There was no stopping him now and Wilson demanded that we go back to Top of the Pops immediately.

We arrived back at the club and were enthusiastically greeted by the head doorman. Pascal was a Basque. He was handsome, huge and fair and the only face in Benidorm I recognised from my previous visits. We shook hands and entered the raw basement venue. I bought Pascal a drink and chatted briefly. He said he was surprised to see me. I told him I thought the place had changed and he nodded in agreement. Wilson and Tommy headed to the edge of the dance floor and stood ogling at the strobe-enhanced beauties strutting their stuff so provocatively on it. Top of the Pops was rocking that night.

I was enjoying myself now. Live for the day. Wilson certainly was. I ambled back and stood beside the pair of them. "How's it going?" Wilson shook my hand hard. His face was contorted and covered in sweat. He smiled at me without speaking and then hurled himself on to the middle of the dance floor. I was shocked, as he was no dancer, but not as shocked as the dozens of startled clubbers who were now forming a semi-circle around the sweat-soaked man who looked like he was having a fistfight with himself. Wilson's huge freckled fingers formed into a heavyweight's fist and punched the air all around him as he grinned and shook his head. He smiled at me and Tommy and gave us the thumbs up. I smiled and gave him the gesture back. I turned to Tommy and spoke into his ear.

"Ha, he's enjoying himself now, mate. You wait until that acid kicks in."

Tommy and I looked back over to the windmilling Wilson and smiled. Until now the Ecstasy in Wilson's system had overridden the acid. The pills were strong and he was feeling euphoria that his dreams were being fulfilled. After years of work and marriage, he was finally liberated. The dance floor calmed down as the clubbers realised that the man with the freckled fingers was only attempting to dance and not fight with them all.

"Enjoy that, mate?"

Wilson had made his return and was standing beside me looking extremely bemused.

"Seen that?" he said.

"What?" I chuckled as I said it. Wilson had danced the E out of him and the acid was now taking dominance.

"What?" Transfixed, he pointed. He was definitely tripping now because as hard as I looked I just could not see a six foot tall dancing Rastafarian Statue of Liberty with dreadlocks to his arse and playing a guitar whilst smoking a reefer.

"Good in here, innit?" Wilson agreed.

"Hello lads, how's it going? Those things alright were they?" It was the lad from Coventry with a couple of his mates.

"Yeah, not bad, cheers. My mate's having a good time anyway."

"Listen, I was just wondering if we could buy enough for a couple of spliffs off you?"

"Why? Danny not got any yet then?"

"No, he's back tomorrow though."

"Yeah well, if he's had no luck, tell him we may be able to help him out."

"OK, will do."

I handed them the lump of draw I had in my pocket, and the three of us returned to Aquarius to continue with Wilson's hysterical first ever trip on acid. We never saw the Coventry kid again and, looking back, there was probably a reason for that although we did not know it at the time.

Top of the Pops was busy. There was Pascal standing commandingly outside, the old charmer making light with the ladies as they entered the club. He looked over and we exchanged acknowledgements. The other two doormen remained expressionless but saw me all the same.

The headlights of a silver Jensen Interceptor lit the wall of the club opposite as it rounded the corner and pulled slowly to a stop outside Top of the Pops. We took in the arrival, paying attention to the smooth bodywork of the piece of art parked in front of us. The driver's door opened. He was a dead ringer for a young Nick Nolte but bigger and leaner. He walked to the back of his car and opened the small boot. He had our attention. Still in a calm, relaxed manner, he reached inside and pulled out a wheel brace. Must have got a puncture, I thought. The man closed the boot, then instead of attempting to remove his punctured tyre, he purposefully walked the several yards over towards Pascal and his two colleagues, and in a precise and clinical way, proceeded to knock the living daylights out of all three of them.

I had seen a man battered to death before and it left a lasting impression. What I saw here was just as dreadful. The man executing this unprovoked attack was an animal and the sheer number of unnecessary head shots to the three incapacitated men was shocking. When there was little if any life at all left in his victims, he walked away, tossed the brace back inside the boot, got in, adjusted his rear view mirror and drove off.

We looked at each other in silence until Tommy spoke. "Ermm, don't mind where I go, mate. Don't fancy Top of the Pops tonight, though."

I couldn't get off without first seeing if Pascal was alright. I walked over and joined the gathering crowd. They looked a mess. All three were out cold, one in particular looked a ghastly grey colour and concern for him was mounting among the shocked onlookers. Although I did not know Pascal that well, I was thankful it was not him slumped in that awful state, even though he looked bad enough.

What the hell was that all about? I said to myself. *And who the hell was that psychopath? He certainly wasn't here last time. I definitely would have remembered.*

We were later informed by a street peddler that the man in question was Crazy Danny from Belgium. He was the wayward son of an international crime boss from Antwerp who afforded his boy enough money and protection to go and set up wherever he pleased, and obviously do whatever he wanted. Apparently everybody, including the Guardia Civil, was petrified of him. *No shit.* I could see why. Putting two and two together, Danny was obviously the geezer who the Coventry kid worked for, the geezer who was supposed to be bringing in some hash. In my bed that night I remained thoughtful for some time.

Within a matter of days things become a lot clearer to me. The unprovoked attack on Pascal and his door staff seemed more like a warning to us rather than a message to them, one he had executed ruthlessly. All three of us agreed that Danny had obviously taken the Coventry kid's message from me to him as an infringement on his business and, no doubt, his town. I think I had pissed him off a touch.

When the summons arrived, it was delivered to me personally via a bent policeman known to me from the old days. This in itself carried weight, showing us how much power and influence he held and buckling us at the knees in the very first round.

"Crazy Danny wants us to meet him on the roof of the Penelope at twelve on Tuesday night."

"What day is it today?"

"Friday. He's making us wait." Second round and we were cut badly and panting for breath.

Tuesday eventually arrived. We got to the Penelope at eleven, an hour early. I used to know the management and door staff at the club, but no longer. On that basis I found it unnerving when we were called directly in and then taken towards the steps leading to the roof.

"How the fucking hell did those doormen know who we were?"

"I know mate, the cunt's got eyes and ears all over the place."

This was more psychology being used on us by the Belgian Brute. Third round, winded a little but finding our feet in the ring.

It was serene up on that rooftop. The moon was magnificent and smiling reassuringly, and I reckon his money was on us for the fourth and fifth. I winked back and sat down with Tommy and Wilson on a large ceramic flowerpot.

"Do you think he'll come?" Wilson's tongue-in-cheek humour took the edge off for a minute or two. Then, as the clock struck midnight, the big man appeared. He was alone.

I stood and walked to meet him. The closer he got, the bigger he grew, so the more I looked for an opening somewhere on his body to make my move if it came to it. He stopped. I stopped. There were several strides between us. He looked only at me. And then he spoke.

"Me Crazy Danny from Belgium. Aaarrrggghhh!"

His mammoth roar erupted as his rigid body pumped and grew bigger still. Fists clenched beside him, jugular bursting from his neck, his face was contorted and evil. An insane rush went through me. *Right, come on Jasp, get in him now while you've got the opportunity. Which part do I go for? Kick him in the bollocks. No. Go for the kneecap instead, yeah, cripple the bastard.*

Danny had given me the chance if I'd wanted to take it, but I didn't; instead I was going to see it through. His introduction over, he looked me directly in the eye and waited. *Oh well. He has left me no choice whatsoever here. I'm going to have to do it.*

I held the man's fierce stare and introduced myself back.

"Me Crazy Jasper from Stoke. Aaarrrggghhh!"

I was bursting my lungs and brain cells as I stood staring back up at the moon to see if he was still smiling at me, and all the while thinking, *Jesus Christ, I have left myself so wide open here. If it is going to come, it will be now.*

But it didn't. Nothing came. And when I had stopped screaming into the heavens I looked Danny straight back in the eye. His facial expression gave away nothing, but the two-second pause before he spoke told me that I had surprised him with my reply. Instead of seeing me as a cheeky bastard, I think he admired my style.

His instructions were plain and simple: to meet him on a beach north of town the next night. Then he departed without another word. We three left too, with much to think about.

"Skin up, Jasp."

"Good idea mate, pass us the skins."

Was it a set-up or was it straight business? None of us knew the answer. Were we going to meet him or were we going to do one? Only one answer. Yes, I was going to be on that secluded beach at 8pm that very next night.

"You coming mate?"

Good, Wilson was coming too. Tommy? Well Tommy didn't say much, he looked somewhere else, so I didn't push it.

My tongue was stuck to the roof of my mouth. I didn't fancy getting out of bed and walking to the kitchen but I was dehydrating and needed some liquid. I opened the fridge door. The bright glare from within cast a different light inside the silent apartment. A movement outside on the balcony caught my eye. I took a bottle, slowly slid open the door and walked out.

"You OK, Tommy?"

My friend was hunched over the balcony looking out over the orange glow of the coast. He seemed caught up in his moment. I moved next to him and took the photograph he was holding out of his hand. He turned and looked at me as I gazed at the most important things in his life, his children.

"Listen Tommy, you don't have to come with us tomorrow night mate." I handed him back his photograph. "Get yourself back home. This is Wilson's fucked-up adventure and I'm in it for him. You don't have to be."

I put my arm around the big man. I didn't feel sorry for my old pal as he left us that next morning, not one bit. In fact I envied him in a way. Tommy had something to go home for, something special, the love of his children, a love I have never had the pleasure of embracing. Wilson and I were just a pair of cunts loving each thing that life had the audacity to throw at us. Benidorm was the first leg of a nine-country adventure that was about to stretch out over the next twelve months, a year fraught with tension and excitement.

Tommy's taxi got caught in traffic at the end of the street. We stood watching until it was out of sight.

"Right, what are we going to do about this meeting tonight?"

"I don't know but I'm putting my trainers on and polishing my new duster."

The puzzling thing was that at no time had I told anyone exactly how much cannabis we had with us, which was a bit disconcerting. This looked all the more like a set-up. I opened the bag with the weed in and emptied the solid slabs noisily on to the table. The measly two kilos we had started out with was now more like one and three-quarters as we had already smoked a nine-bar of it. We decided to go for a couple of beers. Weighing it up, we could be getting ourselves in a whole lot of trouble for a whole lot of nothing here.

"Doss sevecas po fo voa."

Wilson's Spanish tickled me, especially when they answered him in their own lingo and he embarrassingly reverted back to speaking in sign-language-enhanced broken English. Eventually, two large beers did arrive and we continued our discussion about the meet with Crazy Danny. Did we really want to put ourselves in a precarious situation again? The meet with the Spanish gypos had been bad enough and I thought we were lucky to get out of that one. I wasn't too sure about Danny, and neither was Wilson. But then there was the question of bottle and were we shitting out? Even though this mischief was bordering on madness, we had no choice, as we would never forgive ourselves for denying each other the buzz we needed so badly to live off.

"Fuck it, we're Stoke City, let's go."

Two high-powered motorbikes rolled up to the junction of the street. A visor slowly lifted and the mischievous smiling eyes of our friend Animal glared at the pair of us. The cavalry had arrived – and on time for a change. Animal was en route from Amsterdam to Ibiza with one of our friends from the Leeds Service Crew. The two bikes they were riding weighed heavy with goods. They spent the night with us at Aquarius, where we told them about Danny and the meet. Interesting, Animal and our Yorkshire friend agreed.

We arrived on that secluded beach as sunlight was beginning to fade from a warm, inviting cherry red to a chilly, eerie inkwell blue. We used the lights from the bikes to see, but stood well away from the vehicles in the darkness. The powerful sound of the approaching fast moving rig could be heard but not seen. All the same, we knew it was Danny. He was clever in his psychology, we will give him that. The last place we expected to see him arrive from was the sea itself.

He came alone again and immediately shouted at us to extinguish the lights. We did and he strode imposingly across the beach towards us. We began to look around in the darkness as the sound of approaching footsteps could now be heard worryingly on crunching gravel. It was now obvious that Danny had only arrived alone from the front. We were in fact surrounded. I reached for my cosh, knowing full well it would be a hopeless retaliatory weapon against anything these fellas had. We glanced over our shoulders and counted five, maybe more, thickset heavies lurking and looking menacing. More psychology, I hoped. *Let's get down to business for Pete's sake, we already know the score.*

Danny stood and counted our numbers, taking in the new faces intently. We remained silent and probably compliant as well.

"Why two more?" he nodded at each of our friends.

"Because we have got something you may like as well as the hash." Animal was cool and deliberate.

All four of us were now bang on with our thoughts of how this meeting was going to progress, and they were worrying. *All this for one and half kilos of cannabis resin? I don't think so.* The only way to get out of this was by doing what Animal had instinctively done: make it worth his while.

We got off that beach that night by off-loading a tank full of acid tabs bound for the clubs of Ibiza. A slight dip in profit for the lads, obviously, but money back and with it, thankfully, our lives. We all agreed that Danny was planning to get rid of Wilson and me that night. Whatever means he intended to use, I'm glad to say I don't know. I guess the unpredictable nature of the man worked in our favour. Animal had given him something to be unpredictable about. Imagine his evil face if I had pulled out just six bars of hash to offer him. It didn't bear thinking about.

The next day, glad to hit the road, we all headed over to Ibiza, where we spent the next couple of months smoking dope and arguing over whether I should have kicked Crazy Danny in the balls when I had the chance. Personally I think I made the right choice.

Fast bucks, fast rucks and fast fucks, we chased them all. On reflection it wasn't just Benidorm or any of the other places we lived in that had changed, it was life in general, and me in particular. It's called life's progression, and as I hardened and matured I could better see the dangers that had always been out there. It was just that now I was sailing a lot closer to them. So that was it for me, I had exhausted Spain – or had it exhausted me? After Ibiza, and Wilson being able to say that he had been and done it too, I was going home. It was time to watch some football and spend some quality time with my Naughty family on the terraces.

I remained open to offers and would go anywhere at the drop of a hat if it was with the right set of lads and it sounded different. For now, I did not know where or when that would be. One thing was for sure, though. My liking for the odd line of cocaine was becoming more than recreational. Warning bells were ringing, but how the hell do you keep a lid on it when you are partying seven nights a week? In the circumstances, heading for the party capital of the western world was a bit of a bad idea.

Chapter Seven

The Lads' Tales

THE FOLLOWING FOUR stories illustrate different aspects of the football hooligan culture and life that I am trying to portray: taking drugs (sometimes to excess), following England, and serving time. All of the N40 have experienced at least one of these, and some all three. The first of these tales was told to me by Barry Sargeant, the lad who experienced it; the others are told directly by those who were there.

Graham and Pauline Sargeant were strict parents but also loving and supportive to their three children, Jody, Stephen and Barry. Nothing strange about; the vast majority of families in 1970s Britain were no different. Is that not what put the Great into our old country? When neighbours would stand at their gates and chat a while.

"Oh they are a lovely family, the Sargeants. I think Pauline has got her hands full with the eldest Barry, though. He will end up in prison one of these days, you mark my words." The housewives' sentence. The black mark. The teachers' curse. They were right though. Barry was going to go to prison. Several times.

Milton, on the east side of Stoke, was not that rough a place unless you wanted it to be. Gang culture was nearly a decade away from the adolescent Barry, who spent most of his early childhood days playing football and building dams in streams at the nearby Bagnal woods. The theft of a car or tooting of a pipe? Kids did not do that type of thing in those days. Barry's crime was being mischievous.

The early to mid Eighties saw the rise of one gang in particular that changed the street scene of the city of Stoke-on-Trent. A new, vicious identity was being forged among the foundries and pot banks and pits. Young, disenchanted teenagers were hearing the myth and spreading the word. "Get down to Stoke on Saturday, it's going to go off. The Naughty Forty are planning an attack. There is going to be blood spilt. Lots of it."

It was not long before similar gangs were forming all over the suburbs. Milton was no exception. Lynchy and Mellor were several years older than Barry. They were the founder members of the MGC, the Milton Game Casuals. It was they who introduced the bright lights of Hanley to a young Mr Sargeant. They used one pub in particular, Leadbellies, the headquarters of the N40. You only drank in there if you were accepted.

It was not long before Barry was. Tough street fights and inter-estate warfare had seen a teenager gain respect and enforce a reputation on all bar none. Like so many others in our city a nickname came with the turf. "Fucking hell, that's Mad Barry Sargeant over there. He has just got out of young offenders for fighting with some blokes twice his age." And so on. During his apprenticeship with the N40, as with so many of the other youngsters, he was picked up and nurtured by one of the older, more established members. Barry's mentor was Lee Carter, a legend in his own right and now a sadly missed member of our extended family. Carter saw in Barry what we, the "old school", had seen in him. From then on, no questions were asked. It's as simple as that with a football firm. You either make it in or you don't.

The pair of them became inseparable over the years. After one particular night of heavy partying, Barry suffered a brain haemorrhage and fell the full flight of Carter's stairs. He landed badly in the hallway. An ambulance was called and Carter performed resuscitation, actually keeping his friend alive until he was taken to hospital. It's fair to say that these two would have died for each other.

Eventually Barry's football antics saw him start his second prison sentence, and so he found himself in HMP Strangeways, Manchester, in June 1990. Those of us old enough to remember the Strangeways Riot that summer, one of the defining events in the history of the British penal system, will no doubt visualise the roof top demonstration and the carnage that preceded it. We as a nation were permitted to see what the Government allowed us to, whereas Barry saw events at first hand.

Barry came to my home and stayed with me for several days. We sat for hours at a time. Barry spoke and I listened. At times we fell silent. I could see it was more than difficult for him to put into words some of the painful memories. I too at times felt shocked. I also believe every word he told me about his ordeal. Why shouldn't I? I'd trust him implicitly to watch my back in a row. Barry's family and that's that.

In 1990, Barry was nineteen and could drink as much as anyone. He would fight any man. And he loved his mum, Pauline, more than anything else in the whole world.

"Barry Sargeant, I sentence you to nine months in a young offenders' institute." The magistrate was already looking at the papers for the next case as Barry was being led away. He was hardly fazed by another little stint at Werrington YOI, close to Stoke. Barry accepted his sentence and the street cred that went with it and disappeared with a wink and a grin down to the cells below.

But when the door shut behind him, all of a sudden he was hit by loneliness. His mates had all left the courtroom and headed to the pub to salute him, but he'd just been informed by the screw that it wasn't cushy Werrington he was going, but a week in Manchester's Strangeways gaol whilst being allocated a place at a young offenders' institute elsewhere in the northwest. *Get your head round that one, Mister Cocksure.*

He was confined in a twelve-foot cell for twenty-three hours a day with three other people he'd never met before. It smelled of body odour and human waste. He was given one small bowl of water a day with which he was to wash, shave, clean his teeth, and swill the mess off his eating utensils. If he wanted to have a piss or a shit, it came in handy for that purpose as well, as long as you did not mind having an audience. These were Victorian prison conditions at the end of the Twentieth Century. Barry was shattered by it all. He was not so cocksure anymore, and was looking forward to having a visit from his mum the following Sunday.

Sunday eventually came. It had only been several days but it had seemed like an eternity. Time crawls by in jail. That morning Barry woke, slopped out, ate breakfast, returned to his cell and waited for his visit. His heart hung heavy. He was pleased he was going to see his mother but also deeply ashamed that he had to put her through all this. Why should she have to come inside this filthy place? She had not done anything wrong, ever. But that's what mothers do for their sons. That's if you've got a mother who loves you.

With it being Sunday, a day for religion and peaceful reflection, each of the cells was opened and the prison officers offered the convicts the opportunity to go to the chapel. On this particular day, requests to visit the chapel were abnormally high. Why alarm bells didn't start ringing amongst the staff, Heaven only knows. Barry chose to be the heathen he is, and refused a visit to church and a chance to get out of his cell. In all probability he was too scared to venture out amongst the hardened villains that he could hear but not see through his closed cell door.

It was at this point that Barry made it clear to me as we sat in my living room that he could only give me his version of events after what took place in the church. He also made it clear that at no time did he get physically involved in the rioting. He almost looked like a scared nineteen-year-old boy as he remembered the sadistic acts of barbarism he faced that day.

Barry sat back down on his bunk after pacing the cell a dozen times. He was lost in his confinement, pressure heavy on his brain. At least he was getting a parental visit. His cellmate wasn't going to get one. Howard never got visits.

The prison takeover started in the chapel pulpit. More than 300 men had attended the service that morning and many had smuggled in weapons. It was fair to say that these human beings had come to the end of their tether with the inhumane conditions in which they had to survive. Treat people like animals and expect them to behave worse. Their commitment was undying. The power of their takeover was unequivocal.

It was the noise that got the attention of Barry and his friendless cellmate. The church door was in direct view from their meshed cell window. They both crammed their faces into it and attempted to digest the scenes that were unfolding down below them. Prison warders were being stretchered out of the building. Some were covered in blood and looked in distress. Others stood silent, watching in shock. Although slightly muted, the noises they could hear from within the church had them gripped in sheer terror. Neither spoke but each knew the other had never witnessed violence on such a scale. "Jesus!" Barry was wishing he had never got into trouble now. They both wanted to hide.

It had been a well-thought-out plan, and the cons secured several vital parts of the prison before the riot police and emergency services attempted their arrival. The kitchens and an accommodation wing were two key targets, but most important was the hospital wing and its greatly desired pharmacy. It was not long before a percentage of the cons were completely out of their minds.

Neither Barry nor Howard could speak a coherent word. The noise from the rioting prisoners began to haunt the landings as the carnage moved inside. Sat quietly on their bunks, they were almost like condemned men waiting for the priest to appear and read them their last rites. The hysteria outside their closed cell door was getting worryingly closer.

CRASH. The steel-plated door was almost smashed off its hinges. Barry and Howard both let out a hollow gasp and remained seated on their bunks.

"Out."

His instruction was blunt and he looked like the meanest motherfucker they had ever seen. They rose gingerly and stepped slowly towards the open door. Barry likened it to standing at the gates of Hell. Everybody was enveloped in a destructive, Satanic orgy as they tore the prison apart.

The two youngsters said little but thought exactly the same thing. Both were on short sentences. It would be a lot easier for them if they went back inside the cell, closed the door and let it blow over a bit. They had no idea that what was unfolding before them was going to be the worst riot in British prison history. Their plan to sit it out was shortlived. No sooner were their arses back down on the bunks than the command was given again, only this time it was even more forceful.

"Fucking out now, you cunts. Out."

Barry stammered in panic back to the demonic rioter, "I'm just getting my letters." He would have cringed at his own remark if he had not been so terrified. Given no choice at all, he then stepped out onto the landing. The noise was deafening as the mayhem had stepped up a gear. Tables, doors, televisions and piss buckets rained down from the landings above. Cons took the law into their own hands and butchered their enemies. It was impossible to tear your vision away from some sort of barbaric act without looking at something else that was twice as bad.

Just as Barry was about to close his eyes and wish it all away, he saw someone on the landing opposite, casually walking through the mayhem with a ghettoblaster on his shoulder and smoking a £20 note. As he strolled by Barry, without even giving him a glance, the boy could see how completely out of his mind the Rasta was. He had obviously been at the forefront of the attack and the capture of the pharmacy. For thirty seconds or so, Barry's train of thought left the violence. It gave him much-needed time to get over the shock and get his wits about him.

Back in control of his mind, Barry took stock of his surroundings. More and more cons were appearing as keys taken from injured wardens were used to open cells. In what seemed a little under ten minutes, the prison had fallen completely under the control of the belligerent convicts. Barry was reluctant to get involved in the destruction. Naively, he thought the trouble would be under control in no time. Then, hopefully, he would still be able to have his visit from his mum. He began to worry that his mum would have to wait and would worry about him. He was thinking like a boy in a man's world.

He was later to learn that whilst helicopters were circling the prison, fires raged uncontrollably and police and emergency services were frantically trying to regain control. His dear old mum Pauline was indeed outside the prison gates, frantically waving her visiting order in the face of a screw and having none of it when he told her that the inmates had taken over the prison. She demanded to see her son all the same.

The destruction of the wings moved to another level as the safety netting was dragged down and all the collected debris on them crashed to the floor below. It was no surprise that most of the young prisoners stood in silence, frozen with fear. A gang started to form. These, according to Barry, were the most ruthless of anyone seen so far. Barry was ushered, along with some other rioters, up some scaffold and through a hole on to the roof. Blue skies and fresh air at last. Yeah, right! Barry once again froze with terror as he viewed the scene around the perimeter of Strangeways.

Crowds gathering. People baying. TV crews filming and smoke billowing. Through it all he hoped he could see his mum. If she managed to see him, at least she would know he was alive, despite the fact that he was standing on the ledge of a roof with lifers who had no care for their own lives, let alone Barry's. One could take a dislike to him and throw him off with no remorse. What could they do, add another life sentence to the three he already had? Barry thought it might be a good idea if he got back down inside. So he discreetly did.

Back on the floor, things had turned even uglier. The gang had now made it up to the nonces' (sex offenders) landing above Barry's. Piercing screams came from their under-siege cells and blood ran down the walls. It was harrowing.

Barry sat forward and inhaled deeply on his cigarette. He paused for a moment before looking me in the eyes. His face looked strained and I felt an overwhelming sense that what he was about to tell me was going to be far worse than anything he had told me so far. I sat silently and awaited his interpretation of insatiable bloodlust on an unprecedented level.

176

"Jasp believe me when I tell you. The gang had turned quite literally into a pack of bloodthirsty animals. I have never seen anything like it in my entire life. You know me, mate, I will have it all day long. And not much fazes me at all. But what I saw next has haunted me until today. It's blighted my life, mate, honest."

Nailed to his spot, the next sight Barry witnessed was a white middle-aged sex offender who came stumbling at speed down the metal stairs in front of him. He fell the last couple of steps, but kept on going. His eyes bulged out of their sockets. His terrified look was imprinted on Barry's mind. The man's trousers were wrapped round his ankles. Seconds behind the offender were a dozen rioters carrying chair legs, pieces of twisted metal and carving knives.

"Teach the cunt a lesson before we kill him. Cut his fucking bollocks off."

Barry winced as the nonce was caught and took numerous blows to his skull. The noise and ferocity of the attack turned his stomach. The nonce's screams for mercy were wasted in the intense uproar as scores of inmates cheered on the apparent attempt at cold-blooded murder. A knife was plunged deep into the man's leg, the handle protruding, covered in blood. Still he fought, dragging his assailants with him, battling for his life. He fell down another flight of stairs and Barry lost sight of him. Some might say that a child molester deserves to get all he gets, but Barry assured me that as much as he agreed with that principle, it was not a pleasant sight. The men pursued him out of sight.

As if fuelled by blood, the riot continued. New faces carried out new atrocities. Barry continued to watch. Fires began to blaze on different parts of the landings. Sex cases' cell doors were flung open and burning material thrown in. Those doors were then shut and locked. On the landing opposite, a member of the gang was walking along it holding a scaffolding pole with what appeared to be a foot connected to it. His face remains with Barry to this day.

The con entered a nonce's cell and disappeared from view. Even above the consistent noise, the sobbing and blood-curdling screams could be heard. Seconds later the con appeared, holding his victim at arms' length above his head. His victim's blood poured over him running down his bare arms. He then threw the beast over, down two floors on to the remaining safety net. He landed on top of all the collected rubble, his body limp and spread-eagled.

Missiles rained down. Solid steel doors, beds and masonry all found their target, adding to his injuries. There was a lull in the bombardment of the helpless nonce until someone saw an arm move and it started up again and continued until the body was nearly covered. Two now climbed over on to the net and began to beat the pieces of flesh still visible. They were not going to stop. Nobody wanted to. This was their justice and if you were a sex offender, you were getting the full penalty. It was as simple as that.

"It's all gone hazy, Jasp." We had a cup of tea at this point. Barry went on to say that it was at that moment that he thought his mind had stopped functioning. A safety mechanism had triggered in an effort to prevent him from becoming insane. Amidst the swirling of it all, he was sure he could hear more cheering as a sex case was taken up onto some scaffolding and then hurled off. He did not see it happen. He just knew it was taking place.

The siege was to continue for twenty-nine days but the riot burned out after about five hours. Later that afternoon, hundreds of prisoners managed to make their way out of the prison. They were leaving the rest of it to the staunch, hardcore protagonists up on the roof.

For Barry it was over too and he was mightily relieved. Police advised that those who left immediately, through a door they were protecting from missiles from the roof, would not be prosecuted. Anyone who chose to stay was in deep shit. The vast majority of the inmates chose to leave through the designated exit, even though they knew that doing so made them targets.

On reaching the door Barry faced lines of riot police using their shields as a barrier to run under. Roof tiles thundered against them and policemen screamed orders. One at a time the cons made their dash to the waiting vans. "Move, move, move," was the yelled order. Most received a boot up their arse, which was pretty much unnecessary at the time.

After boarding the waiting prison vans and coaches, the inmates were cuffed together, sat down and told to shut up. Anyone who spoke was punished with a baton. They were ferried to different establishments, Barry's being Hindley YOI. There he was granted a thirty-second phone call to his mother before being cut off by a prison officer. He heard her crying. It was all over the news and thank God her son was safe. Barry was then taken away and locked up, left alone to contend with his nightmares.

The next morning, Barry slipped right back into prison life. No counselling was offered, no fuck all. Get on with it, criminal. As Barry said, the authorities don't give a shit about anybody who goes inside. Every day you are reminded you are just a number, not a human being.

Barry did end up doing another stretch in jail. His cell had a toilet and even a television to watch. He could play five-a-side and even buy a phone card and ring the lads.

He lit another cigarette and sat back in his chair. "Do you know what, Jasp," he said. "Prisoners today don't have to swill out their buckets of piss in the mornings. They don't have to eat

179

pigswill either. They fucking owe that to those lads that went up on that roof, mate. That's a fact."

THE VISITORS

By Marcus

"Back to mine lads, my mum's away."

Having a few mates back for cheese on toast after a heavy bank holiday weekend shouldn't be a big issue, should it? It is when you've got "mates" like mine. Looking back, I should have known something was wrong when they volunteered to make the food, then congregated in the lounge doorway to witness me drunkenly wolf my share down.

"What?"

"Nothing. It's just mad finally seeing you eat, that's all."

It was a plausible explanation. Over recent years I'd become notorious as a speed freak (unfounded I might add), and fellow indulgers will know it makes a poor *hors d'oeuvre*. By the time I'd finished my second round, everybody had disappeared back into the kitchen, where they were respectful enough to keep the chatting down to a whisper. Half an hour later, behaviour that I'd interpreted as thoughtfulness took on a dark, conspiratorial aura.

"They must be talking about me, the bastards."

I ambled self-consciously into the kitchen and their whispering came to an abrupt halt.

"Alright mate?"

All five asked me at the same time. For five people I'd done nothing but take the piss out of all day to suddenly be so concerned about me was a tad unsettling, and now I was up on my feet, I noticed my senses were shooting through the roof.

"Who was that?" I exclaimed.

"What? Who was what?"

"There they are again!"

"They" were everywhere. Whereas before there had been only us six, now there were twenty people standing in the kitchen – or so it seemed to me. What was going on? I went out into the hallway. There were people all around the house. I went back into the lounge. The television was changing channels by itself so I took control of the flicker, but still it wouldn't obey. Something was definitely not right. As I stood, transfixed by the TV, three of the lads came into the living room for one last gawp and giggle on their way out. With work the next day for all of us, Lisney got his head down in the spare room, leaving me with my brother.

"Are you sure you're going to be OK, Marcus?"

I was too focused on the TV to reply. I plonked down on the settee, burying my face in my hands. Suddenly, through the gaps in my fingers, I caught a glimpse of myself on the screen, which was now a mirror image of the living room. I was petrified. Especially when I stood up to leave and my TV image did the same.

Before I could leave the room, my image was usurped by that of a lady who announced herself as Gloria. Gloria conformed to the blonde, Hollywood stereotype of the power-dressed businesswoman. She looked about forty and I liked her.

"Hello Marcus," she said.

"Fuck me. Who are you?"

"You what?" A voice said behind me. I'd completely forgotten my brother was in the room.

"I'm talking to the woman on the telly."

He raised his eyebrows. "The telly ain't even on mate."

I turned back. He was right. All that was there was a blank, grey rectangle.

"I'd get to bed if I was you."

The next thing I heard was the sound of the front door slamming shut and I was all alone.

"Marcus?"

Gloria flashed back onto the screen in full effect. She'd not only returned but brought a stern-looking bloke with her, who she claimed was going to sort out my life. I sank back into the sofa while episodes from my recent past were screened. Then, *flash*, I was being shown the negative consequences of my present lifestyle through images of my future life, ten and twenty years on.

Then the two of them returned with advice on how to turn my life around. I tried to deceive them by agreeing to live the rest of my life differently, but they knew. They bloody knew everything that was going on in my mind. Every time I lied, they'd take the film right back to the beginning, so I'd have to suffer the torture of watching my own embarrassing antics all over again. Every time I told the truth and genuinely considered their advice, coloured balloons would float up from the bottom of the screen to a fanfare of trumpets.

I must have been doing this for three hours, as Lisney said it was exactly 4am when I came into the spare room, naked, and pissed all over the carpet. By five past he'd fled and things got really berserk.

Moving to my mum's room, I became engrossed with my reflection in her tall mirror. I could bend my body into every imaginable form, and after half an hour had the physique of the hulk and a cock the size of that white painted man's emblazoned across that hill in Devonshire.

By now I was donning tight, blue and silver, futuristic lycra and was about to sprint the two miles into town. Then, suddenly, "Ding dong." The doorbell rang. "Ding dong," it rang again. Somebody started calling me through the letter box.

"Mr James? Mr James? Are you alright Mr James?"

It was the police. They were responding to a report on the computer that said, "Marcus James has flipped his lid." On opening the door, I saw their jaws drop. They could see no lycra-clad super hero, only a naked nutcase who still had one foot caught in his jeans, which were dragging in his wake. Not only that, but I had a plant stuck on top of my head, with its muddy roots hanging down over my face.

"Is Emma home?"

Is Emma fucking home! Having convinced myself I was a time traveller, I'd been under the misapprehension that my sister was only three years old and upstairs in her bed. She was in fact twenty-one at the time and had left home two years previously.

"Are you alright Mr James? We've had a report of a disturbance at this address and we're aware that your parents are away. Is Emma home?"

Now I'm in trouble, I thought. *How do I explain that I'm from the future and just here for a visit?* Worse, I started to believe they thought I'd killed Emma, so I made my excuses and shot upstairs to get back into the future, quick.

"Get me out of here," I said, over and over. "I need to get back."

Then I reclined on my bed. *Fucking hell, that was a mad trip*, I thought. Until:

"Mr James, are you OK?"

The voice travelled up the stairs. *Fucking hell, it's not a trip, it's real.* Heavy feet rumbled up towards my room, so I quickly tried to get dressed. Hastily rummaging in my wardrobe, I must have excavated a pair of old school trousers, for they were too small and tight to pull any further than my lower thigh. As PC Harper and his colleague entered, I was shuffling across to meet them like some half-free Houdini, my legs glued together in those ridiculous strides. With a look of bewilderment and a plant still on top of my head, I'm surprised I wasn't sectioned right there. I began to speak.

"Emma is not here, I have not done it."

"Done what, Mr James?"

"Killed her."

"Were not saying you have Mr James. We're just trying to establish if you're OK. Would you like to see a doctor?"

See a fucking doctor? What the fuck for? I was starting to come down now and could see everything in the cold light of the dawn. Amazingly the police left as requested and for the next couple of hours I wandered round the house, surveying the damage. Somehow I'd managed to snap my mum's bedroom window off its hinges, and it had to be retrieved from the front lawn, along with a dented frying pan. What had I done? Mud from upturned plants was smeared across ceilings and walls and the kitchen was carpeted in two pence pieces and shards of glass from a shattered whisky bottle. What a mess.

As my brother popped in on his way to work, the neighbours were out talking. They told him how I'd woken them in the early hours shouting, "The deaf man from the top of our street is not deaf any more, he is healed." As he told me this, things started coming back. I'd been waving the frying pan around and pointing into the sky to conjure bolts of lightning that exploded on the street in front of me. I remembered being convinced the police had surrounded the house and so turned myself into a digital image to escape. It was when I'd finally gone back indoors that the neighbours actually called the police.

"You OK mate?" my brother enquired contritely as I sat

trying to tidy the kitchen floor, hands bleeding from the tiny fragments of glass.

"Not really."

Ten fucking acid tabs the bastards had spiked me with. Strawberries, five on each round of toast.

It was an indescribable relief when my girlfriend walked through the door, having been contacted by Kevin. Though it was the least he could do, it was also the best. She ran a lovely, oiled bath and soon got the house looking half presentable. When my parents returned, she and my sister sat either side of me on the sofa to provide moral support. My mum, swinging from fury to dejected disappointment, nearly kicked me out and only softened after I'd apologized to all the neighbours. That was a good laugh I can tell you.

Within a few months I'd be communicating with the voices again, this time on a coach coming back from an Anglo-Italian cup in Padova. It's no surprise I had another episode, as I'd already consumed three grams of a sixteen-gram bag of whiz before we'd even reached Birmingham. Poor Mick the Pole had been waiting for his bus to work in Stoke an hour before when Cossack talked him into coming. How he must have regretted that decision, sitting next to me as the coach entered Italy and I began my twenty-eighth hour of incessant waffle. My lips had turned blue by then and every time they moved I sprayed the poor fella, who I'd never met before, with spittle. All credit to him, this blond giant of a gentleman with a Wyatt Earp moustache didn't so much as verge on a sour look, but he did walk straight past me to another seat as we started the journey home.

I tried shouting to him, "Mick. Mick. I saved your seat for you. Mick!" He obviously didn't hear me.

By the time we started our return, cannabis, cocaine, speed and Ecstasy were stewing inside me. Whether any more acid had been smuggled into my bloodstream we'll never know, but by the time we reached our first hypermarket things were getting scary again. Somebody asked me to hold a bottle of champagne for them, and while loitering I suddenly noticed a CCTV screen featuring ranks of security guards all heading in my direction. *Here we go again!* As I ran down the aisle to escape, shelves were growing really tall all around, right up to the ceiling, then bending over at the top like waves coming to crush me. I flew straight out the fire exit and threw the bottle. There was no way they were getting me for theft.

Back in the sanctuary of the coach, I was sweating and shivering when the lad came up to inquire after his champagne.

"I got rid of it mate. The fuckers nearly had me."

"Eh? That cost me twenty quid, you fucking idiot."

Word must have got round that something wasn't right, as Jasper came down the coach shortly after and sat in the empty seats across from me.

"Hello Marcus. You OK?"

I said I was, but I wasn't. Far from it. I seemed to get back on an alright buzz, briefly, when a film came on the coach TV about a giant dog named Beethoven and then, *flash*, Gloria was back.

"Hello Marcus," she said crossly. "You haven't taken much notice of what we've shown, have you?"

She was right, I hadn't. I'd thought it had all been just a mad trip, but was it? Why was she here again?

"Come back tomorrow," I whispered. How was I going to keep this from everyone?

Next, the stern fella appeared. "We are going to go through your life scenes again, and this time we want you to take note."

I begged him to come back another time, but he said that having to perform the exercise in front of my friends would teach me to listen in future. I kept looking around to make sure no one had spotted me as we went through the same scenario as before: fanfare and balloons when I told the truth, back to the beginning if I lied. This time, though, I did listen and my life changed on that day forever. They'd come to help me and help me they did.

Having sorted my life out again I began to relax. I could still hear voices but now they were coming from somebody on the coach, only this time telepathically. It was a female voice and so could only be one person: Tony the Axeman's wife. I had to think about the best way to approach this. I couldn't just go steaming down the aisle and announce myself to her, after all her powers might have been a secret. No, I played it cool and told her, telepathically, to turn round and look towards the back of the coach. I would be the one stood by the window with my hands shaped in a triangle on the top of my head. I did this a number of times to make sure I wasn't imagining things, then, once I was positive we'd connected, made my way down the coach and tried to talk to her about our psychic relationship.

Of course, everyone looked at me like I was a weirdo. But I knew I wasn't weird, I was beginning to evolve. Tony and his partner evidently hadn't reached my stage of evolution yet and he was repressing his own psychic aura with hostile vibes, so I returned to my seat and, mercifully, slept for the first time in seventy-two hours. The whole coach breathed a huge sigh of relief.

———————

ITALIA 90

By Millsy

England beat Belgium on June 27, 1990, with a stunning volley from David Platt in the last few seconds of extra time. Jasp, Gwilty, Wilson and I decided that if we got past Cameroon we would make the trip down to Turin for the semi-final.

We still hadn't made any definite travel arrangements on the night of the Cameroon game. We were all buzzing about going, but Cameroon were lighting up the tournament. Although they were the underdogs, they were everyone's "second team", plus, as usual, England were not performing to their so-called potential.

The game was unbearable, a true nail-biter. Phone calls were made throughout the game by the four of us, each with a different version of how we should be playing or who should be subbed and so on. I don't think any of us had ever screamed so much at a television screen in our lives. At the end of 120 minutes of excruciating football, including extra-time, England had secured a 3–2 victory with the help of two penalties, calmly slotted away by Gary Lineker. The whistle blew and before I even rang the lads, I rang my boss at home.

"Bob, is it OK if I have next week off to go to Italy for the World Cup semi-final?"

I got on with the fella sound, and he had given me time off to go to a previous court date and I knew there wouldn't be a problem. The four of us arranged to meet the next day at Eddie Hurst's shop in Hanley, where we bought a couple of new tee-shirts for the trip and we were all definitely in character. We were about to set off on a football crusade, to slay the Germans and anyone else who wanted it or got in our way on foreign soil.

We'd booked on the 10:30pm ferry from Dover to Calais and now all we had to do was get down there in one piece in Wilson's red Escort. It was a decent car, but I don't think Wilson was one of those fellas to be found doing a bit of home mechanics on a Sunday morning, probably because he was too busy counting the money he had made from running away match coaches on Saturdays.

After a couple of hours on the road, we decided to pull in at the services. We had plenty of time to get to Dover and we were all a bit peckish. After feeding our faces with over-priced, under-cooked slop in the usual shitty motorway service station "restaurant", we bowled back to the car. It was at this point that Jasp asked Wilson if he'd done any checks on the vehicle prior to us setting off from base camp Stoke-on-Trent. I think Jasp knew what the answer would be and the burst of laughter that came from Wilson was the only answer Jasp needed.

"Lift the fucking bonnet, Paul," Jasp said, with Wilson still laughing. Water and brake fluid were OK and the windscreen washer reservoir was full. Gwilty attempted to check the oil level but without success. The dipstick wouldn't even come out of the tube. Wilson took control and eventually yanked it out. The dipstick was in a dreadful state. It was impossible to even see the minimum or maximum markings on it and dried, burnt oil had pitted it along its entire length. I don't think the oil had been checked or topped up in all the time Wilson had owned the car. Wilson bought two bottles of oil and I'm sure I heard the engine breath a sigh of relief when it was poured in.

We arrived in Dover with plenty of time to spare, so we went for a couple of beers in the town. Surprisingly, there were no other lads about; we'd thought there might have been one or two with the same idea as us. Soon it was time to board the ferry and I was glad I hadn't taken my turn to drive yet. I'd had a few beers and didn't fancy it, my back seat was getting comfier and comfier.

There weren't many England fans on the ship, so we settled back for the ninety-minute crossing to France. We had decided to drive through the night to get as many miles under our belt as possible. Wilson and Jasp had driven all the way down from Stoke and Gwilty, being a long distance lorry driver, volunteered to do the night stint. When daylight finally broke the scenery was fantastic, huge mountains and valleys everywhere you looked. As lunchtime approached it was my turn to take the wheel.

Everyone settled down to get some kip whilst I plodded along the French highway at a reasonable speed. After an hour or so I noticed the fuel was getting low, so I pulled over at a service station. There was no-one else filling up and I could see the attendant clocking me as I got out. The other three lads remained asleep.

As I took the nozzle from the pump and started to fill up the tank, I could see the attendant waving his arms, gesturing at me and shouting something in French through the glass. I didn't have a clue what he was on about and I was too tired to care. So in true Englishman-abroad style, two fingers were raised and he was told, "Bollocks." I went in to pay the man and he took my money whilst muttering some foreign tirade but I didn't give a shit. I got back in the car and had forgotten about him before I'd even shut the door. I just wanted to get to Turin.

I pulled on to the dual carriageway and off I went. I say went, but what I mean is I got about half a mile up the road and the car started coughing and spluttering and eventually came to a halt on the hard shoulder, waking everyone up. I didn't have a clue what was wrong and neither did anyone else. I'm sure Jasp was dying to point the finger at Wilson for keeping the vehicle so badly maintained. After lots of head scratching and staring at the engine, I said I would call for help from a nearby phone box. Luckily, the lady on the other end spoke a little English and half an hour later a fella in a truck rolled up. He fiddled about with a few things under the bonnet and then made us aware that he was towing us to the nearest garage. At this point we didn't know if this was the end of our World Cup trip or not.

Three or four men spent an hour in the garage looking at the car. We were becoming increasingly agitated at their inability to find the problem and even more pissed off with their lack of understanding of the English language. We were contemplating leaving the car there and hiring one for the remainder of the journey to Turin when suddenly one of the Frenchmen bent over and started sniffing the exhaust. They spoke to each other and then somehow one of them made it clear to us that the last person to fill it up had put in diesel instead of petrol. Oops!

Everyone turned to look at me. I felt like a wilting flower and tried to make myself look as small as possible. I attempted an excuse but there was no denying it was my fault. The mechanics in the meantime were chuckling to themselves and if it wasn't for them being our World Cup saviours, I'm sure we would all have been up for wiping those silly grins off their faces. The other lads were really good with me about the whole episode and everyone chipped in to cover the £50 fee for draining the fuel tank and getting back on the road.

After those shenanigans, the rest of the day's journey was a piece of cake. At 4pm we rolled into Chamonix, one of the top ski resorts in France, alpine chalets and snow-capped mountains all around. We managed to get a four-bed room in a hotel next to the train station. I don't know what it is with England lads and their choice of accommodation next to railway stations.

The French landlady was very pleasant and told us that if

we were out after midnight, the security code for the door was 4807, the height in metres of Mont Blanc. We headed into town that night for a few beers and a meal, very low key. The town seemed full of couples and families so we decided to crash in the hotel for the last hour or so. We were four football hooligans on a mission but the relaxed family atmosphere of Chamonix sent us back to our room where we could feel at home in our own moodiness.

Jasp and Wilson had a couple of joints and started to relax after their slight dispute about the car. Gwilty and I had a couple more cans of the shitty French lager we had brought up from the hotel bar. Stoke-on-Trent's finest dope in the air of this cramped hotel room soon had my eyes fluttering and before long I was asleep, in what seemed like the most luxurious bed in the world.

Before we left the next morning, we took a few photos on the monument outside the train station with a Union Jack Jasp had got whilst in the Army and a big Stoke City flag. We set off on what was to be another long drive which would see us motoring through Tuesday night. From Chamonix you have to go through the Mont Blanc tunnel, passing through French customs on one side and Italian customs on the other. There was a long queue to pass through the French side, so we pulled over to take some more photos of the extraordinary scenery, then set off again with Jasp driving, Wilson in the passenger seat and Gwilty and me in the back.

We could see the French customs officers were being quite strict and checking virtually every car. What we didn't see was a flat-capped policeman with a sniffer dog at his feet. Wilson had the gear stashed in the glove box and we had figured that unless they got us all out and searched it, we would be OK. Unfortunately, as we pulled up alongside the checkpoint, the shit hit the fan. As the car came into view of the dog – and the mutt was still at least twenty feet away – the damn thing came alive as if it had been struck by lightning. It jumped up on its back legs and was trying to pull its handler in our direction. The car windows were open and the smell from several joints smoked on the way from Stoke had fastened the attention of this super mutt on Wilson's car.

Guards and policemen came piling out of the Passport Control Office and surrounded the car, shouting at us in French. We couldn't understand a word but all four doors were dragged open and we were ordered out. Wilson had managed to get the dope out of the glove box in the mass panic but as he threw it on the ground, a nosey French copper saw him. We were all cuffed and had to stand together whilst the mutt was sent into the car and jumped from the front seats to the rear like it was possessed. Of course nothing more was found and as we were led away to the cells at the back of the Passport Office, we could see the dog being rewarded with a game of throw and fetch with a rubber dumbbell. Bastard thing!

Each of us was strip-searched and questioned individually about where we were going, where we had bought the dope and who from and so on. We were kept apart for a couple of hours and left to stew. But we had all been through similar shit after being nicked at football back in the UK, so these officers were given the bare minimum of co-operation, just enough to keep them happy. When they considered our statements they would find our supplier was a six foot three inch midget, half black, half white, with a French/Moroccan accent who was clean shaven with a beard. We were all dealt a £20 fine and, surprisingly, let through the border into Italy. Maybe it was not so surprising, as I think they just wanted rid of a bunch of lying English fuckers.

We sailed through the Italian customs with no hassle, as they were clearly not in any sort of contact with their French counterparts, not back then anyway. Out through the Mont Blanc tunnel, it was only a couple of hours to Turin and it passed very quickly. I wasn't really surprised not to be asked to drive again but I did manage the last hour or so up the M6 a few days later. Trust in my driving skills had evaporated in France.

We arrived at the Stadio delle Alpi, home of Juventus and Torino, before midday and parked up on one of the massive car parks adjacent to the stadium. Even though it was still early and it was an evening kick off, there were a fair few people knocking about, mainly Germans. The Turin authorities had shut all the bars for this game because of various little "offs" at most of the England matches and one mini-riot at Rimini a few days earlier. It made getting a beer very hard indeed. The Krauts had brought their own and were sitting happily outside their cars on deck chairs, laughing and joking.

The next thing on our agenda, and even more important than beer, was getting hold of a ticket. To our surprise, after an hour an Italian came along and offered us tickets on the lower tier, right behind the dugouts. Me, Jasp and Wilson snapped them up. They were £75 each but it was the World Cup semi-final against the Germans, games didn't get much bigger than this. Gwilty was less thrilled though and decided to wait and see if anything cheaper came along. Gwilty had a wife and four kids to support back in Stoke, so the most fertile man in the Midlands disappeared to look for a bargain.

While Gwilty was away looking for his ticket, Jasp, Wilson and I got talking about what we were going to do if England won the game and got to the final. We all had plenty of time but a limited budget. The final would be in Rome four days later against Argentina, so an even bigger game was on the cards and we were already two-thirds of the way there. It was an experience not to be missed. A plan was hatched, though the only way we were going to make any money was illegally.

There is nothing but car parks around the Stadio delle Alpi; in some parts they spread as far as the eye can see. At this time of day, Italian ticket touts and normal fans were trying to offload unwanted tickets. We listened to lads trying to barter a fair price, but the Ities weren't having any of it. Almost all of them were asking four times the face value of the ticket. We thought this would be our way to make a bit of travel money and do a few English lads a favour at the same time.

Over the next few hours we must have relieved a dozen extortionate Italians of their tickets, some of three or four tickets at a time. One of us would pick out a tout and approach him, then ask if we could have a look at the ticket to make sure it was genuine. I feel no remorse for those thick twats as they were getting them out and waving them in the air, more or less saying, "Look at me, look how many tickets I've got." As soon as they started this shit, out of nowhere one of us would come flying by, doing a Linford Christie, grabbing the tickets and scarpering into the distance. These massive car parks were brilliant, you just disappeared over the horizon and left the one of us next to the tout acting as bewildered as he felt. The snatcher would appear half an hour later, tickets in pocket, adrenalin still pumping and we were all laughing like fuck.

As we already had our tickets, we sold the spare ones to England lads at face value. Wilson did a cheeky one on his own just before kick-off. About twenty lads were around this Italian, trying to haggle down the price of the tickets and you could see he was getting slightly nervous. His tickets were in his hands, so one or two English tried to relieve him of them. At this point he placed both hands behind his back with the tickets still between his fingers. The English lads in front of him had no chance but the Italian didn't count on Wilson, who snatched them quick as a flash. He didn't run, but just looked around as if some invisible thief had brushed by him. I nearly spat my can of Coke all over the poor Italian, it was that funny. The greedy prick was left flabbergasted and everyone dispersed except a couple of English lads who had seen Wilson. They got their tickets and we got a few more beer vouchers.

Our £75 tickets were worth every penny, the seats were exactly where the tout had said, right behind the dugout. We couldn't have asked for better. You all know the outcome of the game and that those bastard Germans beat us again on penalties. Pearce and Waddle missed ours and, to be honest, everyone knew that Waddle was going to miss by his demeanour. Useless, long-haired Geordie twat.

Krauts tried to come up to us and shake our hands after the miss, all apologetic like. A "go fuck yourselves" was delivered back. There was a bit of fighting in the top tier away to our left where Gwilty was sat. He said that as soon as the whistle went, England just steamed into the Germans and ran them out of the end. Outside the ground there were various little skirmishes, ten on ten between English, Germans and Italians, but no riot or running battles. I think this was mainly down to there being virtually no segregation in the ground. England lads were all over the place rather than in one huge mob.

We met Gwilty, found the car and managed to get out of the car park fairly quickly. We could see little offs happening as we drove away from the arena. We were all tired, gutted about the result, and pissed off that we'd had very little beer and no rowing. Jasp brought up the idea of going into Turin and seeing if we could park the car out of the way and have a bit of a tear-up before we set off back towards France. Wilson and I were bang up for it but Gwilty didn't want anything to do with it at all. I think he was pissed off about our fun and games with the touts and being on his own during the match. We didn't want to upset him any more so Jasp decided to drive out of the city while me and Gwilty crashed out in the back. Gwilty promptly curled up in his sleeping bag but it wasn't much fun being next to him, as the bag had got wet at some point of the journey and was starting to stink. It was christened "the Shroud of Turin".

I'd been asleep for what felt like a few hours when I was suddenly woken by the car being rocked back and forth and banging on the roof. I didn't have a clue what was going on and we were all awake now. As we looked outside we could see a mob of lads surrounding the car. We were in a built-up area and we could tell these Italian fuckers were after us. The traffic lights changed and cars in front started to move. Jasp put his foot to the floor while steering the car as if we were on some sort of slalom. A hundred yards up the road, we all burst out in fits of laughter.

"What the fuck was that all about?" I asked.

Jasp replied, "When you and Gwilty were asleep we turned round and headed back into Turin for a row, we knew you'd both be up for it."

"Cheers Jasp, but you could have woken us up," I said, as we burst out laughing again, all except Gwilty, who was not a happy bunny and curled back up into the Shroud once we were a good distance away from Turin.

We passed through the Mont Blanc tunnel again into France and back into Chamonix. It was gone 3am and nowhere was open. It looked like we were destined to sleep in the car for the night but the state of the Shroud had us feeling grim at the prospect. We tried the hotel we had stayed in before but there was no answer. We all tried to remember the door security code but to no avail.

As we walked back towards the train station car park and Wilson's red Escort, we could see the dreaded Shroud rolled up on the back parcel shelf. I looked towards the sky as Mont Blanc came into view.

"Yes! I remember the door security code lads, it's the height of Mont Blanc." I searched around in my bag for a leaflet I'd picked up a few days earlier and there it was, 4807. We were in. We got into reception and found one set of keys left, which was better than none, and the landlady had also kindly left the till unlocked, which provided more fuel money. We crept up the stairs and into our room, laughing and giggling like kids at summer camp.

It was a double room with one double bed but we were all too knackered to care so the four of us piled in and got our heads down for a few hours. How the Old Bill back in Stoke would have loved to have a photo of that and blown it up to put on the canteen wall on match days. The landlady's face was a picture the next morning as we came down the stairs. I don't think she could quite place us but she knew we had paid her once a few days ago. We bid her good morning before she twigged or looked in the till.

The journey back was a lot less stressful than the one going. We stopped off in Paris for a couple of hours and had a nosey around the red-light district. Before long we were back over the Channel and driving northbound on the M6. We arrived back in Stoke after four days in a confined environment, which had taken its toll on all of us, and with it now nearly at its end, I think we all felt a little emotional. We decided to head down to the old Victoria Ground, maybe to compare it to the Stadio delle Alpi or just to return to our "home".

To our surprise, when we rolled up at the Boothen End gates just after 5pm, they were open. This was unusual as it was so late on a weekday evening. We made our way on to the terracing, stood behind a crush barrier and looked out over a proper English football ground, one that had experienced so many great games and superb players. I think we all felt a bit choked; I know I did. We were home. We took a few last photos of ourselves and our flags draped over the barriers, and very slowly made our way out through the huge red gates that led to Boothen Road.

ROME, 1997

By Penfold

AS ENGLAND HAD failed to qualify for the 1994 World Cup in the USA, the campaign for the 1998 tournament was deemed as one of the most important in the national side's history. The added kick to our crucial qualifier in Italy was that a draw would send England through automatically and the Italians into the dreaded play-offs. It was this scenario that saw 10,000 English fans make their way to the Olympic stadium in Rome.

Stoke didn't take a mass firm to Rome, but different pockets made their own way by various routes. A mate of mine, Mirko, was well in with a couple of Sunderland's main faces, who had organised a charter flight to Rome. This seemed to be a decent idea but turned out to be a pain in the arse, as these Sunderland were some of the moodiest, grumpiest fuckers you could ever meet, with their FTM ("Fuck the Mags") tattoos and constantly going on about getting stuck into Newcastle (Magpies, hence the tattoo) as soon as they saw them. I just wanted to get over to Rome, hook up with some Stoke and have a mooch for the Ultras. Fourteen hours after setting off, we were showered, dressed and ready for what we hoped would be a lively night in the Eternal City.

As the English congregated at the bars around the bus terminus, it soon became known that the Italian youths were gathered around the Spanish Steps. After a few beers, England started to get restless and the next couple of hours was a bit cat-and-mouse as small groups of English tried to negotiate the back streets of Rome, trying to find the Spanish Steps along with any Italians who wanted to know.

We were continually thwarted by the local police and, after several clashes with them, the police soon had reinforcements on the streets. It was like the cult American gang film, *The Warriors*, with the English northern lads in the role of the Warriors as they were chased by the police in superior numbers around the streets and on to the Underground network. After several hours of this, the majority of English got bored and retired to bars and hotels. There were the odd rumours of English lads being stabbed, but nothing was substantiated whilst we were out there.

On the day of the game there were more rumours, this time about no beer being sold in the centre of Rome, so me, Mirko and the Sunderland decided to stay on the outskirts and ended up drinking a bar dry. Three hours before the game was due to kick off, we marched into Rome, where every bar was packed full of lads. The Sunderland were now in overdrive about confronting Newcastle, and there was a small stand-off as a very tidy mob of Boro came out of a bar. Nobody knew what was happening until a couple of faces from either side had a quick chat.

We carried on together. The mob grew to about 100-strong and at every bar a few more lads joined us. With an hour to kick-off, everyone was of the opinion that we should march to the ground, the mob had swelled to nearly 300, all boys: Everton, Sunderland, Boro, Spurs, plus some other Cockney groups and countless northerners. To put it bluntly, this firm was unstoppable.

There was a token Italian showing by the ground that was swept aside. The sound coming from inside the ground was immense. As luck would have it, we ended up at the place where the Italians paid to get in the ground. The few police were pushed aside as England infested the area. As one, we steamed the Italians in their part of the seats, running them right down to the front and battering any brave enough to stand. There weren't many takers.

We entered one of the areas of the ground reserved for the England fans feeling like heroes. I bumped into Elliott and Tim, who were with a good-sized mob of lads from Nottingham and Mansfield. They were top drawer, and offered me a floor to doss down on for the night, since we had been chucked out of our hotel after some of the lads got carried away with fire extinguishers.

A few minutes after kick-off, irate Italians who had now found their bottle behind the Old Bill and plastic fencing began to throw coins, seats and open bottles full of piss into the English section. This went on for a few minutes until England lost their temper and decided to return serve. Surprise, surprise, the Italian riot police took their cue to steam into us full bore. But they did nothing when the Italians were throwing everything but the kitchen sink at us. The battle with the riot police ended as a stalemate with neither side giving much away, although they did have the advantage of batons and shields. Anyway the police had a surprise in store for us later.

The game itself, from the little I watched, was superb, with England playing brilliantly to secure the draw and a place in France '98. Before the match English fans had been promised a DJ and entertainment in the ground after the final whistle. Nothing materialised as Italian police cleared the streets of Italian fans. After a couple of hours, England were allowed to make their way into a forecourt below the stand, which is where the Italian police gained their revenge.

They allowed English fans to congregate near the exit, then

steamed into us big-time from behind. They used batons, horses, the works, and English fans picked up barriers to defend themselves. This was sweet revenge for the police. They were getting paid for the privilege of dishing out a beating to Mr Englishman.

Rome was on lockdown after the game as the 10,000 English fans began making their way back to their hotels or the airport to toast the team and plan for France '98. Shame about the Italians having to face the play-offs.

Chapter Eight

Those German Bastards Shat in Me Flannel

IF YOU EVER want a good row away with England, the older lads used to tell us, go to Poland. "You'll have it all day long with that lot, they're nuts and the Old Bill don't give a shit. And those Polish birds are fit as fuck as well." That was all we needed to know. A guaranteed fight and fit women to slobber all over; shouldn't have a problem filling a coach for this one then.

I was right, there was no problem at all, and my idea of taking a fifty-three seater coach over to Eastern Europe in 1991 to savour its unknown delights, as well as cheer on England in a European Championships qualifier, was met with a mob-handed, "Fucking too right, I'll go to Poland, I've fucking hated them Poles since Jan Tomaszewski fucked us in the World Cup qualifier at Wembley in '73." That was the general opinion of most of the lads as I scribbled their names down in my pocketbook, and saved their seats for a trip that would be looked forward to with much anticipation for the next six months, and spoken about for the rest of our lives.

I did agree with the lads, Mr Tomaszewski had pissed me off just as much as them. But as I rolled up a bundle of £20 deposits, I silently fell back to my childhood. I was at school, listening intently as my teacher, Colin Mellor, read out loud from the pages of the novel, *The Silver Sword*. How would I ever forget the passion in his voice as he read on through gritted teeth, embedding into our tiny, inquisitive minds the cruelty and resolve in human nature as the German occupation of Warsaw squeezed the life out of the burned-out Poles who lived and fought gallantly from the basements of the buildings which were once their homes. And all that in the middle of a cruel winter. After lessons Mr. Mellor would sometimes chat with me about his wartime experiences. Like thousands of other brave and sadly now unappreciated young men, Mr. Mellor landed on the Normandy beaches and pushed on through until Liberation. He often spoke of the relief of it all coming to an end, and the sadness as they counted its costs.

"Some of the bravest soldiers I have ever come across, Mark, were the Polacks. Gentlemen, all of them. They had it tough out there on the Front, the punishment they received was relentless, but they never gave up, you know, fighters all of them. And they like a drink, too." He likened the Poles to ourselves.

I returned my pocketbook to my jacket, pulled out a ready-rolled joint, lit it and filled my own bit of space with a pleasant cloud of smoke that brought the attention of other itchy fingers sitting beside me. Another long deep toke was inhaled as I turned to look into the face of Wilson. His impatience, normally the source of my entertainment, was cured as I handed him the smoke and coughed my question across the table.

"You on this coach to Poland or what mate?"

"Yeah, I'll have it with the Polish, I'm not fucking paying though," he retorted.

"Do you ever fuckin' pay? Just make sure you turn up, eraight."

Wilson was my best mate, nothing surer than that, though our relationship was strained. In his day he was a committed football hooligan and well respected across the city. Not only that, he was probably one of the hardest lads that lived in it. I not only wanted him on this one, I needed him. I knew that with the climate the way it was, it wouldn't be too long before the police cottoned on to our coachload of tasties heading across the continent to not only represent England in the true spirit of the game, but in their misguided loyalty to St George and his cross, have it with any foreign fucker who wanted it. Wilson, I hoped, would be my second vision and help me prevent any unforeseen circumstances ruining our plans along the way.

Refraining from even bothering to share my memories or knowledge of the Poles with a best mate who rarely listened to much anybody had to say, unless it involved himself, I looked forward and tried to envisage the type of mob we might come up against. My gut feeling told me it would be a tough one.

Putting a trip together of this magnitude took hard thinking and endless deliberation. Firstly, I'd have to find a coach company willing to take on such a task, as lying to them by saying we were a bunch of monks heading to Eastern Europe on a pilgrimage of self belief and a quest for Tantric fulfilment would be out of the window the moment the driver saw his rear window obstructed by a cross of St George with "Stoke N40" emblazoned across it. Secondly, as this wasn't your usual package trip and we would be on the road for a week, I'd need to find suitable accommodation to cater for everyone's budget – cheap but still of a decent standard.

That done, I had five months to get forty-six passport photos, along with details, and collect varying deposits, before heading to Edinburgh and the Polish embassy to wait on their decision as to whether they allowed us to travel. I suppose I set double standards: it was as important to me that the lads were well behaved and respectful en route as it was imperative that we met up with some formidable fighting opposition, be it German or Polish. I've always thought things should be done with a certain decorum rather than crashing through someone's town gates, howling and brandishing burning torches. It was always important to me for Stoke to have that fair but firm reputation. Perhaps it was a little part of my subconscious that tried to justify the socially unacceptable culture I came from. If it was managed in a gentlemanly fashion, it could be at least half acceptable, surely?

Our adventure started on a piss-wet Sunday afternoon in November. Minstrels wine bar was owned by one of our main faces, Mad Ant Walford. It was a plush place and the fifty or so casuals stood about in an easy manner. A mountain of sports bags were piled by the door. I grinned as I walked in from the storm. I'd only hours before got off a flight from Los Angeles, chuffed that my stash of stun guns had remained undetected.

"Ay up lads." I shook off the rain as a dozen hands slapped my back and a spliff was placed between my lips.

"Ged, how are ya mate?"

The embrace was long and meant. It was good to see the lads. Although I'm a loner and to this day feel the need every now and then to isolate myself, it's a charged experience to walk into a place and be hit with a rush of love, trust and admiration from such a scale of people. That in itself could be addictive.

Ged and I pulled up a couple of bar stools and started to chuckle about the upcoming trip. Looking around, there was just about every conceivable character you could imagine amongst such a bunch of rogues. The leg-breakers, the tea-leafs, the cards, they were all there, including seven who hadn't booked but had just decided to come on the day. Not a problem as far as I was concerned; none of them were bothered about not having visas, and amongst the seven were two of the funniest lads in the firm, Martin Hallam and his one-eyed best mate Sid Stringer. These were two of the five firm strippers, and I looked back at Ged to share that little glint of acknowledgment. *Fuck me, this trip is gonna be a pisser.*

Laughing, Ged reached into his inside jacket pocket, pulled out his hip flask, unscrewed the cap and offered me a swig of Bushmills, "You sure the driver of this coach isn't Old Bill then, mate?" The whiskey burnt as it coated my insides.

"Couldn't say, Ged, I've not met the geezer yet." Turning over my shoulder and then back to Ged, I said, "All I know is, if he is Old Bill, they've hit the jackpot with this load of loons. I'll suss him out as soon as we set off."

I'd used Leon's of Stafford several times before. Their coaches were always of a good standard, and the drivers easygoing. Mind you, none of them had spent a week away with us before.

"Jasp, it's here mate."

The observation aroused the lads and we all leaned out of Minstrels and smiled at the waiting coach parked at the end of the cobbled street.

"Nice one, it's got a bog on it."

Flags were pulled down from above the bar and bags were thrown into the luggage space. A short and slightly overweight man in his forties smiled sheepishly as he acknowledged each of his boarding passengers.

"Ay up mate, are we allowed to smoke on here or what?"

The driver nodded his head, perplexed at the size of the cigarette hanging from the man's lips.

"Nice one mate."

The hazy-eyed passenger left the scene, leaving me, hand

outstretched and smiling, to make my introduction before it became an explanation.

"Good evening." The palm of the driver's hand was firmly embedded into mine as I took hold of the situation. "I'm Jasper, I've organised the trip, is everything OK?"

It was too late by now, I'd got him. Pete, as he introduced himself, was caught by my towering frame. Immediately, my huge open smile seduced him, and by the time he'd moved his look up into my piercing blue eyes, I was already deep inside the man's mind. I calmed him and cautioned him with one straight look. Although he may not have liked the demeanour of his other fifty-two passengers, Pete knew there was no turning back and the man holding his eye was his only connector between the life he knew and the life he was about to embark on.

We both climbed the steps of the bustling coach, and I listened intently as Pete, in a broad West Midlands accent, explained to me that he worked to a tachograph. This meant he could only legally drive for ten hours a day, with a couple of stops in between. He sat down behind his steering wheel almost as if that was his spot, and the only place he felt safe. Once again I towered over him, clocking his shoes, hands and attire. Pete didn't know it but every man on that coach was burning him alive as we all deliberated whether he was a copper or not. My thought was, *Sit down, let the man do his job, and later on have another chat with him. Who knows? He could turn out to be a good laugh*.

The coach departed from Hanley bang on time at 6pm. By 6:20 we were on the M6 motorway heading south and ten minutes after that came the first request for the driver to put on the TV. The lads had brought some home entertainment and the tape was passed eagerly down to the front. I had decided to sit in the courtesy seat at the front, next to Pete, reassurance if you like that I was a conscientious trip organiser who would be there at all times if need be.

"Pete, the lads have got a video, can I stick it on mate?" Pete nodded to the VHS recorder up above him.

"Nice one."

No doubt he was expecting to hear a cumshot compilation, with loads of lewd remarks being hurled backwards and forwards, or something along those lines. Instead he was treated to complete silence as the lads settled down to watch the 1980s documentary *Hooligan*, a cult classic if you were of that persuasion.

How he must have wished he was heading home for the night as Birmingham came and went, and the coach began to smell like an Amsterdam coffee shop. I didn't feel sorry for Pete as I watched his reflection in the windscreen, he was never going to be in any danger from us. I could just tell he was wishing he was someplace else. I decided to open up a conversation.

"It's a fair journey this for one driver, Pete." He agreed and went on to tell me that normally a trip of this kind would have two drivers to share the load. I wasn't surprised when he added that none of the other drivers fancied the job, and they had drawn straws for it. Pete had obviously lost.

The M25 was a good time to go and have a chat with some of the lads on the back seat. I was pegging for a joint, and I felt that I'd got more of a feeling for our driver by now. "If he is Old Bill, he should be treading the boards." I began to think to myself that he was really alright and just a bit unfortunate to have been landed with us lot. I sat down and lit a skunk spliff kindly prepared for me by Wilson.

"He seems alright, just a bit nervous that's all."

"Go and ask him if he wants a toke on that then," Wilson laughed.

"Fuck off, how much have you brought with you?"

"Enough for the journey, there's a few Gary Abletts knocking about as well."

I'd been there and done that in the 1980s; Ecstasy wasn't for me. I could never understand why everybody wanted to love each other on that shit.

"No thanks, I'll stick to this. Besides, Batto's got a big bag of beak on him. I'll have a line of that in a min."

The coach was rammed from front to back with pissheads, potheads, 'phet heads, pillheads and charlie heads, and all of them with violent tendencies when sober, let alone smashed. Three guests had been invited on this one too. A lad from Preston, who we'd nicknamed Taters because of his accent when describing his favorite food, was one of the lads who had stood with us in a bloody brawl in Dublin before one of the other qualifiers a few months back. Darren from Derby's DLF firm was a good friend of Minstrel, one of our older, more prominent faces from England away games. He sported a long ponytail and the conventional Stone Island; he also looked a bit of a rough fucker. And then there was Terry, a well-respected face with the Villa. Terry needed no introduction as he'd spent a lot of time in jail with some of our lads, and was respected, full stop.

The white cliffs of Dover, and there's a new air on the coach. Very shortly the lads would be let loose, and they could get some serious drinking done on the ferry. I just hoped the crossing would pass without incident.

"Oi, I hope there's a fucking firm on here. Let's have it!"

They were only winding me up, I knew that. I'd made it plain that there was to be no brawling with any other English unless it was brought to us. I just couldn't wait to get to France and back on the coach. We lost sight of Pete as he headed up the ramp to join the ferry. We all stood, passports in hand, eager to get on board.

"Mr Chester, can we have a word please?" I fucking knew it. An uneasy silence came over the lads as two plainclothes police officers took me from Passport Control into a one-way mirrored office. I could still see the lads frowning and passing comments outside as the Football Intelligence officer commenced.

"Mark, we don't have a problem with your coach travelling over to Poland at all. It seems that you've catered for everything quite well. Although it is our duty to inform you that we have the addresses of all the hotels that you will be staying at. This information has also been passed over to the local authorities."

I was a bit gutted, but at least we were still able to go.

"And Mark, the other thing, we will be monitoring your coach all the way to the game and until you arrive back in Stoke-on-Trent next Friday. OK?"

"OK." I was tempted to ask about the lads who didn't have Polish visas, but thought, *Fuck it*.

It was a boozy but trouble-free crossing with no sign of any other English firms. France was a blur, and we arrived in Neuss, on the outskirts of Dusseldorf, mid-afternoon. I'd booked all the accommodation blind over the phone, and breathed a sigh of relief on seeing that our first night would be spent in a quality hotel. The concierge was an attractive woman in her mid-thirties, a typical German looker if you like, blonde spiky hair, stern features, silver-rimmed spectacles perched across the bridge of her nose. Proper wanking material. And that was probably written across the faces of the forty or so men now jostling at the reception in front of her.

The first problem flashed into my head. *For fuck's sake don't give anyone a key to their rooms until you've locked the mini-bars*. The small lobby became congested as I pushed my way towards the desk. The manager appeared from an office behind the counter.

"Group leader, where is group leader?" she spouted. Laughter. "Group leader, group leader, where are you?" The lads liked that one a lot.

I smiled as I pressed against the desk and offered the woman my hand. A brief introduction preceded my concerns about the mini-bars and the problems that may cause at checkout the next morning. She assured me it would be no problem. I raised my eyebrows and sighed quietly to myself.

"I'm sharing with you." Wilson was in my ear immediately. He grabbed the key from my hand and headed with Dave Baker to an adjacent staircase.

"Right lads, shower and out then, eh?"

After fourteen hours in the confinement of the coach, we were all dying to get out and see what the German city had to offer. Different people had different agendas, some wanted to go straight on the piss, others wanted to go robbing tracksuits and designer wear, and a couple of the lads actually wanted a meal and maybe a museum. But most wanted the red-light area and some pure sleaze. I was amongst that fraternity.

Twenty minutes later the lobby was full to the brim once again. It was decided that we'd all travel from Neuss into the city centre together. Nobody wanted to get split up, although we knew it was inevitable. Mobile phones were the size of house bricks in those days, and none of us owned one anyway. It was down to your instincts to remain in touch, and not get lost.

A twenty-minute tram journey took us straight into the main square of Dusseldorf. We exited as one tight unit, each man playing his own scenario in his heads. *We are English hooligans everybody, we are on our way to Poland to have a brawl, but if any of you would like to take us on in the meantime, please feel free to do so.* Opposite was a large pub that was designated immediately as HQ in case of problems and if anyone became detached from the rest. Anything else would be taken from there.

Late afternoon saw a change in the climate, the crisp temperature dropped significantly and darkness fell. Neon lights replaced singing birds, and office workers headed home. After a few beers the group split into the aforementioned categories and we arranged to meet back up a little later on in the same pub in the square. I was with thirty of the sleaze-seekers.

"Someone ask a taxi driver where the red-light area is," suggested Billy Burton. Everyone agreed, enough beer had been consumed for now. A line of white Mercedes taxis was pointed out, and we headed towards them at pace. "Just pile in them. We'll meet up when we get there." Finbar had already asked at a kiosk where we were to go. In broken English the vendor had explained that the area we desired was called Ban Dam.

"Ban Dam please, mate."

Five of us dived into the Merc and slid across the shined leather interior. I was in the middle of the back seat, and stole a glance at the cab driver's expression as he adjusted his meter and pulled out into the Dusseldorf rush hour. Six more cabs followed suit and a collection of cheesy grins and thumbs-up salutes disappeared into the black German winter. Ten minutes on and the driver indicated and pulled to the side of the road.

"Ban Dam," he pointed as he turned towards the back seat, cutting short the spurious conversations. "You want Ban Dam, yes?" His voice was deep and gravelly.

"Yes my mate, Ban Dam. That is where the girls are, yeah. You know, fucky-fucky." Laughter filled the cab. We all knew the driver could speak perfectly good English and would probably take us around the block a few times to make up the fare. We were more than likely squaddies to him, why else would we be out in force on a freezing Monday night in the middle of November?

"Okay you can get out now," he replied. "This area is not good, you have to walk that way. Twenty Deutschmarks please."

That remark coincided with the concerned look I'd previously clocked in the rear view mirror as he pulled off to start the journey.

"You what, you? What you on about, walk from here?" It was the first aggressive remark I'd heard since leaving the hotel.

"Fuck it, let's get out and walk," I chirped.

The driver was adamant, and several hundred yards along into a dark narrow side street I could plainly see a fluorescent light, the only light, clearly reading Ban Dam, with an arrow pointing down at a small doorway in the wall. All five cabs arrived within seconds of each other, it looked like the other drivers had also chosen to drop their passengers off on the main road rather than turning into the dingy street. Their caution in their own city heightened all of the lads' excitement and a tidy mob of thirty moved at speed in the direction of the neon light.

The doorway was just about big enough to let one man through at a time, causing a slight congestion as several German businessmen in overcoats and carrying briefcases hurriedly made their departure.

"That's it lads, off home to the wife and kids now."

It was an uncalled-for comment, but it was inevitable. We filed through like a viper and arrived inside a small, enclosed courtyard, almost certainly the one depicted in the sitcom *Auf Wiedersehen Pet*. To the left, a few dirty Turks hung around inside a bus stop-style shelter, their eyes and filthy thoughts now fixed firmly on us. Had there not been four floors and sixty windows of women to look at, they almost certainly would have had a slap. The Turks scurried off as we filled the shelter and took up places as if on a terrace, and with wonder gazed up at a multitude of temptresses, all of whom were role playing perfectly.

Amyl nitrate filled my nostrils and several purple-faced lads next to me roared with laughter as Billy Burton, a fast character with a face full of reminders, took it upon himself to be the first one through the doors. I joined in too. It didn't matter which girl Billy had chosen, collectively we all knew she'd be fucking gutted when Billy turned up at the door with a toothless grin and dripping right nostril. I decided to take my time and have a closer look. I stood with two of my close mates from my home town of Alsager, Stan and Finbar.

"What do you reckon, Stan, you havin' one or what?" Stan liked his women busty. He was a big lad himself, almost like Lenny in Steinbeck's *Of Mice and Men*. I wasn't surprised when he pointed immediately to the top floor second window in. "Nice that Stan, I might have the one in the next room." Predictably, he'd gone for the only window to have a pathetic display of Christmas lights, and a voluptuous-looking young woman wearing the full hit in white lace. Stan couldn't contain his delight as he rubbed his hands and headed off to the main door of the brothel. A wink at Finbar and I was straight through the door with Stan, not giving a fuck what the girl in the next room looked like. It was more about bonding and having a laugh on the way up the stairs.

We entered the landing and separated our cash into different pockets. Pausing for a last giggle, we both then rapped on each of the doors. Stan's opened first. I looked towards it and the thing was standing side-on, over-exaggerating her stretched tits. A glance at Stan's bitterly disappointed expression brought a belly roll from inside and I let out a laugh. My door opened and the smile immediately left my face. Both women were well into their forties, both looked like they needed a good wash, and both spoke little English. The only difference was that Stan's had turned out to be black and hugely overweight, and mine was the colour of a milk bottle, with carrot hair, tar-stained teeth and weighing about six stone. A right pair of mingers.

It must be a man thing, or if not, definitely a Stoke thing. Stan and I stood hijacked. The red-carpeted corridor suddenly seemed to be a mile long as I started to trip out at the situation. Neither of us fancied a fuck anymore, but then "he" appeared. Just ever so slightly over your left shoulder, you'll see him there, perched roaring with laughter, calling you a wanker and goading you on. Lucifer himself. Two acknowledging winks preceded two closing doors and we were in.

The woman smiled hesitantly and introduced herself as Petra. I frowned back, taking less than a second to dismiss the shabby burgundy bra and knickers. She had calluses on her toes, and as she pulled out a selection of vibrators from the bedside drawer I noticed a stab wound under her rib cage. A second glance around the room revealed blood splatters around and above the headboard.

"Erm, it's OK sweetheart, I'll just settle for a blowjob if you want. How much is it?"

In the courtyard below, the strains of "Rule Britannia" became less audible, as by now most of the lads had chosen their quarry and were most probably banging the back end out of them. *Fuck me*, I thought, as she undid the buttons on my fly, *I'm not even turned on here. Male bravado or what. She's pig ugly and to the tune of forty Deutschmarks to boot. Oh well.*

She started telling me I was a bad boy. "I already know that, luv, just suck the fucker, eh?" The noise in the corridor told me that most of the three pumps and a squirt firm had shot their fat and it would soon be time to hit the streets again. Stan was already waiting as I left the room.

"Any good yours, Stan?"

"Apart from a couple of bruises on her thighs, she didn't do much for me, so I just did her from behind, mate."

Quality Stan, quality. We exited and met up with the lads outside in the courtyard. While we'd all been inside, one or two unsavoury characters had started to show up and hang around by the exit. One in particular caught my eye. Leaning against the wall with eyes as sharp as a hawk was Germany's Lily Savage. I can't honestly say if this was actually a man or a woman but it had the traits of both. From the peroxide bobbed hair, plastered-on make-up and visible lip and chin stubble, down to the mink stole and black hot pants, it looked iffy. Mr Perversion in me took a second sharp glance as I passed outside into the street. The Thing didn't give me a second sniff. Samson had found his Delilah and they were talking. Samson was one of the younger Alsager lads, a six-footer who said little unless questioned, a respectful lad. A dirty chuckle rattled round in my thoughts as I picked up my place in the waiting congregation. *Nah, he wouldn't do that. Surely not.*

Seconds later we were all back at the top of the alley, and trying to flag down several uninterested taxis. Many lads were exchanging vulgar accounts of sodomy and the like. Dusseldorf was a bit of an anti-climax after Ban Dam. The numbers dwindled as we all strove to find our ways back into the city centre, which in itself was quiet and lacked any scent of excitement, be it a club full of girls or a vanload of patrolling skins scouting for any English passing through.

It was going to be up to ourselves to provide our own entertainment, and Wilson had the answer. Mid-evening and our numbers were down to twenty, it was cold and we seemed to have been walking for miles without getting away from the business quarter. Disorientated, we slowed up and moved towards a small supermarket. Most of the lads entered and bought chocolate and a couple of beers. I stayed out on the street cupping my hands as Baker skinned up in them. Now was a time for vigilance; I didn't need a disgruntled shopkeeper yelling and chasing a bunch of shoplifters up the street. I stared in through the open door and immediately caught sight of Wilson removing a case of Johnny Walker whisky from a shelf and casually walking out on to the street and across to where I was standing. Wilson pulled out a bottle, cracked open the cap with his teeth and the night degenerated from there.

"Ask those tramps which way it is to the bars," suggested Baker.

Wilson's bollocking was shelved as I followed Dave's nod. Three smiling tramps sat huddled in an office doorway, I handed them a bottle of whisky and asked them for directions. The next half an hour was spent walking and drinking. Three German tramps and twenty hooligans made the journey into town, swigging whisky and passing it on. All that on empty stomachs, and pretty soon the night would take a turn.

Here we go. Who are these? We'd just entered the main square at last, and a mob on the move brought us to our senses. They were Stoke, some of those we'd lost after Ban Dam. We ditched the tramps and our numbers were back at thirty. The new arrivals were pumped up and buzzing and my guts told me that we'd missed out on something.

Among these lads were two real hotheads, not the types that you like to see go off and do their own thing. Donavan, the landlord of our local boozer, was psychotic. The other, Nidge, was one of those where everything is either black or white, with no in-between. Fucking hard work if you want the truth, though still a valued member of the firm. These two Boswells commenced their tale of events. On leaving Ban Dam they'd caught a tram straight into town, went immediately to an Irish bar and set up stall in a snug. They'd got chatting to several local girls who were half up for it. Donavan was convinced he'd pulled the young blonde with freckles and a gap between her two front teeth. They'd told him the name of a nearby club that was busy on Mondays and said we could meet them there.

The girls seemed charmed by their new admirers, even warming to a cheeky line of chizz. That was until Nidge, who could never sit down and felt the need to continually patrol any strange premises we might be in, found a wall on the other side of the pub with some commemorative IRA plaques of Michael Collins. Nidge freaked and began punching each one, smashing the glass with his fists. Donavan and the rest were up out of the snug and bounced across the spacious themed pub. Slightly bemused at the sight of nothing at all except Nidge having a blowout, they eased up and started to head back to their pints, only to discover the girls had upped and left in the commotion.

Donavan went back into the main bar. Nidge's outburst had left the violence stage and was now becoming an enraged verbal explanation for why we should all remember what "those Irish bastards" had done to our lads. Inevitably the door security arrived. There were two of them, and events then happened so fast that it was difficult to recollect what they looked like. Each made a grab for Nidge and each received a stomach-churning blow, one a punch, the other a butt. The third blow was a bit unnecessary, but the biker sat at the bar shouldn't have got involved.

We moved on to a shabby-looking place off the main drag, and devised a plan to get us all into this club where the three girls had gone. Donavan relayed the details and we staggered our arrival over the next hour. Everyone was calm again. The club was only two streets away. I remained behind with Finbar and voiced my concerns that we might not even make it to Poland if it was to go off again that night. He agreed and we made our way tentatively to the nightclub.

More than an hour had passed since the first group of four had advanced to the club, and no negative reports had come back. *Everything must be sweet.* We approached an open street-level doorway, and peered inside. A balcony looked down over a set of red-carpeted winding stairs that went down two levels and finished at a set of double-panelled glass doors, through which you could see inside the club. The place looked heaving and inviting.

However, the two huge skinhead doormen dressed from top to toe in black did not look inviting at all. Worse still, ten of the lads, including Donavan, Nidge and Wilson, were on the bottom step. They'd been refused entry point blank, and were not about to turn around. Finbar was quick with his observation, "Forget it J, we've got no chance of getting in there." I agreed, but didn't take my eye off the situation below.

There was obviously the language barrier to get over, so most of the communication between the doormen and the lads was aggressive hand gestures. It brought attention from inside the club, and the glass doorway filled up with the faces of the lads who had already got in. I knew there was no turning back now, and the night was about to be over. Finbar and I settled in our ringside seats. Nothing we could do would prevent it from happening, and getting involved was unnecessary, as Stoke had overwhelming numbers and it was going to be a slaughter.

Both doormen read the situation immediately and made an attempt to get inside the club. Donavan read them, and hurled himself from three steps up, crashing his forehead into the side of a German's face. Both doormen fell inside the foyer, retaliating with karate kicks. Nidge and Donavan led the charge inside the doors and were joined by several of the lads already inside.

After only fifteen seconds of the vicious fight between two karate-kicking German doormen and seven or eight football hooligans, reinforcements emerged from the bowels of the club. Another huge skinhead, wearing knuckledusters on each of his hands, ploughed into the middle of the fight, sending bodies flying. He bought enough time for one of the other two to pull out a handgun, but his arrival also brought a new attack from both the stairs and inside. Still less than half a minute in, the entrance to the club was going berserk. Light fittings were ripped off the staircase and hurled at the Germans.

From our elevated position, we could see everything clearly. The first flash of a gunshot lit the glass inside. I heard the second shot as it was aimed outside, on to the staircase. The retreat was pure panic. Thirty lads fought each other as they headed at pace up the stairwell towards us.

My main concern was for Wilson. I saw him running with the rest and slamming a right-handed peach into Nidge's kipper. He was also pissed off that the night was over. Happy that Wilson was going to make it out of the club, I grabbed Finbar and yelled, "Run!" We did, blind. My first thought was to head into a nearby bus stop, just become German and hopefully blend in.

"English, stop!"

The command was being screamed into a handheld loud-speaker, and not from within the club but from outside the building. Two more shots rang out as clear as day and more shouting became audible over the panic now spilling outside onto the street.

"English halt, English halt!"

Dogs barked viciously and the street echoed as high-powered vehicles screeched along it. A side glance showed me bodies exiting the vehicles at pace and blocking off the street. Finbar and I were fortunate enough to have had that thirty second start on the rest of our number, as the plainclothed police officers who had tailed us since the fracas at the Irish bar laid down the law in no uncertain terms.

Sprinting, Finbar and I moved away from the melee as fast as we could, our hearts pounding. Hopelessly lost, we carried on along the street, making a left turn and running blind along it. Everywhere looked the same. We piled inside the doorway of an office block, panting heavily.

"Fuck me, J, we were lucky there. They've all been nicked for sure."

I tended to agree. The adrenalin rush had sobered me up and a decision had to be made fast. It had definitely been undercover cops that had tailed us to that club, and they had been bolstered by the local uniformed police as well as a stream of meat wagons that hurtled past us towards the scene. Getting off the street would be a good idea, but to where?

"Let's not fuck about hiding in a doorway," I said. "We'll get sussed. Let's just stroll along casually in the direction that all the police vans are going."

Finbar's normally gormless expression turned to bemusement.

"Trust me, run away, you'll get lifted. Walk towards it and they won't pay you any attention at all. Come on."

Finbar disagreed, and thought an adjacent park area was a better option. Against all our ethics, we did the unimaginable and split up. I pulled myself together, straightened myself up and casually walked back along the street. Pandemonium faced me up ahead. A blue, flashing light display bounced amongst the buildings, the sound of dogs snarling and men screaming filled my head. Still I walked on. The scene gutted me. The lads were strewn out across the ground, face down, hands on the back of their heads. Each one had a policeman stood over him, brandishing a gun and yelling persistently into his ears. Dog handlers allowed their animals enough slack on their leads to terrify their captives.

I walked on, mightily relieved that I was able to do so, hailed a taxi, fell into the back seat and huddled down, saying, "Neuss," in my whisky-enhanced German accent. As we drove, I cringed at the sight of plainclothes snatch squads running about in a determined attempt to capture any escapees. I shook my head and tutted out loud, hoping the taxi driver would share my sentiments and get the fuck out of there. He did and I was safe, for now.

The small park that Finbar had entered was pitch black, and he lost his night vision immediately. He fumbled through bushes until he found a small play area with a couple of benches. Sitting down, he regained his composure. His night wasn't over for sure, he was on his own and his adrenalin rush had his senses pinned and alert. He too could still hear the distant echo of the continuing police operation.

"Fuck that," he said to himself. "I'm going to sit here for an hour." A minute later, three casually dressed figures ran inside the park entrance and immediately broke into a stroll. Finbar breathed a sigh of relief, reassured by the appearance of some of the lads who had obviously made it out too.

"English, don't move."

Their accent chilled his spine, and winded Finbar as would a blow to the abdomen. He stood and the three figures ran towards him. "Shit." Finbar's cumbersome, six foot three inch frame darted about like a condemned turkey at Christmas, running blindly for any kind of unlikely exit.

The blow that felled him came from the butt of a handgun. Wincing with pain he lay flat out across the grass. Both hands were immediately cuffed behind his back, and he was unceremoniously dragged to his feet, frog-marched out of the park and thrown into a waiting van. Saturated in his own blood from a gaping head wound, he sat on a bench, gutted, and awaited his uncertain fate.

The van containing Finbar pulled into the street where the lads were being held. The door slid open and several other injured men landed in heaps in front of him. They were taken to the local station, where they were processed and then removed to hospital to be treated for a variety of wounds, Finbar's needing twelve stitches across the top of his head. Luckily for them, they managed to slip the net after being treated and nipped off from the hospital in taxis, feeling a bit sore but mightily relieved not to have been taken to Dusseldorf's main prison, where the remaining fourteen captives had been transferred.

Completely unaware of the unfolding events, I sat alone still in the cab, mulling over the consequences. Dover and the Football Intelligence officer came to mind, and I was sure there would be a reception waiting back at the hotel. A fleeting glance in moving traffic of Fig, a doorman from back home, on a stolen pushbike told me I wasn't the only one to escape. Despite the fact that Fig had been heading in the wrong direction for the hotel, the knowledge gave me hope that not all had been lost. Even though he obviously was.

There was a reception waiting at the hotel on my arrival, but not the type I'd feared. Gibbo, my old school mate, and Ged had spent the whole day on the rob and missed everything. Eager to hear of the day's events, we headed with Gwilty and Bradley to their room and trashed the mini-bars that I'd been so worried about on checking in.

After four hours' kip and with a mouth like a buzzard's crotch, I headed to the restaurant and breakfast, where there was little noise but the sound of scraping of spoons on crockery.

Several tables closest to the hotplate held most of the night's survivors. An array of bandages, swollen hands and black eyes caught my attention as I calculated the damage. Pete, our coach driver, sat alone, staring into his bowl and stirring his cornflakes over and over.

"How's things Pete?"

I don't know how I had the gall to ask that really. His reply was hollow. He told me that the hotel manager had woken him during the night and informed him that the police were holding fourteen of his passengers, and that they would be appearing in court that morning. He was concerned about his tachograph, and breaking the law. He urged me to leave the lads behind. I refused.

Checkout went without a hitch. Everyone was too hung over and concerned about their mates to want to arse about with mini-bar bills. A handful of cash was left on the desk and we headed to the prison. As expected, Dusseldorf's main gaol was a grim place. Built like a castle, it had rusty, reinforced metal shutters across every window and looked cold. Ged, Wilson and I explained at the reception who we were, and asked if there was any chance of our friends coming out to play.

A stern German officer gave us a stern reply. He said that ten of my friends were going to be released immediately and that we could take them with us. However, the other four were being detained and would be appearing in court later that day. He gave me a piece of paper with the names of the four. I wasn't surprised at all to see that Donavan and Nidge were among them.

It took me less than ten minutes to get the released men back on the coach, collect a whipround, and gather their passports and bags together. That still left me time to take Nidge's washing and shaving kit out of his bag and shit in his flannel. Placed neatly with the rest of his kit, the rolled-up turd

225

was taken inside the prison, and left with some instructions how to get to the hotel in Berlin.

The atmosphere on the coach as we left Dusseldorf was surprisingly upbeat. Yeah, we were all knackered and hung over and most of the lads stank a bit, but all in all we were well ready for the next stage of our adventure. I took my seat at the front and pacified Pete with the fact that we were only two hours late setting off and that if we were lucky he would make up the time on his tacho. He accepted this in his Brummie drawl and with a nod and a wink. "No probs, Jasp." Pete looked tired. I smiled back at him as I stood up to check on each of the lads. It was more than obvious to me that Pete was resigned to his fate and was going to take each mile as it came.

Now we were settled I felt it necessary to spend some time speaking to the lads. After all, they were my priority, and I wanted to hear their thoughts on the trip so far. I'd hardly had time to start a conversation when anguished shouts from the back seat could be heard above Wilson's *Shelley's Mix* rave tape. Pete gratefully turned it off at my request, as I stood to and listened to a worrying question.

"J, where the fuck is Samson?"

It was only on leaving the gaol that had it been noticed that our numbers were not all present and correct. Stan, who had been sharing a room with Samson, had assumed he had been locked up along with the others, but he hadn't. The mood fell flat and the laughter changed to concern. Heads were scratched hard, and faces frowned as we all remembered where it was that any of us had last seen the lad.

I hoped I was wrong, but the sick feeling in my stomach churned up the image of Lily Savage. I shared the thought with the lads and they agreed. Samson was missing in action and the last place any of us could remember seeing him was Ban Dam, standing at the exit talking to Lily. My guts fell even flatter and my thoughts turned sinister. *Fuck me, he's either been mistaken for a squaddie by some IRA sympathisers and has ended up in a binliner at the bottom of the river, or even worse he's manacled face down on a bed biting a fucking pillow.* I kept my thoughts to myself and went into Sherlock mode.

Pete was less than impressed with my next request, though he remained silent and accepted the fact that I needed a police station as quickly as possible. Wilson and the lads took the opportunity to go shoplifting while I presented myself to the desk sergeant. Luckily Stan and Samson had doubled up on their luggage, and his passport details were immediately faxed to local hospitals, radio stations and the three hotels I'd booked us into. I then rang home to see if his parents had received word from him. They hadn't. All of a sudden the shine had gone off my trip. I was worried for the lad. Wilson had been less than helpful in keeping his eyes on the lads, and was one of the released detainees that morning himself. *Cheers mate.*

Berlin was the eye-opener we had expected. The Sport Hotel I had booked was nothing more than a converted block of workers' flats that resembled an open prison. The place was dull and shabby and the lads had their first chance to have a real moan.

"Fucking hell J, it's minging."

They were joking, I knew that, but Samson's disappearance was weighing heavily on my mind and I snapped back, "Oi, have you come here for a fucking holiday or a row with the Germans?" I was awarded the twenty minutes space that they knew I needed at times like this, bless them.

Half an hour later Donavan, Nidge and the others arrived by train from the gaol and lightened the mood with their story of the court proceedings and Nidge's outburst in front of the judge, claiming that he'd been picked on for no reason and that he would never return to Germany again. That was appropriate, as they were all awarded four-year bans from the country and heavily fined. It was a good job I'd left a tidy whipround at the gaol.

The English turnout in Berlin was moderate. Most were congregated below street level in an Irish bar opposite a weapons shop. Knowing that Berlin was most probably going to the best place for an encounter with German hooligans, most of the lads bought coshes and tins of CS gas.

"J, can I have a word?" Finbar was persistent as he pulled on the sleeve of my jacket. "That fucking China from Stockport is in that Irish bar with some Man City. Let's do the cunts."

Finbar and six of the Alsager lads had had a run in with China and thirty Stockport County late one night travelling back from a fixture at Oldham. They'd passed through Stockport's manor and had been spotted. The attack came on the train station. It was swift, vicious and uncalled for, but I suggested we bide our time. We had superior numbers in Berlin over any of the other English. I played the psychological game by entering the bar, exchanging a few pleasantries with China and his mates, and leaving. Finbar wasn't happy, but China wasn't either. They would have to travel into Poland the next day not knowing when or if a revenge attack was going to happen. *That's right lads, you sleep on it. Have a nice night.*

During a slight altercation between some English and locals, CS gas was let off, arousing the attention of the local police. That was our cue to mooch off into the back streets and find some fun of our own. It wasn't long before we left the city centre behind. We were all together, a tight firm saying nothing, drawing no attention to ourselves, prowling in the cold and damp of sleaze city, the part of town we felt most at home.

"Ay up lads, red lights up there on the right. Looks like daddy's coming home tonight."

Gooey had been scouting ahead and informed us that he'd found several local bars and a brothel. It was bitterly cold and a good time to get off the street and warmed up. Several lookouts were posted and Stoke's firm disappeared from view.

The majority of the lads went straight into a couple of the bars. The younger members, under the guidance of Mad Ant Walford, sat supping strong German lager and listening to Ant's tales of the Eighties: of how he would go to bed early on a Friday night so he had a clear head for the next day's fighting, and how, sometimes, before a major off he would piss his underpants because he was that excited. Ant was dedicated to the culture and had earned his nickname tenfold.

Knowing that the younger lads were in good hands, I went with fifteen others to what turned out to be a very dingy brothel. The door was so thick and solid that we expected Boris Karloff to answer it. Instead the small peephole opened up and a piercing blue eye scrutinized us from within. Seconds later the door opened and we were beckoned inside by an overweight madame in her sixties, with bleached blonde hair, huge tits and smoking a long menthol cigarette. She wore black gloves with diamond rings over them. I almost fell in love.

The place was dark and damp and the smell hit us instantly. We liked it, and no-one complained at the fifteen Deutschmark entrance fee. Inside was cramped, the size of a terraced house knocked through. We were shown to a cluster of leather beanbag chairs by the madame and a slightly younger Oriental woman, who nodded persistently and avoided eye contact. Happy with our surroundings, we sat down and ordered a round of drinks. Billy Burton was told to remain on a bar stool near the door. He knew immediately why, and remained perched on his stool, eyes like a hawk.

"Fucking all right in here, J. This will do us for an hour." Bradley leaned towards me, scooped a huge pile of cocaine on to a coin from his bag and shoved it up my right nostril. The lighting in the room grew dimmer and the lads shuffled in their seats as if preparing for a Saturday matinee. In front of us was a raised six-foot stage covered in a sheepskin rug. Behind it, a projector screen lit up and a Seventies-style colour-climax porn film began, to a dodgy soundtrack. The lads happily chuckled amongst themselves and slurped hard on their cheap supermarket beers.

She appeared from behind a crimson curtain. To most of the lads she brought a squirm, but she was just how I like 'em: big, black and ugly.

"Giz another scoop, Bradley. I might have a go on that in a min."

The lads knew what I was like and all the usual innuendos commenced. As the show began, the room started to fill up with more women, mainly Oriental and east African. Another round of beers was shouted up and the lads started to relax, treated to head and neck massages by the girls.

"Fucking love it here, I do. Better than Hanley any day." Nidge was happy.

Wilson came and sat next to me. "Have you noticed any type of security in here?" I hadn't and glanced over to see if Billy was doing his job properly. Transfixed, Billy was more interested in watching the mamma on the stage as she filled both holes with a double-ended dildo.

"Looks casual to me, but there's probably a room full of minders upstairs or something. It'll be all right, just stay on your toes."

Every one of the lads was now engaged in deep conversation with a woman, all with that love-sick puppy look. I checked my pocket out of instinct to see if my wallet was still safe, then returned my attention to the stage. To the left of the stage was a doorway covered with a net bead curtain and one by one the lads disappeared behind it.

More than an hour had passed since our arrival in the joint, which we had now aptly named "Madame Twang's". Beer had been swapped for vodka and our huddled whispers had become bellows of belly laughter as the antics inside had become more and more slapstick. We were all completely off our nut.

"Ay up Charlie, I think the momma's took a liking to you."

Ged was right. The huge Nigerian woman smiled as she sat down on the arm of my chair. I offered her a drink and she accepted as she wriggled in close, pushing her huge breasts towards my face.

"Be careful with the powder, sir, I see you like it a lot." She glanced towards the madame and whispered in my ear. "Is there some coca for me, handsome man?" Of course there was. Six different arses had been plugged full of it on the journey over. There was more cocaine than we knew what to do with. I slipped my left hand down her back and over her huge ass, pulling her cheeks to one side. I stroked her moist pussy with my finger. Circling her sphincter, I whispered back, "How would you like to snort a big fat line off my chunky cock?" Our eye contact remained hard and head-on as we played with each other.

"AARRGHH! She is dead! He has killed her!"

The moment was gone in a flash as the screams from the terrified woman behind the bead curtain sobered us all in an instant. She ran into the room in tears of despair. For a moment I was panic-stricken, wondering what the fuck had happened. That was until he appeared naked from behind the beads. Jimmy Two Steps was the firm's Italian Stallion, a real Pacino looker with a cock nearly as big as mine. The woman was obviously over-reacting as there was no look of panic on Jimmy's face, more one of disgust.

"Mine's fucking collapsed on me," he shouted.

He stood there like a rampant rapist, bollock naked, hands

on hips, sweaty hair stuck to his head, wearing nothing but a Durex and a pair of mountain socks. He looked more like Rigsby from *Rising Damp* than the Italian Stallion, and demanded another woman or his money back.

The madame lunged from her position behind the bar and an almighty row erupted. She claimed that Jimmy had broken her girl and demanded compensation, while he insisted he'd been ripped off and declared he was never coming back. I decided it was time to get off and meet up with the rest of the lads, and the signal was given. Before leaving, I had to have a look at what all the fuss was about. Entering the narrow corridor behind the beads, I leaned my head inside a doorway. Kneeling on the floor were two Asian women with a bucket of water and a sponge. On the bed with her legs up the wall and her head being mopped was an exhausted-looking young Thai girl.

One of the women looked up at me and said, "Arghh, your friend, he fuck too hard."

I smiled back and replied, "That's Jimmy Two Steps from Stoke, duck. He's a football hooligan."

That was Madame Twang's over for us. We pulled up our collars and hit the frost-bitten street in search of the rest of the crew and the main agenda. It was time to get down to some real business. We exited the brothel as a unit. No one was left behind. I made myself the last man through the door, half smiling at the Madame in an apologetic manner in acknowledgement of her broken hooker, but firm in the fact that she had taken more money on a Tuesday night than she normally would. The door closed heavily behind us.

A biting Berlin wind sobered me with every step. The temperature had plummeted significantly during our hour or so off the streets.

"Ay up, here's all the dirty bastards."

The remark came from a shadowed side street to our left. Mad Ant and the rest of the lads were tactically spread out, impatiently awaiting our arrival. They were all heavily drunk by now. Some looked bloodied and all had that rabid look to them. They had obviously been brawling.

"Has it gone off lads, or what?"

"Gone off? It's gone fucking mental."

A couple of skinheads had come up to the pub windows and peered in for some time, obviously counting the English numbers. Tommo stepped forward and showed us his broken and bleeding knuckles. He'd been alone outside, hidden in a doorway, having a knee-trembler with a street hooker, when he noticed an old Merc pull up alongside the road. The car was rammed with skins and two of them had got out and started to spy on the lads through the windows. Tommo observed their behaviour, keeping one eye on the skins and the other on the hooker, in case she decided to rifle his pockets while she was blowing away.

The lads assumed that someone from inside the pub had called the skinhead gang and informed them of the English presence. Tommo proceeded to tell everyone how he decided to forsake his carnal pleasure in favour of a good punch-up instead and after putting his hard-on away, still sheathed up, he charged from the shadows and tore into the skins from behind. Within seconds, Tommo had been joined by backup from the pub. They made short work of the Germans, beating the two spies to a pulp and managing to hurl a bar stool through the back window of the car as it sped away.

Everyone was sure that a massive backlash was shortly going to hit us on our route back into the city. We decided to march instead of stroll. The Stoke firm was now like a primed grenade ready to go off, all senses pinned and alert. Little conversation unless necessary. Breathing was controlled and heartbeats heavy. This was the buzz, the thrill that was so sought after, and we hoped for a major confrontation soon in the darkened streets before we hit the neon haze of the Berlin city centre. We were well out of our manor by choice. All of us present knew the dangers we might face. The excitement could hardly be contained, but instinct pushes you on. *Come on you German bastards, you know we're fucking here. Where are ya?*

We numbered around forty-five. It was a tidy mob and everyone was time-served and trusted. Nevertheless the order was given to tool up. We needed some heavier armament than the gas and coshes we'd obtained earlier in the evening. It didn't take a scientist to figure out that if we did cross paths with the Germans after the car incident, they would most probably outnumber us and be significantly better armed. Scaffolding poles were pulled from a derelict building and a skip emptied of planks of wood. Still we marched on into the darkness, slightly disorientated but keeping the orange-hazed sky up ahead as our guiding light. Adrenalin was abundant, you could almost smell it on people's breath. Fuck, I was turned on.

"Wow! Wait here in the dark a minute, spread out."

Every man heeded the warning and disappeared into small huddles in the shadows. The street fell eerily silent. We were being watched. I ran with Wilson and two others across the darkened street to a corner. We stopped and cautiously peered around the corner. The question was, "Why are there no local people about the streets when it's not yet midnight?"

The area we had walked through certainly was depraved. If an ambush was coming it was surely going to be in this vicinity, before we made it back into the city centre. We decided to wait and watch instead of making a break for the main road several hundred yards away. That main road spelt the end of the excitement and a chance of a passing police patrol latching onto us. I hadn't witnessed this, but several seconds before we'd gone to ground, a bald-headed figure had been seen running sharply across the street junction where we were now. Still we waited. Then it happened.

"Fuck this, let's fucking go."

The tension had become so unbearable that we all blew at the same time. It was a collective spontaneous combustion as we roared from the shadows, screaming at the tops of our voices and brandishing our weapons. Down into the blackened street we marched. As tightly as possible we filled the blackness with our light of defiance, daring anyone to come and take us on. Fear had crept in ever so slightly, fear of the unknown, fear of being pushed to your mental limit, the fear of remaining sane before insanity took you away with him forever.

"YARGHHH!" The roar sounded a million decibels louder than it actually was, as it echoed amongst the dimly lit, worn out tenements. "YARGHHH!" We surged on towards the light of the main road yards ahead, now our focal point. We reached it still tightly compact as a unit and turned immediately right towards Berlin central. The shouting stopped and laughter followed, mostly from relief.

The ambush had not materialized. Indeed the shadowy figure of the skinhead was most probably a figment of imagination. In our drink and drug-fuelled state, we had taken ourselves on a huge paranoia trip, with such a thin line between reality and fiction that it had become unbearably surreal. The consequences could quite easily have been so much more than an anxious laugh and a pointed finger. This was living life on the edge.

Time elapses and pales into insignificance when you're completely out of your senses. You feel comfort and strength from the unity. The feeling of being in a minority mindset, yet with so many unusual and powerful minds to place your own with. Your minority becomes an overwhelming majority, making you dangerous to the rest of normal society. Powerful is the word to describe the collective mindset of a firm of football casuals who are on foreign soil and completely off their heads.

We arrived in the jewellery quarter quite by mistake. With most of the weaponry long discarded, we marvelled at the brightly lit, gem-filled windows, a complete contrast to our surroundings of less than an hour ago. We found ourselves weaving amongst a throng of late-night revellers and clubbers. The aroma of frankfurter sausages filled our nostrils and expelled the stench of the ghetto. Those of the lads who had something of the Urchin inside them stood eyeing up a window full of Breitling watches. My gut told me that the night was very nearly coming to an end. I looked for an alibi and immediately struck up conversation with two fur-clad women. They responded in broken English. I glanced nervously over their shoulders as their remarks were followed by synchronized laughter.

The tube of scaffolding the lads carried was three and a half feet long. It had started the evening as a potential weapon. Its purpose was now as a battering ram to smash a jewellers' window. Four stood waiting with itchy fingers. Two stood as lookouts, the other two clasped each end of the pole and took six decisive steps backward. They straightened themselves up and prepared to charge.

"Ha, ha, ha." I joined in with the women's laughter, faking my understanding of what was so funny. Crash! The pole hammered into the glass, creating a small, round hole. Onlookers turned to observe as the word "again" was screamed several times. People began to run from the incident, others crowded round for a better view. I hung on to the fur-coated women who now stood watching, speechless.

Five times the jewel thieves attempted to breach the reinforced glass. Whipped into a frenzy of frustration, they attacked the window with dropkicks, punches and metal dustbins, all to no avail. I had already turned and walked away, hailing a cab, before the sirens could be heard. The jewel heist, for all its ferocity and determination, had been a failure.

In no time at all the police had mounted the pavement, spewing bodies in all directions. Riot police arrived in three vans, each officer carrying a small, round shield and brandishing a truncheon. They pretty much smashed anything and anybody. German or English, if you were within range, you suffered, yet nobody was arrested.

I arrived back at the hotel alone. The room key was not at reception so I knew someone else would be in. A sign said the lift was under repair. I doubted that it had ever worked. I walked up the seven flights of stairs to my spacious six-man suite. The music and noise found me as I turned on to the fifth floor. My only concern was that Pete the driver would be disturbed. Apart from that, I was glad the lads were all up and having a party. The hotel really was appalling. I doubt anyone had the intention of getting between the sheets and catching scabies. I was up for the night and by the sound of it, everyone else was as well.

There had been no news of any arrival by the name of Samson at the hotel desk. I knocked on the door of my room. It opened immediately. Inside a quiet discussion was taking place between some of the older, more senior members of the group. I walked inside and considered the expressions on several of their faces. Wilson sat quiet, not giving a damn about how poor his surroundings were. Yeah, we were all tired and needed a kip, but as far as Wilson was concerned there would be time enough to catch a couple of hours on the bus the next day. His face lit up when he saw me.

The six single beds were placed skew-whiff around one

metal framed table in the middle of the room. Some of the carpet tiles were missing and the windows had no curtains. I fixed my gaze on the face of the main protagonist, Mad Ant.

"What's up, Ant?"

"It's crawling, Jasp. The place is a fucking dump, mate. Disgusting."

He was right, it was, and I couldn't agree with him more when he suggested we'd be better off in some nice five-star gaff. But while we could afford to do that, not all of the lads could. We were booked in for two nights and, as scummy as it was, I'd decided to stick it out as part of the adventure. Wilson was up for staying as well, the first time he'd backed me up since leaving Stoke.

The atmosphere was a little tense. On the table in front of me was a paper cup. I leaned forward and dragged the cup towards me. I gave Ant a wry smile. It was time to relieve the tension. I undid the buttons of my jeans and jumped up on to the table. Still smiling devilishly at Ant, I dropped my pants. Holding the paper cup, I bent right over, shoving the cheeks of my arse towards Ant's shocked expression, and proceeded to squeeze hard. The huge black Guinness shit took its time to appear. I'd been wanting it all night. Unbelievably Ant remained motionless, watching in total disgust as the black turd hung heavily before dropping into the cup. Wilson was in stitches. I found it hard to contain my own laughter too, as I handed Ant the cup and said, "Ant. That's fucking disgusting, mate." I jumped down from the table and flicked the shit onto Ant's pillow. Everyone in the room by now was gipping with laughter, including Ant, who had seen the funny side. We all decided to stay up. *Fuck it, let's party.*

Breakfast was another sorry sight. Everyone looked completely haggard. The continental breakfast was meagre and most just sipped at black coffee. Pete had again suffered a sleepless night. His room had been next to the Under-Fives, our younger element, who had spent most of the night pulling the train on two exchange students from the States. Pete had heard it blow for blow. The man looked to be in shock.

Crash! The restaurant door was flung open and smashed into the wall. Enter an enraged and perplexed Nidge, holding his pink flannel up in front for us all to see.

"Those dirty German pigs have left a shit in my fucking face cloth. The bastards!"

Everyone fell about laughing, even Pete. It was a good start to the day. Everyone was happy and I'd been reunited with some old DNA. No-one ever did tell Nidge the true source of the turd. Most agreed he did deserve the present. Plus, he enjoyed the attention. We boarded the coach, itching but upbeat.

"Right, Pete, ready when you are. Let's get to Poland."

Not one of us got a wink of sleep on the two-hour journey to the border, Wilson saw to that. I hated that rave music, I think we all did by the end of the trip. Worryingly there had still been no word on Samson.

The German-Poland border post was in countryside and not in a town as we had expected. For as far as the eye could see in either direction, scratching a mark across lush fields, stood a sixteen-foot metal mesh fence with barbed wire running along the top. Few comments were passed as we drove slowly towards border control and the armed Polish guards. Patiently, Pete pulled his coach into line and queued with the Ladas and trucks. One other coach caught our eye, an official supporters' coach from the England Travel Club. They closed their curtains and avoided any contact with us, fearful of being infected from the disease that we were.

I sat next to Pete at the front. "How's it looking Pete? Do you think we will be here long?" Pete raised his concerns about the seven passengers he was carrying who held no valid visas to enter Poland. I assured him it would be alright and no comebacks would land on his lap. He disagreed and pointed out for me to take notice as several unfriendly-looking soldiers mounted the England supporters' coach.

I paid a lot of attention. An exuberant Polish Army officer looked to be enjoying the sight of his troops taking each of the English supporters off their coach to an office in the bunker, and identifying them individually with their passport photographs and visas. Locals sat patiently in their vehicles saying little about their annoying hold up. The Poles were taking their time, and the search of the other coach was meticulous. I decided to heed Pete's concerns and warn the lads to stash things and have a quick tidy. I headed towards the stowaways at the back and explained the situation. It looked dire for them; in truth their journey ended there. I told them to discreetly jump out of the back exit and walk the several miles back to the last town we passed through and catch a train back to Berlin. My suggestion was met with disapproval, but I said, "Oi, you had six months to get your visas for this trip. You're not fucking it up for the rest of us. Off the coach now."

That was my final word on the matter. I was gutted, to be honest. I'd been made up when the likes of Billy and Sid Stringer turned up at Minstrels. They made me laugh, especially Sid with his scarred face and NHS glass eye that remained bright blue and motionless in a face full of character. Yet the eye seemed to follow your every move at all times. Weird. Sid and his glass eye were the last to disappear off the coach. In seconds we'd lost sight of the stowaways in the long queue of traffic to our rear.

"Fucking hell, Pete, how long now?"

The lads were getting impatient. It took the best part of an hour before the troops appeared next to Pete at the front of the coach. Everyone sat quietly, eyeing up their armoury and listening to their harsh dialect as they ordered us, with quickfire gestures, off the coach four at a time.

I got off first with Wilson, Finbar and Chief. We were pushed to one side and told to stand by a wall. All four of us stared at two concrete towers, which we could now see were gun emplacements. Each of the heavy machine guns either side of the road was manned by what looked like young conscripted troops who were doing their best to shit us up. Pricks.

The official England coach had disappeared over half an hour ago. Obviously some snidey bastard on it had said something to the Poles about us. Several alsatian dogs appeared, along with a dozen or more heavily armed soldiers. They seemed very concerned about our party. Pete did his utmost to smooth things over with the Polish officer who took little notice. We noted his efforts, though. Pete was starting to warm to us. The Poles gave us the third degree, which added a couple of hours to our journey, but eventually they let us enter their country. I sat next to Pete as we were beckoned through. Slowly the coach drove over the border, past the now grinning guards, barking dogs and machine gun posts. We all sneered back in silent defiance, knowing full well they had made a mistake letting us in, and by the afternoon we would be brawling somewhere.

After the barbed wire fences were several hundred yards of thick undergrowth before a dense line of forest darkened the sky. It was pitifully bleak. I knew one thing: I didn't fancy getting nicked this side of the border. The thick tree line lasted for about a quarter of a mile before we hit the open road again. Poznan was now only a couple of hours' drive away. The lads were excited again and the smell of marijuana and sounds of excited chatter filled the coach. Amazingly, the sun appeared and the landscape became bright and fresh. We were still out in the sticks but we could see people walking along the road, heading towards wherever. Horses pulled carts of hay, which children and the elderly alike hitched a ride on. Poultry ran wild. It was like a scene from *Poldark*.

"Jesus Christ."

Pete slammed on the brakes causing us to skid and veer slightly off the road. Pete started effing and blinding out of relief at not losing control of his vehicle. His outburst was directed at a peasant stood in the middle of the road in front of us, waving his arms frantically. I started a tirade of four-letter abuse too. "Silly cunt, you could have fucking killed us. What's up with you?" The coach followed suit, erupting into aggression combined with relief.

The peasant took no heed as he dashed to the door of the coach and banged on it desperately. I looked down at the man, half wanting to give him a slap. Dressed in what looked like rags and covered in shit and grass from head to toe, his blood-splattered face looked up at me in a knowing way through the door windows. I controlled my anger and stared harder. Somehow I felt a connection with the waif. Still banging hard on the glass, nodding and staring at me, he wiped away the stream of blood trickling from a cut on his forehead. It appeared, shockingly, from beneath the crimson, a bright blue National Health Service glass eye. I almost immediately wet my pants with hysterics, as did everyone else when we realized who the frantic peasant actually was.

Sid Stringer had managed to crawl on his hands and knees across a border that people had been trying to breach since the end of the Second World War. Plenty had died in the attempt. He climbed on to the coach a mightily relieved man, to a tremendous reception from the lads. Even Pete was in uproar. Sid was a mess. He stank of shit, was soaking wet and his clothes were torn to shreds. He was also bleeding heavily from barbed wire cuts.

Off he went towards the back to tell one and all about his

escapades. I shook my head at Pete as he composed himself and pulled off. I kept a thought to myself for now. Yes, it was hilarious that Sid had been so stubborn and determined to break into Poland, but how the hell was he going to get back out again?

Laughter and fresh banter filled our short journey into the Polish city of Poznan. Pete's first question was where did we want him to drop us off? It was decided to get as near to the ground as possible, jump off the coach and disappear into a bar before we were sussed by the police. It was still only just after midday. Getting into the city undetected was imperative for the success of the rest of the day. We didn't want to end up with any unwanted attention. Pete was told to lose us, park up at the ground and wait for us there. It would be almost ten hours before he would see us again.

We drank in a bar for a short time before heading off in search of three things: the city centre, match tickets, and the local hooligans. We found the first two easily. The match tickets we bought from touts for as little as £2 apiece. So cheap were the tickets we decided not to rob the touts and give them a slap, as we would normally. In Berlin most of us had changed £50 into Polish currency and it was looking like we'd find it hard to spend a third of that. It was cheap but you wouldn't want to purchase anything from anywhere other than a bar. Even the fruit on the market stalls looked old and wrinkled, and with no visible fast food joints, we all decided to drink vodka to kill the hunger pains. What a great idea that was.

By three o'clock most of us had wandered round the centre of Poznan a dozen times. There was nothing to it and we were getting bored. We'd spent the afternoon looking for a firm to fight. German or Polish thugs would do or, failing that, China from Stockport and his Man City mates, but no joy, so on we carried with the vodka. We were getting blitzed.

Sex, Drugs and Football Thugs

The first real English crew we met were the LTE, the Lincoln Transit Elite. They had a vanload of tasty-looking older lads. With no bad history between us, we enjoyed their company for several hours. They told us that most of the English were on the other side of town, drinking in a hotel. Chelsea had a crew there and were a bit moody towards any northerners. Fine, we replied, that suited us. They added that the previous night had been eventful and the Cockneys had been battling with some tough locals. That was a sobering thought. We all started to feel a bit happier at the prospect of some fireworks after all.

Dusk fell early and quickly, and with it the mood darkened. We decided to get on the move. We said goodbye to the LTE and headed on foot towards the stadium a couple of miles away. It was time to make our presence felt. As we set off for the long walk towards the ground, Wilson decided to nip into a shop, pick a thirty pence bottle of vodka off the shelf and walk off without paying for it. It was an insane thing to do by any standards. He was promptly arrested as he left the shop by undercover police, who were tailing us. A scuffle ensued as some of our lads tried to free the struggling Wilson but more police swiftly arrived, bundled him into a van and attempted to arrest several others as well. We made a dash for freedom and suddenly we were well and truly split up. I was fuming with my best mate for that act of absurdity. *A thirty pence bottle of vodka, for fuck's sake.* After keeping it tight all day, our numbers had been decimated in seconds. Angrily I headed on into the night with ten of the others.

For most of the day we'd seen little if anything of the locals. That began to change the farther we got away from the centre and closer we got to the football stadium. It wasn't a rundown town like parts of Berlin, it was just bland and tough-looking, rather like the local men who stood around in small huddles in their hob-nailed boots and dirty work clothes.

"I'll tell you what lads, some of these look as though they've just come straight from the pit."

Stan was right, they did look as though they had just come straight from work. We half fronted them, not sure if they were the right people to start a fight with. They stared at us with blank expressions. Nothing happened, so on we walked, slightly unnerved at the lack of resistance we were facing. I started to think to myself that perhaps they were letting us walk on towards something more dangerous than themselves. The adrenalin kicked in bang on cue, and on we marched.

We arrived at the stadium and immediately met up with fifteen of the others. Together we circumnavigated the ground looking for some local resistance. Again we found none. With a little over an hour to go to kick-off, we decided to just keep on the move around the stadium, firm in the belief that sooner or later it would happen. And as we began a second lap, it did.

A stocky fella emerged from the crowd and started shouting, "Polski, Polski," towards some English who had gathered by the away supporters' turnstiles. He was wearing a ski hat, one with a long tail down his back. A Huddersfield Town fan walked towards the man and spread his arms open saying, "Come on, I'm English, I'll have it." We watched in silence as the one-on-one ended with the hat-wearing Pole pulling out a can of gas and spraying it into the Yorkshire lad's face, saying, "Fack off you mug. I'm fackin' Chelsea and we're fackin' England."

Impressed, we side-glanced each other and headed off again. We walked away from the ground on to a car park covered in little barbecue stalls selling hot food, mostly big fat greasy sausages. Each of the stalls was covered in little fairy lights that ran along the roofs connecting the stalls together. Rising from the burning hot plates were clouds of smoke that rose up above the lights, giving it the look of a shanty town from a *Mad Max* film.

Most of us bought some hot food, our first meal of the day and stood eating, keeping one eye on our sausage and the other on our surroundings. The whole area was becoming busy, with thousands of people filing past us towards the ground. It was a strange atmosphere, almost like the calm before the storm, the Poles apparently walking around in slow motion yet slightly animated. As I munched on my food, I took a look over my shoulder towards a garage that was being built. The mist rising up from the food stalls had blown over towards it and hung thick under the forecourt canopy. The bright light from the floodlights gave it a density that was difficult to see through. I stopped chewing as I caught a sound and listened hard. I remained transfixed, staring under the garage roof and deeply into the mist.

"Hear that lads? Hear that?"

It was definitely a chant. It sounded deep and aggressive. We all stopped eating and looked towards the dense, white mass. Excitement and fear hit us all at once, and what was left of our sausages was discarded and replaced by our weapons.

"This is it. This is fucking it. They're here." Ged was excited. We were all excited, as we moved slowly towards the garage, straining our ears. The sound of a marching mob grew louder as the twenty-five of us prepared to do battle. We had travelled a long way for this moment. Slightly disappointed with our numbers, I looked at the quality of the men beside me: Ged, Gibbo, Cragg, Batto, and so on. I knew we wouldn't budge and a surge of excited anticipation lasered through my body, making me tremble from head to foot. This was the addiction being fed whole-heartedly. This was the main course.

The busy road directly to the left of us was a matter of yards away and still visible. Gibbo spotted them first. "Hey lads, look on the road over there. That's a film crew. Come on we've got a chance of getting on the news here." The news crew had already been filming for several minutes. They had followed alongside a combined mob of Polish and East German skinheads numbering well over 200. Their front line was just about to cut through the garage forecourt. The skins had a heavy police presence with them and were also aware of the camera crew. They were putting on a bit of a show. The one thing that the skins were not aware of was only yards away, hidden in the mist. Twenty-five members of Stoke's N40 were frothing at the mouth. Tooled up and ready to go, we stood, straining our eyes. The first fifty appeared seconds later. Dozens were wearing orange flight jackets with black arms, all had tight, short-cut jeans and wore German Para boots, some with the leather cut out of the toe to show gleaming steel caps.

For the first time in my life, I have to admit, I pissed my pants slightly. I was so terrified and excited at the same time, and I knew there was no turning back. I exploded.

"Yaarrrgh!"

Into the mist we charged. Hate-filled, we clattered our enemy with coshes and knuckledusters, every one a head shot, aiming for maximum destruction. Within a split second in the mist I had lost sight of everyone I knew. It was like being on the battlefield at Culloden. Images all around me hacked at each other bitterly. I aimed my blows at anything that had orange on it. Several times I was knocked sideways as I too received direct hits. I could taste blood. It spurred me on.

As more bodies entered the garage the mist started to disappear. I could see clearly now, we all could, and the skins could see they were being routed by inferior numbers. They charged again with renewed ferocity, gaining a slight edge.

Sirens could be heard and riot police appeared to my left. Still the battle raged on. To my right Gibbo and Ged were back to back, staving off an assortment of attackers. One, a geezer in his forties, almost looked out of place he was so casually dressed. What made him different to an English casual was the length of his ponytail. Even so he was game as fuck, and leathered Ged with a telescopic cosh.

Bang! I fell to the floor, sent reeling by a blow to my left shoulder. I scrambled to my feet, frightened of being over-whelmed and taking a serious beating. The battle continued. It was close-quarter combat at its best. Regaining my composure, I could see that we were starting to come unstuck. Most of the skins had been split and driven backwards away from the garage by the riot police, who mainly concentrated on them to prevent an escalation of the situation. Even so, there were still at least fifty of them plus the casual with long hair left on the forecourt. It must have been brutal viewing for anyone not involved, although I bet the news crew was loving it.

I picked another target and aimed a punch at one of three skins getting the better of Gibbo. Crack! A cosh hit me again. Crack! Another blow from a cosh leathered across Gibbo's head. I rushed forward, trying to grab the cosh to prevent a second and possible fatal blow. It was pulled back with such force that it broke my left thumb, leaving it dislocated and hanging oddly off the side of my hand. I screamed in agony. Luckily, I still managed to pull Gibbo free. We were picking up injuries now and most of us were hopelessly out of breath.

"Come on!"

It was a sweet sound. The white Transit van screeched to a halt and the twelve Lincoln lads piled into the garage with unforgiving venom. What a feeling it gave us all, as well as a fresh wind. Our reinforcements turned the tide and the English were getting the better of it again. Still in agony, I tried one more attempt to relieve Ged, who was trading punches with the cosh-wielding casual. Luckily, most of the blows on Ged were to the body, and it was so cold Ged had four jumpers on, so he was hardly feeling them.

Nursing my broken hand, I placed a well aimed kick into the thigh of Ged's attacker. The man, who was obviously enjoying himself, gave a smile and pulled a neck chain out from under his jumper. On the chain was a police ID card.

"Stop, polize, polize."

Ged and I turned and fled back down into the shanty town. Breathless, we stopped and looked back. The battle was over. The only bodies left on the forecourt were horizontal ones. Police officers with long sticks became silhouettes as Ged, Gibbo, myself and several others legged it away to a bar in a side street at the other side of the stadium. We all needed a stiff drink. Plus I needed someone to try and put my thumb back in its socket. We agreed without doubt that had it not been for the Lincoln Transit Elite, we might not have got out of that garage.

I put two pairs of tight gloves on over my broken thumb to try to give it a bit of support. Even so, I was still in agony as I stood behind the goal watching the lads filling the fences with their Stoke flags. The English turnout was bigger than I first thought. As I read a multitude of slogans, I counted the number of firms present: Leeds Service Crew, Pompey 6.57, Chelsea Headhunters, Birmingham Zulu Warriors and the West Ham Inter City Firm. None of them had the numbers that Stoke had but all were there that night.

The stadium was huge, open and packed. England needed at least a point, Poland needed a win. The atmosphere was tense and highly aggressive. More and more of our lads started to show up behind the goal. All had stories of exciting skirmishes they'd been involved in outside, a couple even witnessed the aftermath of the garage battle. We'd done better than we first thought, as reports counted at least a dozen injured skinheads.

There was no animosity between English firms inside the ground, as we had at first expected, although just after kick-off the end opposite us erupted with fighting between what we were led to believe were Nazis and Communists. This continued sporadically throughout the match. I took time out to nurse my injury and have a look at some of the faces there from other firms. I walked around the away enclosure on my own throughout the first half, chatting briefly with Harold and some of the Villa lads, and promising China of all people a lift back to Berlin on our coach. *Finbar's gonna love this*, I thought.

Half-time provided one of the funniest sights of the entire trip. I could hear my name being called by several people, headed down to the fence at the front, and climbed it to see what the fuss was all about. Several groundsmen, one on a motorised roller, were busy at work, filling divots around the goal mouths.

"So what's all the fuss?"

"No, no, not them, look over at the centre circle."

Bradley had tears streaming down his face as I followed his direction to the centre of the pitch. Recognition had me shouting and waving with the rest at a bemused and disoriented Wilson as he walked around the pitch, completely off his head. He looked mindless. After seeing him arrested for the theft of the vodka, I'd already arranged to stay in Poznan for the night with two others to wait for his release. As pissed off as I was with him, I would never have left him. Now, seeing him free and making us belly roll with laughter, he was my best mate again. We beckoned him over.

Ever the jammy bastard, Wilson on being arrested had been taken to a gaol not far from the ground. He was taken to an interview room and told to wait. In his pocket was my quarter of hash that he'd been about to skin up with before his arrest. He decided that theft was a bad enough charge without possession of cannabis so he ate the lump and sat waiting for his fate.

An aggressive police captain returned with a lady several

minutes later. She was the owner of the shop he had stolen from. An intensive interrogation began in broken English, resulting in Wilson finding the word "sorry" in a translation book on the desk. He said it to her while pulling a suitably sorry face. She took pity on him and spoke to the captain. Reluctantly, he told Wilson he could go. He gave the woman a handful of Polish notes and floated out of the gaol. Minutes from the ground, he followed the noise and light from the stadium. Somehow he managed to crawl under a turnstile and ended up in the middle of the pitch, looking for me to apologise for not making that joint I'd asked him for a couple of hours before. I was over the moon to see him, but still bollocked him for losing my hash.

The second half kicked off, and so did the Poles. To our left, a mob of several thousand had gathered during half-time. They all looked rugged and up for a fight. Ripped up terracing and lumps of concrete hurtled down at us from their elevated position. All the time firecrackers and flares illuminated them and a red mist gave them the look of devils. They hated us, and you could quite clearly see that they wanted to kill us.

We responded by hurling the concrete back at them over the twelve-foot fences. Stood with us in hysterics at the antics of a bunch of drug-addled northerners, were several prominent members of the ICF. They roared with laughter at the site of Wilson driving the motorised roller into the fence in an attempt to smash through it. Police appeared in numbers to pull us down off the fences and whipped the backs of our legs and shoved us away with their rifle butts. They paid little attention to their countrymen, who continued their onslaught with renewed vigour. We incensed them even more as we stood, defiantly holding handfuls of their currency aloft and burning it with our lighters.

This also upset the riot police who donned their helmets and took a tougher stance against the English. For most, the fun and games were over. They had had enough of us and wanted us gone. And most of us acknowledged the fact that a night in Poznan after the game could get a bit hairy. Our group was rounded up immediately after the final whistle and shepherded back to our waiting coach. Pete was sat, engine running, looking mightily relieved it was time to head back over the border to Berlin and his pit. It must have been a long day for him, sat around waiting for us. The lads acknowledged this by quickly taking their seats and staying reasonably quiet on the journey back to the Polish border.

China and his mate from Stockport also remained quiet on the journey. The only time I saw them speak was to marvel at Sid Stringer being dropped off the coach several hundred yards from the border and rejoining us slightly out of breath on the other side. Twice in one day, in and out of a closed border. Amazing. It was amazing too that China and his mate didn't get any grief off any of the lads for their attack on the Alsager boys that night on the train station. But the lads were better than that. The point was made the right way.

Slightly disappointed on our arrival back at the hotel that there was no sign of Samson, I called it a day. We were all knackered. It had been a long one, and the vodka and drugs had us all looking like old men. I think most of us slept all night and most of the next day before Pete pulled his coach into Amsterdam and the finale to the trip. Sleaze city once again.

I was truly thankful that the third and final hotel of the trip was of a decent standard. Most of us spent at least twenty minutes under a piping hot shower before heading to the arranged meet in the hotel foyer.

"Mr Samson? No, I am afraid no one of that name has checked in here Mr Chester."

"OK. But if he does turn up, will you give him a key to room 138 please. We are all eager to see him."

It was more out of hope than expectation that I made my request before heading out into the red lights of Holland's legalised Babylon. It almost makes it less attractive when what you are about to indulge in is within the law. All the same, we headed to our favourite coffee shop, just off Dam Square, and purchased some super skunk and a couple of grams of oil, something that was an acquired taste to most and usually hard to obtain.

Cocaine, marijuana, strong Dutch lager and compliant women of the night were to take the edge off what had been a grueller of a week. With no visible police presence and no other moody firms to keep a track of, the lads relaxed awhile and spent some time to reflect on what we had all been through together. Much laughter was heard that night, and still is to this day.

Even Amsterdam wasn't incident free. How could it have been with that lot in town? Gooey kicked off in a brothel because the momma had promised a gangbang for himself and four others. She took their money and the five all undressed and stood expectantly. Maybe it was a misunderstanding or the fact that Gooey's feet stink to high heaven, but what was promised never materialised. The story goes that as the lads made off, semi-naked, Gooey's outburst grew louder. "I've paid me money, now suck the fucker," was the last any of them heard as they turned the corner and fled. All agreed that Gooey was lucky to get out of that place alive; moody hardly summed it up.

To end it all, my best mate, Wilson, was arrested on the ferry for robbing duty free perfume. Luckily he was allowed to pay for what he had taken and released without charge, and we headed back home to Stoke.

"Cheers for helping me keep an eye on the lads this week, mate," I said to Wilson as we sat at the back of the coach smoking a reefer.

"No worries, mate. I told you I'd give you a hand."

He didn't expect a reply. He knew I would just laugh. And I did, from the bottom of my belly. Anyway, what are friends for?

Pete pulled his coach up outside the Freetown nightclub late that Friday night. He was visibly relieved and also choked. I handed him a blue moneybag with a £700 whipround. He squeezed it and thanked us all for the experience. He told us that we had grown on him and that he had actually started to enjoy himself towards the end. You know, I really believed him too.

A mountain of sports bags was piled by the door, and the fifty or so battle-hardened casuals entered the club to a heroes' welcome. They'd all made it home. It was good to be back in Stoke. Most of the lads' girlfriends were elated to see them, and the N40 who hadn't travelled with us were just as keen to hear of our exploits.

I hadn't even had a sip of my first vodka when the news breached the bowels of the club and was quickly passed along to me. After four days missing in action, Samson had been found by some Interpol officers. He was still in Dusseldorf, and by all accounts was wandering the streets dazed and confused, without a penny to his name and with no recollection of what had happened to him. The club was ecstatic and everyone raised their glasses in jubilation and relief. I raised mine too and took a hard slug of vodka, but I remained silent.

To this day, Samson too has remained silent about his ordeal in Germany. It is a subject that has been left overseas. I would have liked an explanation, as I spent most of the week with him playing heavy on my mind when I would have preferred to relax and enjoy the absurdities. But there you go, at least my initial concerns about him being at the bottom of the river in a binliner weren't true. As for biting a pillow? Well I guess we will never know. Some things are better not spoken about.

Chapter Nine

Road Trip

FROM THE MOMENT I looked her in the eyes, I knew I was a long way from home. Green was always my favourite colour and her eyes were greener than the pastures in God's garden. Nor had I ever seen hair like hers, not anywhere, not that soft and black. Have you ever seen a perfect smile with teeth so white that you went home and cleaned yours for days? Brandy had a smile like that. She even had one of those little black beauty spots just above her lip and to the left of her right nostril. When she called out my name with her soft Latino accent, I lit up inside and turned immediately. I too would always smile; it was hard not to.

When driving her Pontiac, her hair blew across her face and she would smile and pull it from her eyes. The rest of it blew behind her wildly. She would sometimes glance at me when a favourite record was being played on the radio and lick her flushed lips to me in approval. Each time I would slap the dashboard, shout out "Yeehaa," and turn up the dial. Brandy would put her foot down on the accelerator with cute, perfectly formed toes on which she wore silver rings. I marvelled at her slender manicured hands and nails. She used those nails on me, especially her thumb nails.

Sometimes we would sit together amongst the sand dunes on Pizmo beach and Brandy would make fun of my British Bulldog tattoos. She would giggle and occasionally, if I was not seeing the funny side of her jest, bite my earlobe. How could I expect a Mexican-American cowgirl not to find a dog wearing Union Jack shorts and smoking a cigar funny?

Her tattoo I could relate to. It was the first sign that led me to believe that she had lived a diverse kind of life. Below her bikini line on her right buttock was a picture of a war-torn Confederate battle flag. Below it, inscribed in Latino-style writing, were the words, "American by Birth, Southern by the Grace of God."

Believe me, in a previous life I fought as a footsoldier in the Confederate Army. I have some kind of notion that I was killed on the battlefield at Shilo. I died fighting for a cause that I believed in. Looking at her tattoo gave me a feeling that I was back home where I belonged. It comforted me. She comforted me.

Even without a beautiful and intricate woman beside me, California made me happy. I was twenty-seven years old when I first arrived in the States and apart from the fact that I had a mounting cocaine habit, I was still reasonably fit and in good shape. Not a bad catch if you liked the rough type that also knew which fork to use first.

People often remarked on what an attractive couple we made. They may have been pleasantries, but I felt they were true. It is fair to say that I was falling in love for the first time in my life with an insanely beautiful, sultry woman. The only problem was that Brandy was a Hollywood hooker who worked from a phone booth advert.

So fucking what? This was a carefree period of immoral living where the neon signs were endless along roads that stretched forever. I did not give a damn she was on the game.

She wore snakeskin cowboy boots and made me laugh. She also loved The Eagles, my favourite band. Some of their lyrics in one particular song tell of a woman who marries an older man for his money and cheats on him regularly with her first love from the old town where she grew up. "Lyin' Eyes" is about deceit and has an undertone about women and how they put a price on every man regardless of whether he is paying for it or not.

"You can't hide your lyin' eyes,

"And your smile is a thin disguise.

"I thought by now you'd realise,

"There ain't no way to hide your lyin' eyes."

There has never been a truer saying in my mind. For the three months I spent on the road with Brandy, I never once saw that hidden look of deceit in her eyes. Their honest smile always reflected back into mine. Her life was mysterious and carefree and she was as bang up for it as I was. There was no getting off this rollercoaster. Born of mixed-race parents, she had clean and honest morals. She just chose to earn her living on the street, that's all.

The sun had shone for the best part of three days without a hint of a downpour. This wasn't bad for round our way. Most people would say that if you got more than a week of sunshine it was a great summer. But by 1991 I'd had a gutful of Stoke. Apart for the football and the firm, there was little else to hang around for.

I had taken my first Ecstasy tablet in 1987. We, a small group of Stoke lads, had run Benidorm and most of the drug trade in it for several seasons. Everyone in the Spanish resort knew it. They might not have liked it, but nothing was ever said, at least not in the beginning. The pills were clean then and the people pioneering their experimentation were mostly faces in the towns and cities from which they hailed. It was a cool scene to be around and the sex that went with it was as liberal and pure as it was in the Sixties. For a couple of years at least, people felt free.

I blame it on the caps; it was the Scud Missiles and Dennis the Menaces that turned it all dirty. Rammed full of powder with a bit of ketamine, some amphetamine and half a trip. All of a sudden people were sucking lollipops and rubbing Vicks on each other's chests, looking gaunt and filling their sweat-ridden shellsuits whilst gathered in crowded corridors and stairwells. Jesus, even going for a piss was depressing. It can be the problem when you're ahead of the rest: the masses are just catching you up as you're starting to get bored of the buzz. I needed a change.

I'd spoken too soon. The rain began to fall hard and forced me to seek shelter. Well, we hadn't done too badly. It had been over a week since the last downpour. I skipped into the doorway of Minstrels wine bar, exchanged pleasantries with the doorman and ordered coffee. It may have been mid-afternoon and midweek but there was always a chance that some kind of menace could be waiting with a vendetta, so I scanned the place.

It seemed to be clear. A couple of mothers were attempting to catch up on gossip over the demands of a three-year-old, but other than that there was only myself and one other figure, who sat alone in the bottom corner of the room. He faced the other way and paid little attention to his surroundings. Now if that was one of my mates they would be facing the other way, positioned in a strategically advantageous manner. Nevertheless, that posture, the relaxed shoulders, even the colour of his hair were all familiar. I looked harder.

Gibbo was one of my oldest friends. We had sat at the same table at school and served our hooligan apprenticeships together. It had been a long time. I was delighted to see him. Nothing had changed. It was just like we were back in the classroom laughing our bollocks off at Lenny Payne, our science teacher, after we had burned his beard off with iron filings we had hidden in his Bunsen burner. It had been more than five years since we had seen each other, but it didn't matter, when you come from our culture and have lived within our code, you don't change.

"So, what you been up to G?" I spoke in a whisper, almost as if I were expecting him to tell me he was sat waiting for a shipment of Peruvian flake. It turned out that he had just sold his antiques business in Cheshire. He had tried the normal route and had eventually begun to hate it. He too needed a change. He was feeling as down as he first looked. Gibbo wanted to party again and I was just the person to party with.

"I'm thinking about getting off, Jasp. I'm nearly thirty, mate. I want to see a bit of the world."

This was sweet music to me. I ordered up a couple more cappuccinos and asked him if he had anywhere in mind.

"California mate," he said with a wry smile. He knew full well that I had always talked about going there one day. He also knew I would not be able to resist the thought of going with him.

"I wanna go and swim in the Pacific Ocean. Snort cack off a hooker's bare tits and watch *Bonanza* seven nights a week."

My reply was fast and excited. Gibbo chuckled. He knew he had found his travelling companion. He looked chuffed. Nothing ever does change.

"When are you planning on going?"

"As soon as possible."

By chance I had a grand on me. We sank our coffees and

walked laughing through the bouncing rain. Funny how all of a sudden getting soaking wet is part of an adventure.

I paid for two seat tickets to Los Angeles, with a stop-off in Dallas. Yeehah! Six days later we were there.

"Ladies and gentlemen, if you would like to take a moment to look out of the right side windows, the city you can see nestled in the valley between the two mountains is Pheonix, Arizona. Through the left hand windows, ladies and gentlemen, is the Rio Grande river. The mountains away in the distance are in Mexico. Ladies and gentlemen, welcome to the United States of America."

The captain of that plane had no idea who I was or even what I was about. To him that was a routine speech; he was probably picking his nose as he said it. But with those words he had just made me the happiest man in the world. Gibbo and I raised a Coors beer and promised each other that if one of us made it he would take the other with him. When I looked back out towards Mexico I also cried one solitary tear. In a strange way I kind of felt that I was coming home.

We were both nervous as we passed through immigration. For some reason I thought I was going to get turned back. It blew me away when I got in. We beckoned a waiting cab.

"Where are we going to go, Jasp?" Gibbo's voice carried concern.

"Straight to the ocean, G. Let's get our feet in the water and backs to the Pacific and anything we have got to face is there in front of us." These were good football hoolie tactics about getting into space. The ocean felt cool and refreshing, and the Malibu sunset looked relaxed as it said another "goodnight" to the land of milk and honey.

We didn't hang about. LA at night was not the place to get caught out in. We weren't your normal package trip holiday-makers either, with a warm hotel bed waiting for us. Our intentions were to stay as long as we could without being deported. To push life to the max, whilst keeping it within the boundaries of just plain and simple mischief. A decent motel and we were sorted for a couple of days. It was now time to go and announce ourselves.

You could smell the wealth in Santa Monica. It was almost stifling. Jesus, we were going to have to be slick to get it on around this part of town. With little money but a bucketful of ideas, we became predators on the prowl for the first opportunity to make a hit. First priority was to find a place to live or doss. We could only afford the motel for another week, after that we were fucked. I got the raging hump about it straight away and Gibbo said that we should have known better.

Being knocked back at the door of a busy, open-fronted club rammed full of beautiful women because we couldn't prove our ages also had me fuming. We had already walked for more than half an hour to save money on a cab and now I had to go back to the hotel room to pick up our passports before we could have a beer. In all fairness the two cool-as-fuck doormen were sound with us. Let's put it down to jetlag or something but I was a bit volatile, which was unusual for me.

It was no bother, Santa Monica never closed. It was still moving the next night when we pulled up outside the same club in front of the same two doormen. We looked pretty smug in the back of that open-topped Mustang. Shawna and her girlfriend, Isabella, were hot. Gibbo said we were definitely on, and that it was time to start playing our characteristics off against each other to entertain the girls. I agreed and went into my Sir Charles Aznavour Esquire alter ego. He can be a very charming gentleman at times and a complete bastard at others. All the same, his rugged chisel-jawed features always proved a winner.

The previous night, instead of going back into Santa Monica, we'd hung out around Venice, where our motel was. There was a multitude of hip bars to choose from, most with that psychedelic Doors/Beach Boys touch to them. All had available women and some even smelt ever so slightly of marijuana, which was nice.

She seemed delighted and almost broke into a giggle as she pointed at the packet of Silk Cut cigarettes.

"May I?"

"Help yourself, love, they're duty free."

It was as simple as that and we were in. The very next morning we moved out of our beachside motel into a loft conversion in a Culver City suburb where most of the houses had swimming pools and established trees lining their drives. It wasn't a bad gaff at all and would certainly do us for the time being.

Shawna worked as a physiotherapist in Beverly Hills and shared the practice with Isabella's half brother. She had a fiancé, Jay, but he was a heart surgeon living in New York, and she hardly ever saw him. Plus, over the last two Thanksgivings he'd forgotten to call her, at work or at home. I thought they were definitely on the rocks. Her pad was like something out of *Miami Vice*. The thick shag pile carpet, which looked like a sea of clotted cream, led to a sturdy cast-iron spiral staircase that spiralled up two floors. The whole place was open plan, the windows were outrageously big and strengthened to earthquake resistance. We fucking loved the place immediately. *Which way's the pool, love?*

Caswell Avenue became our new home. We had had it bang off within forty-eight hours of arriving in America. After several weeks of our company, Shawna could skin up, loved a line of Charlie and could sing, "We've got Terry, Terry, Terry, Terry Conroy on the wing." She even told Jay to get a life and have a line of coke or something. I had no idea we were so infectious. Well, until Shawna started to call everyone "Duck".

Our time in California was colourful. Life flowed and it was only a matter of weeks before the next two arrivals were introduced to our captivated landlady and made themselves at home with us. After a couple of months, eight of us, including Wilson and Animal, were all staying at the house. We survived by our wits, always aware that one misdemeanour would mean our passage back home.

There were many stories to tell about our times in LA. Some were funny others not funny at all. I mean, if you were going to lose the plot, this was the place to go and do it. We all took shitloads of MDMA and far too much liquid GHB. We snorted copious lines of cocaine and smoked pounds of marijuana. The amount of sleepers we took to bring ourselves down was frightening.

One night we fell out with a gang of Crips at a party in Manhattan Beach. Wilson decided he wanted to try on this black guy's bandanna without first asking his permission to remove it from his head. We got out of that one but only just. Then there was the gay airline pilot that made a pass at Animal. Wilson and he pretended to be gay and allowed the pilot to pick them up whilst they picked him off. It all got messy at the pilot's apartment when the coke ran out and tempers flared. A handgun was produced and used and they got out of there by the skin of their teeth. They were never again to underestimate a fella with a limp wrist.

We all got out of LA by the skin of our teeth. Well, all except one, that is. He over-indulged heavily with some pure E and found his feminine side. He then dressed up in an array of the hostess's under garments and introduced him/herself to us all at a Leeds Service Crew party. It was a hell of a shock, but he wasn't a bad looker, considering. And, for the record, that person is as loved and respected today by those of us that know, as he has always been.

The lads who had followed Gibbo and I over had brought a chunk of Stoke-on-Trent with them. Any more than five of you in my book is a firm, and that's how we all began to behave again. We were enjoying the danger and sleazy undercurrent of LA. I suppose in some ways we had made Los Angeles another outpost for the N40. There are still some of our lads living there to this day. During the following two or three years I was a regular visitor to Sin City.

––––––––––

A female friend of ours who had first introduced herself to the N40 several years earlier in Sydney was now living the high life out of the Beverley Hills Wilshire Hotel. I was told that if I flew over and met her there, I could become involved with a lucrative fraud that was about to take place. My instructions were to ditch the casual appearance of a football firm member and look more like an executive.

It was a dead steal. South West Airlines were celebrating their anniversary by doing a three-for-the-price-of-one promotion on any ticket used within the south-western air space of the States. Our friend had used her contacts in New York to laser-copy a couple of tickets. These two tickets were used on a flight from LA to New Orleans to see if they were acceptable. They were, and the scam began. Ads were placed in papers all over the state of California, offering a whole batch of cheap tickets: stag nights to Vegas, all kinds of group tickets. They were sold via mobile phone and always delivered.

However, before I had a chance to get involved in the scam, there were some complications and my contacts left town. I decided to hang around. I hadn't travelled all that way just to go home after a couple of weeks. I headed down to Venice and chilled out by the beach for a while. The Queen of Hearts Tarot

Club on Venice Beach was a favourite haunt of mine whenever I was in town. Occasionally I would have my crystals read, but mostly I sat around and read people.

I remembered Ruben as soon as he entered the room. He was pleased to see me and sat down on a cushion next to mine. He was just about to off-load an eight ball of cocaine to another customer. Ruben was a small-time coke dealer who wasn't cheap, but his gear was second to none. Out of respect to the owner of the club he never dealt to anyone inside the building. Ruben never mixed business with pleasure. First and foremost he was there to have his cards read.

"Bad karma, Jasp, bad karma. I've had it all week. Something's going to happen, I can feel it."

Ruben was not openly gay, although his mannerisms gave him away, especially when he was upset. He led everybody to believe that he was a struggling actor who was on the verge of nailing the part of a lifetime in a sitcom. He looked like the character that Gene Wilder played in the film *Stir Crazy*. Ruben had red, curly hair and wore checked pants with v-neck sweaters, shirts with fly-away collars and golf shoes. He looked younger but I reckon he was in his mid-forties. He perspired a lot and sometimes spoke with a lisp that could occasionally spray you with saliva. But other than that I liked him. Everyone in Venice liked him.

Most of the people I got to meet through Ruben were either musicians or actors, and all skint. This was the scene I was comfortable around, a far cry from the terrace tear-ups and dance clubs back home. In LA I wore my chisel-toe cowboy boots, chewed gum and listened to American folk music. Ruben introduced me to the sounds of Michael Tomlinson, and I thank him for that.

There was one other thing about Ruben that led me to believe that there was more to the man than first met the eye. He knew some rich people, people that he said were in the industry. He never told me which industry that was. He told me that at certain times he provided entertainment for these people. "You know, the odd eight ball or two, maybe a couple of girls." His hand gestures became curvaceous when he spoke about girls, so maybe he swung both ways. Either way, I made it clear from the off that I only played for one team – and that was in goals! Even so, I enjoyed hanging out with the man, I felt he was trustworthy. When he asked me if I wanted to go to a party in Avalon, I said yes. I rarely said no to a good party.

Fifteen men on a boat, all high rollers and most of them verging on obesity. They got together several times a year, always in Avalon and always for three days. Rich fat Yanks. Should be a laugh.

I got the feeling that this particular party was bigger than normal. Ruben was in his "Sshh darling, I'm concentrating" mode. But fair fucks to the man, he delivered eight girls on time by air, and turned up on board with the requested nine-bar of cocaine. I arrived on Catalina island by hydrofoil several hours after Ruben. He had insisted that he made his journey alone. I'd hesitate to put a price on the yacht I was looking at; it was certainly in the millions. The deckhand manning the outboard that took me to it told me he had been working on it for six months and still had no idea who the owner was. I said nothing.

The party was in some swing. All three decks were lit in a seductive orange tone. Waiters hurried up and down steps carrying platters of food and trays of drinks. I accepted a flute of Champagne and headed to the top deck, where I had seen Ruben as he waved me aboard. He was vibrant. Sweat ran off his chin and soaked his burgundy satin shirt. He felt important, I could tell. In his world he was achieving something by being on this boat with these people. It was a bit like us lot at the match being aired on the news for some pitch invasion that had got a match abandoned. How much we loved the attention. Ruben was getting that attention, even if it was only because he was the cocaine dealer who everyone liked to mock and keep hanging on with a sure-fire promise that pretty soon a role is coming up that will make him a household name.

"Nice boat this, Ruben. Cheers for the invite, man."

Ruben afforded me an eight ball. It was his own personal buzz that for once he was in a position to give me a little touch for zip. I accepted it gladly and proceeded to impose two large lines on each of my nostrils. Ruben did the same. We laughed at each other and then he left me to fend for myself. I'd heard the girls' laughter from across the bay. It was false and over exaggerated, but even so they sounded like real cuties. With a bit of luck Ruben might even afford me a little time below deck with one of them later.

"Are you waiting to use the john, coz I need to use it, and I'd really appreciate it if you would let me go first?"

I believed her too because the drug-taking on board that yacht that night was blase and open. She certainly wasn't nipping in there for a quick sniff.

"Be my guest, it's always ladies before gentlemen."

"Who said I was a lady, eh?" She smiled at me and cocked her head. "You're Ruben's friend. Wait here, I've wanted to talk to you for some time."

My heart started pounding fast. She was a girl that I had seen a couple of times having her crystals read but this was the first time I had got up to her this close. I took her all in, my gaze remaining soft and discreet. Every part of her body was toned and her face was majestic. *Shit, I hope I haven't got any snot hanging out of my hooter*. I lifted my crystal flute and inspected myself in the reflection.

When she reappeared, she'd brushed her hair and glossed

her lips. All the signs were there. I was getting a gut feeling that she was into me even though she was also preparing herself to go back to another man's cabin and entertain him. That was a weird feeling at the time, something I analysed carefully. It was purely a lust-fuelled fascination. The fact that she was a prostitute meant little in reality. I would have had no reservations whatsoever in paying for her company. Here was a person that not only did I lust after, but before I knew what she did for a profession I actually fancied her on face value. I had no idea how to resolve the situation other than let it ride.

It wasn't like a party back home. I didn't see anybody doing the Dance of the Burning Arseholes and there was no sign of the obligatory fistfight. But give them their due, they made me welcome. A couple of the hosts even knew about the English game. They were all in agreement that Gascoigne's knee injury in that year's cup final was his own fault. I put it down to commitment.

Ruben's generosity exceeded my expectations. We were only on the boat for that first night and in the morning we were heading back to Santa Monica and another party, leaving the girls behind to get on with it and earn some dough. His treat came on the stroke of midnight.

"Fancy getting your rocks off, Jasp? I've got a couple of girls who'd like to welcome you to the US of A, LA style."

He led me along an oak panelled corridor towards an end cabin. I poured some cocaine onto my thumb and fired both nostrils full of the powder. My eyes watered and I adjusted my bollocks inside my pants before I entered the room. I was introduced to two teenage girls, one black and one white. They were both sexy and wore tee-shirts with little else. I was even more made up that neither of them was the girl I'd been talking to earlier. The introduction was as quick as it took Ruben to rack out four lines, snort one and leave.

"Ooh, that's it baby, right there. Yeah, you've got it. Nice and slow, that's it. Shit, that's good."

I couldn't believe it. I've got this blonde piece, Bobby Joe, lying underneath me while I straddle her face. She's greedily tonguing my arse and sucking my gonads while the black girl, Tyler, is knelt down in front of me, talking pure filth and tit-wanking my shaft whilst licking the end of my bulbus barabacus. And all the while she is staring me seductively in the eyes. They demanded that I tell them when I was about to explode. I honoured that promise and spritzed the pair of them hard and covered them all over their mooeys. They looked like a pair of greedy cuckoo chicks waiting on a feed. I think I shouted that they were both a pair of dirty bitches as well and that they were to keep licking my Hampton until I told them they could stop. Or I might have just made that last bit up.

I left the boat early the next morning. There was no sign of life anywhere on board. I was gutted I didn't get a chance to talk to the girl who had introduced herself to me as Brandy. Ruben said, "Hey, don't worry. You will see her around." I hoped so but I didn't go looking for her. I had a lot to think about first. One side of my head was saying, *What the fuck are you doing wanting to get involved with a girl who gives sexual favours for money.* The other side was saying, *Well, if I was a woman I would do exactly the same, so does that make me a bad person?*

My final decision was left to common sense. Ruben assured me that Brandy was as conscientious at her work as a dental hygienist would be at theirs. Oh go on then! Funny how another man's opinion can sometimes be the swinging vote. I was up for it, and Ruben reckoned she would be at the Queen of Hearts this Thursday night.

A solo guitarist called Otis Remembered played live that night. He was fancy with his fingers, his music was moving and Brandy looked out of this world. I think we both knew that this was no coincidence and that Ruben had been playing his cards of fate. We both smiled and moved towards each other. She smelt delectable. I clasped her hand and we moved on from there.

There was never going to be any chance that I would move in with a hooker. I was going to keep my bag and belongings in Venice at a friend's condo. You know, just see her three nights a week and get pissed up with the lads for the rest. Four days later I had moved in and was deciding which side of the bed I wanted to sleep on.

She said she had met lots of European guys. A couple of years earlier, before they cleaned up Santa Monica promenade, Brandy worked the tourist trade down there. "But none were ever as handsome as you, though." Every time she revealed to me a part of her past that she thought I may find hard to swallow, she softened it with a cute remark or compliment. I found that a comfort within the context it had been meant, but I still got off on the dirtiness of it all.

Our first sexual encounter was a late-night affair. We parked up on Mount Cahuenga, not far from the Hollywood sign. It was humid and we had both been drinking. Brandy owned a 1968 Pontiac Bonneville, black with a cream soft top. The interior was in red leather and it stuck to my bare, sweating buttocks. She hitched up her skirt and her snakeskin boots felt coarse against my thighs. Brandy positioned herself astride me and slowly lowered her body on to mine. She teased me for a while, taking each centimetre of my swollen head slowly inside her red-hot labia. All the while she kissed and bit my neck and spoke softly in Spanish. Her minky was soft and felt good but lust allowed room for only a short period of foreplay before we succumbed and began to screw each other senseless to Bob Seger's "Hollywood Nights". We then lay silently for a while and shared a joint. She kissed me softly and pulled me in close. We finished off our first sexual experimentation by grinding each other slowly to Steppenwolf's "Hoochie Coochie Man". Exhausted, we slept on the back seat of her car. And, no I did not see a shooting star, although I was up there amongst them.

Filomena Mijares, or Brandy to those of us that she chooses to call friend, was born in Victoria, a Gulf Coast city in Texas. She was twenty-five years old when I met her. Her grandmother told her as a child that Filomena in Aztec meant "Lover of Man" and that it was an important position within their Mexican culture. Brandy giggled when she told me that.

"So you see, Jasp, it was meant to be. I'm fulfilling my obligation to my ancestral roots. I am a natural lover of men, it is my destiny."

She had a look of innocence as she smiled and awaited my reply. For a split second a part of me almost felt a sense of pity towards her. She could have been from a past civilisation, such was her thinking. I held her hand and stroked her hair softly. I told her that I believed that it was what we do with our lives that makes us the person that we are today. I told her that the woman that I was holding that night had captivated me like no other. Brandy laid her head on my chest and sighed lightly. We slept on the floor in front of the fire that night, its dancing shadows flooding our senses with a soft ambience of warmth and security. We made slow love and climaxed quivering together. There was no music, just the sound of the rain.

Her grandparents had taken her teenage mother and both their grandchildren with them via a smuggling operation from the city of Ciudad Juarez, over the American border into El Paso in the late Sixties. From there they headed for the coast to the small town of Victoria. Within weeks of arriving, Brandy was born prematurely. She grew up having never met her natural father; he didn't make the journey. When she was older she found out that he had been sent to jail for a long time but she never wanted to ask what for. Her mother, Silvia, married a local man. He was a good man, a loving man, and they quickly had a child of their own, but he died when Brandy was eight. Silvia became a depressed alcoholic, before becoming addicted to amphetamine sulphate. Brandy reckoned it was the speed that killed her in the end.

When Brandy was seventeen she hung out mostly with white kids in the working class area she lived in with her grandmother. Her stepfather had been white and colour was not an issue with her; she had been brought up white. This caused friction with local Mexican youths and resulted in a vile act of gang rape. She consequently gave birth to a daughter that next year, knowing the father could have been any one of four. It toughened Brandy up and at the age of seventeen she went on the road, leaving her daughter with her grandmother. It was an echo of my own childhood. She reached Los Angeles after two years of working strip bars in Nevada. Never in a million years did she think she'd end up hanging out with a member of one the most revered football hooligan firms in the western hemisphere!

I wasn't one for sitting around in her condo, waiting for her to come home to shower off another man's body scent. I was up to my own thing. Unfortunately, for various reasons I am unable to say what I did to earn money, although I think a whiplash claim was one of the first financial touches to be had. There were many others.

Brandy had her condominium in an area of Hollywood just north of Sunset Boulevard. It had twenty-four hour security and a pool shared by the other residents. It was a pleasant and safe place to hang out. The majority of Brandy's close friends were hookers too. Some I liked, others I was not too sure about. One thing I did notice though is that they were all tough chicks and very streetwise. If one of them had a story to tell about something that had happened to them whilst soliciting, nine times out of ten I listened. Brandy asked them about what they thought of me and they told her, "He must really like you, girl. How many guys do you know who would lie next to a no-good hussy each night without complaint? Especially a guy who is that good-looking." See, there she was with that little cushion again. It wasn't a match made in heaven, but for a short time at least, a couple of lost souls had found their ivory tower.

Brandy's daytime hustling down on Sunset Strip became less frequent. I had known her for over a month now and we were beginning to develop some cohesion. Life was mostly relaxed but the sex was hectic and the drug intake above average. She told me one morning that she had been saving some money for a while and had been planning a journey. She wanted to find her daughter back in Texas and wanted me to go with her. Inevitably, I agreed. That night we stayed in bed and watched back-to-back episodes of *Branded* with Chuck Connors. The programmes were followed by a news update with explicit footage of the Rodney King beating. The pictures we saw shocked us both and we agreed that after that LA was going to be more than a little tense. Early the next morning we loaded our belongings into the trunk of Brandy's Pontiac and hit the road. Leaving behind the confines of Los Angeles lifted us both.

As we sped along the Ventura Highway on that overcast morning, it started to spit warm rain, just heavy enough to use the wiper every minute or two. We kept the roof down anyway. There was no time to stop. We did not even want to look back; there was no reason to. Sat beside me was one of the coolest women I had ever met. She oozed charisma. When she wanted to be feminine she was an absolute diva, so beautiful she looked untouchable. The rest of the time she was wild and free. I was caught in her wind and I wanted it never to stop blowing.

I looked at her as she drove on through the canyon, and then I looked up into the desert sky. I really did pinch myself. I pinched myself hard. This was the best feeling of happiness and freedom I had ever had. The cowgirl, the car, the glove compartment full of cocaine and grass, the Road Trip. I was a happy man. I was twenty-seven years old and it was good to be alive.

We took turns to drive. First Arizona, then down through the arid New Mexico desert. Sometimes she would sleep next to me in the passenger seat. Other times we drank bottles of beer, smoked grass and laughed at the prairie dogs as they scuttled for cover. It took five days to reach Victoria. We could have made it in three if we had pushed it, but there was no point in rushing. Nobody was waiting for us at the other end. Nobody even knew we were coming.

On the third night we stopped suddenly by the roadside. I didn't see him at first. It was mid-evening and Brandy only just caught sight of a man in the headlights. I didn't question her decision. I always stopped for hitchhikers anyway. Lord knows I've spent enough of my life stood by the side of the road, waiting in hope, with no real destination in mind.

Vincent was a motorcycle mechanic. You could tell, he smelt of engine oil. He would have gone on his Harley, he told us, but tonight he was hitching instead. I smiled as I pulled my seat forward to let him in. Now I'm not saying that Vincent didn't really own a Harley Davidson motorcycle, but we only dropped him off about ten klicks up the road, and Vincent didn't look the type to be bothered about picking up a ticket for driving under the influence – that's if there was any kind of law and order around those parts. I thought he was making it up about the bike but he handed me his joint straight away so I liked him anyway, even if he was a bit of a Billy Liar. Vincent told us he was heading for a gig, invited us along, and said that if we got in early we could get a good spot to watch the band. "They are two sons of bitches from down Santa Fe way calling themselves the Tequila Sisters," he said. "Should be a hell of a gig."

There was no way on earth either of us could have driven past that place without stopping. It was pumping hard with Southern Rock tunes. Harleys lined the frontage of the roadhouse. The crowd queued patiently down past the gasoline pumps. It was called the Hot House and I was about to live out a boyhood dream inside it.

There were up to 200 people in the queue outside but not one of them moaned as we strolled past and walked in. We paid a cover charge of ten bucks apiece while Vincent stood at the door and spoke with some of the burly biker security men. He waved us inside and said he would check on us in a short while. I was impressed. It seemed our passenger was a little more than the bullshitter I had first had him down for. The beer was ice cold and poured from a pitcher. Brandy and I were on our second when Vincent appeared at our sides. He drew up a stool and joined us sat at the bar.

"A bottle of Jose Cuervo and three glasses please honey. I'm going to toast my new friends' first ever drink in the Hot House with a bottle of cheap tequila."

That's where it always goes pear shaped for me, when the Tequila comes out. After a couple of shots, Vincent loosened up and we talked over the sounds of the steel guitar. The Hot House had opened as a biker bar a couple of decades earlier. The five men behind it had all served together in Vietnam, seen action in the North and had given themselves the nickname the Hot House Platoon. Vincent pointed at a photograph mounted behind the bar in a glass cabinet of several men, all wearing Army fatigues, pilot shades and green bandannas tied round their heads. One smoked a loose joint. They all sat astride a

Harley. Vincent, I could see, was sat in the middle of the picture. He looked too young to have been in Vietnam. I looked into his thoughtful face and listened to his story about the picture.

"That was the day we buried one of our closest friends and co-founder of this club. We were all aged eighteen when we arrived in Nam. Only five of us returned home. Our other four hometown boys never left that hellhole. What little remains were found were sent home to their families in a shoe box." He went on to explain that there were now only four of them still alive. They stuck together and looked out for one another. They shared a common bond, one that I understood. The club was the focal point of their lives and vets would use it as a stop off on their journeys of guilt. "Most of us keep on running," he said. "Afraid that if we stop the nightmares will soon catch up with us again."

Brandy had discreetly left us several minutes earlier and disappeared into the depths of the vibrant club. It was almost as if she had seen the deep understanding between two men who had seen active service for the country they loved, only to have it thrown back in their faces. Two disenchanted ex-squaddies keeping on the move for sanity's sake if nothing else. Understandably, she left us both to get on with it in our own way, which we did by reciting each of our Army numbers out loud and sinking another slammer straight after.

We hammered that bottle of Jose Cuervo, then smashed it behind the bar, a Hot House tradition when soldiers reminisced. Brandy returned to my side; she had been dancing and looked flushed. Every man's stare returned to the stage as she leaned up towards me and kissed my cheek. She picked a piece of bottle label from my shirt sleeve and smiled. She said nothing but her smile spoke for itself. I felt the same way too.

I have no idea how that brawl started and escalated as quickly as it did. Maybe some of the country hicks had taken a dislike to the band or maybe it was something to do with someone's girlfriend paying less attention than she should be. Who knows? But it went off good style. Within seconds the entire roadhouse was in uproar. It was a pine-panelled place with a big open dance floor at the foot of a staged area. There were three bars the length of each side of it and a narrow balcony circled three sides of the club. The walls were covered in poignant biker artefacts and neon beer signs. Packed with several hundred bikers and their chicks, it was a typical rough hole. My kinda gaff.

I got stuck straight in on the side of the house, firstly because I liked Vincent and it was his club, and secondly because I had always wanted to be in a barroom brawl ever since watching *Cat Balou* as a kid. It seemed to me that the music grew louder as the fight got more out of hand.

Vincent and Brandy had already headed to a back room to take some cocaine. Vincent said the rule of the house was two people at a time, so I abided by it and got stuck into the brawl instead. Wherever their security men steamed in I would follow in with them. Whoever you swung at swung one straight back. *Fantastic!* Tables were up-ended and flung, women jumped on feuding men's backs and bartenders hurdled the bars and crashed straight in. I was starting to giggle at it all.

The brawl was not as gratuitous as it could have been and a lot of the people fighting actually looked to be enjoying the upheaval, as if it were part of their night out. What I am trying to say is that they were naturally enjoying the fight as it was obviously a part of their culture to do so and I likened it a lot to the culture that I am a part of. It all came to an end as quickly as it had erupted. I saw a few bloody noses and a couple of the young bucks had had to be trussed up with a length of rope, but they were just thrown outside to cool off a while. Apart from that, everything returned to being just rowdy.

Vincent was obviously a very popular man and his attention much sought after. He bid us good night and good luck. Brandy and I settled back into our own company and watched the place and everyone in it. We left at 4am and headed back to the car. We thought it better not to make any attempt at driving too far so we drove just far enough away from the club to be alone and pulled off the highway. We parked in the desert under the protection of a Joshua tree. I needed a piss in a hurry and jumped out of the car. I walked several yards and relieved myself. It was a fantastic feeling letting go of all that bladder pressure. That was until Brandy called to me saying to keep still as she thought she could hear a rattlesnake somewhere between me and the car.

Like a fool, I completely shit myself and jumped in the air in an attempt to cover as much distance back towards the car as possible without having to walk it. In mid-air I made an attempt to save my manhood from a potentially lethal snake bite by shoving him back inside my pants. Unfortunately I was still urinating at the time and saturated myself. I dived into the back seat of the open top car and screamed out of relief that I was still alive. Brandy was hysterical with laughter at the sight and sound of me in pure panic and pissing myself at the same time. It was a small blip on my normally ice cool demeanour. I saw the funny side of it soon after we smoked a much-needed joint.

That morning we watched the sun rise and impose itself fiercely high above that arid desert. It was time to either hit the road or die in the scorching heat. I chose the Eagles to listen to that morning, and the first song I played was the aptly named "Tequila Sunrise". It was the first and only one in my life but at least I can say that I've had one. One more dream come true. God Bless America.

I noticed a change in Brandy as we got closer to Victoria. She became subdued and looked lost in thought. I understood where her thoughts might be, and mostly sat quietly, smoking a reefer or two. I only hoped that she was making the right decision. She had not seen or spoken to any of her family since leaving seven years earlier. I was already aware that the longer you leave something, the harder it is to approach it, and usually you find yourself wishing you had left it alone in the end.

I shared her pain on finding out her grandmother, Esmerelda, had passed away almost three years ago and that her daughter had entered the welfare system. The last anyone could remember of her only other living relative, her brother Salvatore, was that he had been sent to the penitentiary for robbery. Other reports claimed he was a crack cocaine addict who lived as a down-and-out with a bunch of others.

I was quite surprised at how rough Victoria was. Brandy had painted a much different picture. By all accounts Victoria in the early Nineties was one of the murder hotspots of Texas. That was mostly down to the crack cocaine industry and the gangs that fought for supremacy. I had picked a proper time to visit the place, especially as I was now in a car cruising the downtown areas looking for a junkie called Sal.

Salvatore was sat with several others. They were huddled around a trashcan fire, even though it was broad daylight and touching ninety degrees. Each held a brown paper bag from which he swigged spirits. Sal recognised his little sister right away. He seemed cautious of me, so I remained in the car until Brandy beckoned me over. All five men had that glazed look and gaunt features, each was painfully thin and none of them could look you in the eye. Sal looked weathered. His face was wrinkled, his teeth nothing but little brown stumps. He twitched a lot and smoked continuously. He was basically a man waiting to die over and over again.

Sal's expensive Nike trainers were at odds with his scruffy denims. Brandy admired them and asked where he had got them from. Without emotion, Sal described how he had removed them from a dead body after a road traffic accident. He joked that had he had more time he would have had his teeth as well. His friends joined in with laughter. They had each lost all sense of morality. I found the whole experience of standing on a street corner and conversing with a small crowd of people who were hooked on crack cocaine very moving indeed. They all had the same distorted look to their faces, yet years before they would have all been individuals with their own identity. The power of that drug really frightened me, though it did not stop me from having a line of coke when I was alone later that day.

Brandy had named her daughter Fate. She told me it was fate that had brought her daughter to her, and fate why she left her. She opened the palm of her hand and showed me two pink crystals. She held them up to me and I noticed they were beginning to change colour.

"You see," she said, "fate was what brought you and I together. The stones change colour when you meet a person that's travelling along the same astral projection as yourself. It does not matter if you only meet them for a brief moment then never see them again in your lifetime, they will still have left their mark with you forever."

It was all a bit deep for me, but I was a believer in fate, so I liked the name. The next morning we visited Brandy's grandmother's grave. She said little. I stood back and waited under the shade of a nearby tree. I could only imagine the pain of losing your grandmother. Mine was still alive and I thanked the Lord for that. When she was finished she hugged me briefly, then smiled and wiped a tear from her cheek. We walked for hours.

She was told it could take several months to trace Fate. Children placed into care are never easy to trace. She seemed disappointed yet a little relieved. I could do nothing other than accept her decision to head back to the road. We hung around for a couple of days, mainly to get a proper headstone for her grandmother's grave. It was while doing this that she stumbled on her daughter. A family that had been close to Esmerelda had become the child's legal guardians. In the interest of the seven-year-old, it was decided that Brandy should see her in secret from a distance. The next morning that entire family of ten, with two dogs, walked along the beachfront. They played in the sand and splashed in the waves. We sat in silence. Fate was a picture of her mother. She was beautiful and happy, her laughter was pure and innocent. She was secure.

Brandy stepped out of the car and closed the door quietly. She said nothing as she walked slowly towards the open sands. She stopped short and folded her arms. I knew she just needed to be alone with this moment. I know I would. The mother stood in silence for several minutes, looking at her daughter play, then turned and walked back to the car. Looking depleted, she got in and said, "I'm ready." I started the engine and drove away. She said little else and not once looked back. It was starting to rain.

America had been everything it had promised to be. I said goodbye to Brandy the day we arrived back in LA. It was over as quickly as it had started. No tears and kisses, just one long hug of acknowledgment. Her agenda had changed, although we never spoke about it. I just knew. I hope that in meeting me, Brandy found the strength that she was missing to make that fateful trip to reunite herself with her family. I don't think for one minute that it had turned out the way she would have hoped, but I'm sure that she found at least a small amount of peace. I hope that developed into the strength to go back again to Victoria and be a real mother to her daughter. Everyone deserves a loving mum.

It was brass plated. It had the head of a bald eagle inside a motorbike chain that encrusted the edge of the belt buckle. Brandy had retrieved it from the aftermath of the Hot House bar brawl. It was the last thing she gave to me and I still wear it to this day. I ran my finger over the texture of the buckle and sat back with my thoughts. They were happy ones and I was slightly sad to hear the stewardess telling us that we would shortly be arriving at London Heathrow.

Or was I? *Nah, fuck it. Lou Macari was working wonders down at the Vic. Twelve points clear and taking 5,000 away everywhere we played. I can't wait for Saturday. Grimsby away with the lads.* I'd missed them.

————————

My love affair with the States came to an abrupt end in the winter of 1996. I was arrested on arrival at Miami International Airport as I stood waiting at immigration. Very politely, the two tall, suited men asked me to accompany them to a room for a short interrogation. It lasted for over eighteen hours and was at times extremely intense, though I had no idea why they had pulled me. Immigration played good guy, bad guy with me and more or less got me to confess to every crime I had ever been convicted of during my lifetime. Satisfied with what I had told them, I was allowed on my journey down to the Florida Keys for a chilled-out Christmas. They assured me that every police officer down there in Key West knew I was on my way and I was promised that if I so much as stepped off the sidewalk they would "can my ass". Relieved that I could go, I had one question. Why had I been pulled?

According to the good guy, in 1994 they had received some information on certain individuals known to be active hardcore football hooligans and were in positions to orchestrate violence from different firms in England. I was on a small list of men who were thought by the English authorities to be a possible problem during the World Cup being staged in America. I wouldn't mind, but England hadn't even qualified for the tournament. They told me I would not be allowed back in if I went again, and so that was the end of my love affair with the States.

At least when I came home I felt alive again. That was the effect that Brandy had on me.

Chapter Ten

The Doc

By Reegez

GLENWOOD SPRINGS IS set in a valley dwarfed by the Rocky Mountains of Colorado and renowned as a stopping point for the skiing fraternity, as it's only a few miles from the famous ski resorts of Aspen and Vail. The Colorado River runs down to the small town alongside the railroad track. There are a few small, up-market hotels and the rest of the town is made up of traditional, old style wooden buildings and a couple of bars and shops, a butcher's, a general store and boutiques.

Considering that the skiing clientele spend a lot of time here, it was nice to see that the town hadn't changed much since the days of the cowboys. One cowboy in particular, the famous gunslinger Doc Holliday, visited here and ended up staying for good, which is the reason I came to Glenwood Springs. I alighted from the train after a ten-hour journey from Sacramento, California, through Nevada, stopping for a couple of hours in the gambling town of Reno, a smaller, more sedate version of Las Vegas.

Bearing in mind my quest, it was ironic that during my two-night stay in Reno I had found a bar near my cheap, Wild

West-style hotel named Doc Holiday's. It looked like he spent time in these parts too and spent quite a few hours in that bar. It was nothing like the saloon I would have liked, but it seemed right to have a few golden throat charmers for the Doc.

Leaving Reno I boarded the night train to Denver. For eighteen hours or more it made its journey through some of the most spectacular scenery a man could ever hope to see. Even in the hours of darkness, the full moon lit up the barren landscape of Utah. The light broke as we were coming into Colorado, and it just kept getting better. At one point, around four o'clock in the morning, the full moon was at its best as the train wound its way through a valley alongside the Colorado River. These trains only travel at 50mph in daylight, and at night they slow down to around 20–25mph.

As the train took a huge bend, the river and its wildlife were illuminated. I saw deer and elk drinking from the river and a huge owl swooping around the dark skies with its wings outstretched. The whites of its underwing looked almost ghostly. As I pressed up against the glass, covering my face to blot out the dim night-lights of the carriage, I saw what could have been a prairie dog or a wolf crossing the river. Its eye lit up as the headlamps of the train shone out in front. Keeping my face against the glass, I looked up and caught a glimpse of sky hiding behind the towering rock face of the Rocky Mountains, as the stars shone brightly alongside the moon. I sat back in my seat and dreamt of what it would have been like to have slept out on the prairie and in the mountains back in the days of the cowboys.

The train slowed down even more as I walked along the silent, dimly lit carriages, when a sudden jolt made me look around. I pressed my hands up on the glass once again. All that fresh air and wildlife outside and here I was, trapped in an air-conditioned but stuffy, man-made contraption. I walked to the door wishing I could open a window at least. The white tips of water breaking over the rocks in the river were so near yet untouchable.

Fuck knows why, but in my mind I could hear the singing and haunting music of the native American Indians, not a war cry or rain dance but mourning chants and mellow drum beats. Just as I caught sight of the owl again, swooping and spreading its wings, I nearly jumped out of my skin as the train guard brushed past me, having silently opened the sliding electric doors connecting the carriages.

The train pulled into Glenwood Springs around midday. Ten inches of snow lay on the ground. I took a long, deep breath of the fresh Rocky Mountain air, slung my bag over my shoulder and walked down the steps onto the snow-covered platform. I took a last look up to the front of the train and then to the back. All I needed now was a shower and a bed.

My journeys were based on a whim, depending how tired or drunk I was the night before. But I had to get to Doc. Not having a driver's licence meant doing it by train and bus or hitching lifts state to state. Through these means, I travelled more than 17,000 miles, taking in all the landscapes and scenery. The US rail system is spartan compared to Britain's, so I had to backtrack through Arizona and California to catch a train to Colorado from Sacramento in east California.

I sat down on the bottom one of bunk beds. The room was for two people but the guy on reception had said that he would let it as a single so long as no-one else turned up that day. "A nice joint of skunk or hash would go down a treat right now," I sighed to myself. It would send me off to never-never land after that epic journey. I needed to shower badly, as I reeked. Before crashing, I got out my washbag and stripped off, emptying its contents on a wooden chair. I noticed the one thing missing was razor blades. Worse than that was my camera film from

San Diego, Tijuana and parts of Arizona was missing. Checking the already empty bag, I put my hand inside a zip pocket searching for a razor blade but felt nothing. Hold on, what's this? Fucking hell, it's weed. Berserk! Where had that come from? I could have got nicked at Customs weeks ago with that.

There I was, naked in a tiny room two metres by two and a half, staring at a lump of hash. How long it had been there I'd no idea? Maybe from last year's trip, island hopping in Greece or the "bedsit mania" days, living in Bristol. It was Heaven-sent from someone, somewhere watching over me. It had been five whole weeks since my last intake of cannabis back in San Francisco. For a man who normally smokes half a dozen spliffs a day, this in itself was a little miracle. After a long hot shower, the first in four days, I set off to buy tobacco and Rizla papers. Upon getting past the onslaught of other travellers asking, "Who are you, where are you going and where have you been?" I eventually made it out into the fresh, cold Colorado night air. The moon was out and shone brightly, only its welcoming light was sporadically broken by thick, heavy dark clouds which were travelling quickly through the night sky.

Trudging through the snow, I called at the convenience store to get what I needed then headed off to Doc Holliday's bar. I got chatting to Dusty the barman with good, quick friendly service. He was a well-travelled man who was into mount-aineering. As I chatted to him over my hot buffalo wings, I got to know more about the well-known, well-liked cowboys that I had had a fondness for since I was a small child. That fondness had now turned into almost an obsession now that I was on their turf. Dusty explained it like this. "Say, supposing we go back a hundred years or more and those guys having a drink there behind you were playing cards and a Doc Holliday or Wild Bill Hickock or lesser known cowboys such as Johnny Ringo walked in, they'd get up and leave."

These cowboys were not that friendly whether in their own town or a strange one. Similar to hooligans today, I thought. Always causing trouble, but mainly misunderstood, decent people with a grievance against the system or its rules and regulations. The hours flew by, especially with Dusty's stories of rock climbing in Italy, Argentina, Mexico, Switzerland and next stop Uzbekistan. Upon leaving, Dusty walked me to a picture of Doc Holliday and an exact copy of the letter he wrote to his best and loyal friend, Wyatt Earp. The next day, after visiting Doc Holliday's resting place, I wrote down the letter word for word and sent it on to my friend Jasper, who still has it to this day.

I'd pre-rolled a spliff and set off down to the station next to the rushing Colorado River. It brought back memories of the wildlife I'd seen the night before, the white tipped river, the moon and the mountains. Then I heard in the distance the elongated horn of a train coming in through the cold night air and saw the headlights. Sucking hard on my spliff, I got emotional thinking how much my father, who had been a railwayman all his life, would love to be doing this trip around America. As a boy in Blackpool, he watched steam trains from atop a bridge, getting laughs with his childhood mates over who had the blackest face from the rising soot and steam as the train passed them underneath. Then he'd return home to a traditional 1950s rollicking from his mum and dad for getting filthy and being late for his tea.

The train didn't stop at Glenwood Springs. It was a freight train heading east. I counted the cars it pulled as I finished my spliff, thinking, *Fuck me, the trains are long over here*. I checked the time, worked out the difference with the UK and thought of my dad and mum sitting down to their tea. They would no doubt be wondering whether their son was eating well and looking after himself now that he'd gone off on another mad journey.

Sex, Drugs and Football Thugs

I rose the next morning at 8:30am, showered and went down to the communal kitchen. I had coffee and three bowls of oatmeal, my favourite being apple and cinnamon. Well you can't get enough of a good thing, can you? Besides, it was free. I set out around 10am armed with a shoulder bag containing a bottle of water, spare jumper, camera, pen, notepad and of course the little nugget of joy I had found in my wash bag. Off the beaten track, I came to the start of a mountain path. There was a signpost and information board telling me about the history of Glenwood Springs. I set off up the icy path, kitted out in Adidas Samba trainers, jeans, sweatshirt and jacket. Not exactly the correct apparel for climbing icy cold, snow-filled mountain paths in the middle of a Colorado winter, but hey, casual.

I started to slip-slide my way up the steep, winding path, grabbing tree branches for balance and to stop from falling flat on my face. At some point I had to literally swing over a treacherous section of path. I asked myself how the hell they got dead bodies up here in the winter all those years ago. I also took time to admire the sheer beauty of the wood-built town, dwarfed either side by the Rockies.

I slipped, cutting my hand on a thorny plant. It was a case of head down, focus on my footing and try not to slip for the fifth or sixth time. My hand started to hurt like hell as warm blood met the cold, freezing air. *Fucksake, what am I doing?* Then I caught sight of the Stars and Stripes blowing gently atop a pure white flagpole. *That's it, got to be,* I thought.

I'd arrived. "Yee haa," I whooped, trying to cheer myself up after all that effort and pain. I tentatively approached the wooden gate and opened it. I felt nervous and then got a sick feeling in my guts. I closed the gate gently behind me and a few inches of snow fell off the ledge on to my cut hand. I walked into the sloping, uneven mountainside graveyard. Old headstones of forgotten frontier cowboys and other folk were indiscriminately scattered around.

"Doc Holliday is buried here in this graveyard somewhere, this memorial testifies to that," read the inscription on a polished, immaculate marble headstone surrounded by perfectly painted black railings. I set up my camera, put it on timer and placed it on the railings before quickly running to the headstone for a snap. Then it was time for a spliff with the Doc.

I told myself and the Doc out loud that I couldn't believe he would have such a gravestone. Well, I mean, the quickest-drawing, hardest-drinking and -gambling outlaw didn't have too many friends. I looked around and started to examine the other headstones, some marked, some unmarked. Not to tread on the dead in these wintry conditions with two feet of snow and uneven ground was becoming impossible. I started to feel really cold. My Adidas Sambas had given in to the Arctic-like conditions, my feet were numb with pain and my hand had become more sore. I walked back to the Doc memorial.

"Well Doc, I know you're here somewhere, it's been nice to come this far, sure would have liked to know you more if I could. Guess I'll be going now." I lit up another pre-rolled spliff and took a deep breath. I pulled my right foot up out of the snow, shoving a finger into my trainer, feeling how wet and cold both pairs of socks and my feet were.

I was saying goodbye to Doc when the wind picked up. *Oh God, that's all I need*. Clink, clink, clink. The ropes holding the American flag banged against the flagpole. The noise went through me and I went cold deep in my stomach. I shivered as the wind started to howl and the flag unfurled into its full glory, then dropped, then rose again as if pointing at me. No, Doc wouldn't be buried under a polished, touristy headstone.

The Stars and Stripes almost angrily flapped in my direction again, pointing once more. I looked in its direction as I walked behind the memorial. There, down what was almost a ditch, were a couple of foot-high headstones. "Doc, is that you?" I wiped my hands over the headstones. They were unmarked. As I looked up, like the noise of a yacht's sail, the loud flapping of the Stars and Stripes blew me in another direction to one more headstone, then another, then another.

Walking then half running, like a madman 800 feet up a mountain in freezing conditions, following the directions the flag gave me, I must have looked like Jim Morrison running round the Nevada Desert tripping his tits off in the movie *The Doors*. Val Kilmer, the actor who played Morrison in the film, also played Doc Holliday in *Tombstone*, which featured Kurt Russell as Wyatt Earp. Spooky or what?

Looking up at the flag as I got to one headstone, I was at six o'clock and the flagpole at twelve o'clock. It kept sending me to seven or eight o'clock, but no further in that direction. Always back to four or three o'clock, which is where the memorial was. I was now in a trance of belief in spiritual assistance.

After twenty minutes or so, I found myself back where I started. "Fuck me, Doc. Are you winding me up or what?" I asked out loud. I wished I hadn't, as the wind stopped, just like that. I apologised and prepared to head for home. About ten yards from the memorial stone, I turned to look back, said goodbye and walked to the gate.

Then, without a breath of wind, the flag rose up from its pole and blew hard and sharp at ten o'clock. I had to follow it. It stopped as I wandered towards the eight o'clock position. Then "whup", the flag gave a cracking sound as if to shout at me, "That way." I went that way then "whup" again. This time it wasn't the Stars and Stripes but my left knee cracking hard against the corner of a stone cross. I felt blood instantly run down my shin. I followed the flag's directions to a couple of trees all bent and twisted after years of harsh winters and scorching summers up in the mountains.

"There's nothing there," I said out loud. The flag, I felt, was getting impatient and gave me one last direction towards eleven o'clock. "There's still nothing here." Picture me now bending down under a tree, wet through, bordering on frozen, feet blue and wet, hand swollen from a nasty cut, and knee bleeding and throbbing like a bastard in the middle of a graveyard all alone. No noise bar my own and the sound of the flag and its ropes.

Just as I thought, *Fuck this*, my left foot slipped as my damaged knee gave way and I found myself looking at a flat stone. I brushed and scraped with my bare hands at the dirt and leaves, some of which were frozen solid to the stone. Kneeling on my good knee, I unearthed two pistols crossed over just like you could see on the memorial stone, similar to West Ham United's crossed hammer or irons. They were hand carved but barely recognisable after 100 or more years lying there.

"Jesus, is that you Doc?" I said excitedly. "Whup." The Stars and Stripes unfurled one last time, directly at me. The cold and pain had gone with the wind, and I sat there, my back up against a tree with my left leg out straight, my right knee upright near my face, smoking a spliff on a snowy Rocky Mountain in a graveyard with my friend, Doc Holiday. I chatted to Doc out loud about how the world is these days, how I'd got there, how me and my friend Jasper loved him to bits, and how he felt about the way he was portrayed in films. I answered a few questions and left some open.

It had started to snow and my arse had gone numb, so I made polite excuses to take my leave. As I stood up to take a photograph of Doc Holliday's true resting place, you guessed it, I ran out of film. Or had I? A twenty-four exposure film usually lets you take more then twenty-four pictures and mine had stopped at twenty-two. I laughed as I took a look up at the dormant flag. It moved gently as if smirking at me. I looked back at the Doc's unmarked grave, walked over and gently covered it over, saying goodbye. I then hobbled off down the mountain path.

That night I told Dusty what had happened. He was unusually quiet with a smirk on his face.

"What's with the smile, Dusty?"

"Do you believe it?"

"Believe what?"

"Believe what you saw and did today."

"Yes," I said, sheepishly.

"You're sure?"

"Yeah I'm sure. Fuck me, I've come a long way for this," I said.

"I know you have, guys like you will."

"Tell you what," I said. "Why don't we ask this guy here, he looks like he'll know?" I raised my left arm out to an old cowboy with a Stetson hat, long ankle coat, boots and Levis who even had longish hair and a droopy 'tash.

"What guy?" said Dusty, polishing some glasses.

I replied, "This guy here . . .?"

The cowboy had gone.

"Where'd he go?" I asked.

"There was no-one there", said Dusty.

Take whatever moral you want from this story. I know mine. Go wherever the wind blows you and live the dream.

Chapter Eleven

I Love You Brother

GED NEVER MISSES. It is the same remark every time he puts down the phone.

"I love you brother, take care of yourself."

Contrary to common belief around our home town of Stoke, I actually did write *Naughty* myself, with no help from a ghost-writer or academic. Just myself, my sordid thoughts and my laptop. Ged's a writer too, only he prefers smaller, hard-hitting jabs to drawn-out epics. Modern poetry and short stories are how he expresses himself. He, along with dozens of others, pulled it all together with me and made our first book a bestseller. If you read it thoroughly it actually tells you who is speaking to you, and if they wrote it themselves you will see their name by it. Just to clear things up, that is!

Many of us like-minded people who were born of our culture will know how easy it is to belong just by actually belonging, but how difficult it is to be accepted if an outsider tries to become a part of it. Especially if they've spent a decade of their life following a culture alien to our own. There is little chance if any of being welcomed in.

Well, Ged was. He and I became good friends working a tough nightclub door. Inevitably, with my background, it was not long before Ged hit the streets with the N40. Some people found it hard to accept a stranger, but my word was their bond. My decision was respected and Ged was in – and loving it. For a man of twenty-three with no prior knowledge of our codes and expectations, he would prove to be either a born hoolie who had finally found his way home, or a very clever mimic. The first big football row would always tell.

An overseas excursion with England and a week-long coach trip to Poland wouldn't be a bad one. Ged loved it and proved his salt to boot. He is also a very sensitive and intelligent man. I got a chance to look inside his mind many times during our days as down-and-out druggies who took each day as it came and any meal that was offered. He remarked once about how for the first time in his life he actually felt like he belonged somewhere. He told me that the buzz of football was more far-reaching than a mere street brawl with a load of lads from another town. He understood that the infrastructure of the N40 was built on love, loyalty and respect. It was face-value to the core, with no room for pretenders and chancers. He and I liked that observation a lot.

When BBC2 contacted me to appear on a hooligan documentary they were working on, we arranged a meeting with them in a discreet part of Cheshire. I searched both of their staff for wires. Then dialogue opened. I knew before I went to meet them that I was not going to give them an interview, and none of the other prominent heads present would have either. We were suspicious. Even so, I still wanted Stoke to get their message over to the audience. With no qualms, I asked Ged to do it. I trusted him implicitly.

Usually when he has polished off his second bottle of Stoli vodka, he rings me. We keep the same hours; most of the old party heads do. "Charlie [my nickname to a certain few of my close friends], I have just finished my latest batch of poetry,"

298

he would slur down the phone and would I chuckle and listen in. I always know it is going to be entertaining and always different. His work can vary from one extreme to another. I have long thought, how could Paul Simon, one of my favourite songsters, write such poignant lyrics at such a young age? And how many times whilst on the road had he had his heart broken in doing so? When I listen to Ged I feel the same. My interpretation may be different to other people's, but I always find a hidden, poignant meaning that satisfies the soul. Ged has a certain way of putting himself over. What may sound unpalatable at first can become a firm favourite. He is an acquired taste. Here is what he would like to say about his life and how he found himself living and surviving amongst the football fraternity.

———————

The Swinging Sixties. That's how it has been viewed ever since. But we all know that some parts of society take longer to catch up than others. We're still waiting on a few. The Sixties only really swung for certain people in certain parts of the country. The year in question was 1968, the Year of the Stone Monkey; according to the Chinese zodiac, the monkey represents a year of war and political upheaval. Those born under the sign of the monkey are mavericks. 1968 saw the start of the Vietnam War, the De Gaulle riots and the beginning of what became known as the Troubles in Northern Ireland. It was the year I was born.

My mam was a free-thinking girl, hungry for knowledge and reaching the end of her teens. She was also a single Catholic girl from a mixed family in a Protestant town just outside Belfast. There was no way she was going to give up her baby. Some of the family were living in Burton-on-Trent and that's where she went to give birth. The place of my birth has become a bone of contention throughout the years, to others not me.

Everyone has their own view of nationality and cultural identity. My early childhood involved various locations while my mam worked and brought me up while learning about parenthood on her own, the path of most single parents. At one point I lived with my grandparents back in Ireland. But Ma couldn't stand being that far away from me and took me back to Burton. She married a man from Burton and he adopted me. He also gave me his name, which was rare.

I never really felt that I fitted in at school. I can't really remember those early years, in fact a lot of what you've just read is what I learnt afterwards. There are, though, two memories that are really clear from junior school, they're what people call life-shaping.

The first happened after morning assembly at the local state school. My teacher asked me if I believed in God. I knew that I didn't but the whole class was looking at me with open mouths. I got enough grief on a daily basis, why should I make myself stick out even more? I lied and said that, yes, I did believe in God. The teacher said that in that case I should have my eyes closed during prayers.

Not long after this, I was sat at the table on a Tuesday lunchtime. All of a sudden one of the kids said, "That's what it's like in your house in't it, you dirty paddy bastard." Another one piped in, "Yeah, shit up the walls." There were a few of them now. I didn't have a fucking clue what they were on about. It was bad enough having glasses and long blond hair, I didn't need grief I couldn't understand.

I used to have to go to bed at 8:30 on a school day. *World In Action* started at 8:30, and the night before it had been about the "dirty protest" on the H-blocks at Long Kesh. That's where the kids got their ideas. I knew then that I would do my best never again to be in a position where I was so outgunned by what other people thought they knew. That was the point when I became political, at the age of ten. As we moved up to secondary school I was reading about Lenin, Che and the Easter Rising.

Mam and Dad had already had a period of trial separation. I can remember being round my mam's flat when the 1979 election result came in. I didn't know much about Thatcher then, but even at that tender age I knew there were bad times ahead. Ma had been at college for the previous few years, she even became the first woman president of the local students' union. Now she had her chance to follow her dream of getting a degree and she moved to London. Cool – I now got to visit her there. This gave me the opportunity to go on demonstrations and dance with her interesting, big-breasted hippy mates. I also got to go to Carnaby Street, which for an eleven-year-old mod from a town called nowhere was pretty fucking ace.

It was over a game of snooker that me dad told me he wasn't me dad, but that he loved me as if he was. Up until then I thought he'd always been there. I wasn't bothered though, I loved him and he said he loved me. Cool. Things weren't going well between him and my mam and soon after he told me they were probably going to get divorced but that it wouldn't affect me and him. No problem then.

Mam stopped her course in London and moved back to Burton. I don't know when Dad started seeing one of his old flames but it got a bit messy. They were still sharing the house for a while. I spent time living with both of them, as there was a period when one was ill, then the other. I never saw this as strange, I just thought that this stuff was nothing to do with me and I couldn't do anything about it. I got on with being a teenager.

I'd tried smoking, had my first drink, my first spliff, tried to lose my virginity and been arrested for shoplifting. Pretty run of the mill for the lads round our way. A few of us spent a couple of lunchtimes cutting ourselves with bits of metal or broken glass. That soon got boring and they went back to sniffing glue. I never tried it.

Not being satisfied with getting grief for being a paddy – and a proud, bolshie one at that – I decide to wander out of the safe subculture of being a mod; I became the only lad under eighteen in town to become a New Romantic. My journey to becoming a dandy had begun. I think being a contrary bastard has always been part of my make-up. I used to get slapped on a regular basis, but the one time that sticks in my mind was after an under-eighteens' disco. A gang of lads held me against a wall and burned my arms with cigarettes. I laughed at them. They stopped. I learnt a useful lesson.

Not long before the end of my third year at secondary school, my uncle came to stay with me from Northern Ireland. It was around this time that I started realizing that I had family on both sides, or what they now call both "traditions". My granda had just died, he was an ex-Regimental Sergeant Major. I hadn't seen him for years but once he died I missed him. He died at Christmas on the same day as Nat King Cole.

My uncle brought me some plastic bullets he'd picked up after a riot. There was this kid at school who'd had a rubber bullet and showed it off, saying that it couldn't hurt anyone. I took the plastic one in and threw it at his head. I made my point. A teacher saw the bullet and took me to the headmaster. He started punching fuck out of me, a grown man punching a thirteen-year-old boy and not holding back. If I saw the dwarf now I'd just laugh at him, the malignant, wee, short Scots bastard. He got so carried away that Mr Ramsbottom, an old-school teacher, strict and fair who never held a grudge, had to pull him off.

When I got home there were two coppers in the front room.

Turned out the Army depot round the corner where they kept the Green Goddesses was also where they stored the plastic bullets. CID watched the house for three days; obviously this could have been a dangerous sleeper group. Mam kept my uncle out of sight, that accent would have had us all down Paddington Green nick.

She decided enough was enough and over the summer holidays arranged for us to move to London. On the day we were going to move, she changed her mind and decided instead to transfer me to the local Catholic school to give me stability, better discipline and a better education. Unfortunately, I just became a bigger fish in a smaller pond. I was promoted from relegation struggler to challenging for a Champions League spot.

The other interesting thing that summer was that I stopped being a pacifist. Through my political readings I had decided I was a pacifist, and that meant I didn't fight. If I got punched I used to take it. Some of the lads told me I was mad and that I could take most of the people having a pop. A dickhead I'd known since junior school thought he'd become a hard man and tried to goad me while I was on my way to the corner shop to get some biscuits. I took no notice and carried on walking. Not taking no for an answer, he ran up behind me and knocked off my glasses.

Fuck this, I thought, and got stuck into him. His mate got me from behind and they kicked the shit out of me in the gutter. All the time I kept thinking, *Is this all you've got?* I had bruised ribs, a split lip and cut ears. Mam wanted to call the police but I just kept laughing. She thought I was in shock but I wasn't, I thought it was funny. That's when I stopped being a pacifist.

Mam and I were really close. She studied for her degree and I helped where I could. When I left school I could cook, shop, clean house and do the laundry. That meant I was self-sufficient, and they were some of the most important things I learned. A man can't be independent if he can't fend for himself. The three main things I remember from Catholic school are that I got into a lot of trouble, I lost my virginity in a potting shed, and there was a posh girl who used to play with my cock in maths lessons.

I left with an O Level in English and a couple of CSEs. The main thing I had going for me was that there was always a senior teacher who'd stick up for me when I was in bother. Mr Shaw did his best for all the lads. Mrs Walters encouraged my interest in drama, which my mum had always supported and nourished. I went to a theatre group on Saturday mornings. My mam had spent some time in the theatre and hoped that I would take it up.

Two teachers really surprised me though. One was Mr Spendlove, who we used to call Aubrey after the cartoon. It was no secret; wee bastards that we were, we said it to his face. He stopped giving me shit for not doing me homework, said it was my choice. The last parents' evening before final exams, my mam was just finishing with another teacher when Mr Spendlove walked over to her. "I'm fucked," I thought. All I'd done for two years was give this poor bastard grief and he was making a point of speaking to my mam. She said afterwards that he'd said that he knew I'd had problems in school with other teachers but that I'd never given him any difficulties. When it came to my exams he helped me get a better grade in any way he could.

The other one was Mr Ballantine. I argued with him regularly; proper stand-up rows in the lesson. I think he sent me to the headmaster more than anyone else. I found out later that he constantly argued with Mr Donnelly, who took the O Level English Literature class, that I should be upgraded to his class because I'd fly it. Donnelly always said no because of my behaviour. I passed Mr Ballantine's course with a grade one CSE.

Mrs Irwin did her best with my love of history and thought it was great that I chose the General Strike of 1926 for my topic instead of the stuff everyone else was doing. These teachers are worthy of respect, as are many others up and down the land for seeing promise and trying to nurture gobby little wankers who think they know it all.

When I left school I got a place on a YTS hairdressing scheme. There wasn't a great deal of exciting things to do in Burton. I'd always been one of the first with whatever different haircuts were going round and had known a couple of cool hairdressers for a couple of years. They had money and girls, cool.

Then the local college announced that a course was starting in Theatre Arts. Drama was one of the few lessons I enjoyed. One of my mates from school, Nicandro, an Italian lad with three older brothers, was going on the course. Nic is one of the most decent men I have ever met and when I think of him it is with fondness and respect. It was during the course that Louise and I got close. I'd known her for a while just to speak to, but we went on to be best friends. It was the first time I'd ever had a really close mate like that.

I approached my college work the same as I had school. That meant that most of it was half-arsed. One of the exams we took was the English Speaking Board and involved reciting a poem and giving a talk on your topic of choice. I learned the poem on the way in and read the back of a book about Stanislavski during the exam. I spoke about him for two minutes and I got a distinction. Louise and I hatched a plan to get into a stage school in London and move down there together. Even if we ended up on different courses, we could still share a gaff.

The most important thing happening at the time was the Miners' Strike. Some of us used to collect for the strike fund and when they made that illegal we collected food. I was amazed at how much anger was directed at us. Even a year after the strike, a geezer tried to have a pop at me.

I'd been going to meetings of the Labour Party Young Socialists. They objected to the fact that a lot of the people that I used to knock about with were skinheads and came out with bollocks like, "How can you talk to them, they're fascists?" My reply was that actually most of them were more like Conservatives and if no-one spoke to them, how the fuck did you expect to change their minds?

When the strike was over I lost interest in sitting around discussing the minute details of political ideology. I still wanted to change the world I lived in but I didn't think constantly trying to work out if someone was a Trot or a Leninist was the most productive way of doing it. The petty bickering of the left-wing splinter groups in the 1980s was what allowed Blair's mob to take over and sell us down the river. That gave them the opportunity to say that the country had rejected anything that even sounded Socialist. The truth is people need to feel there is unity at the top. That's why people kept voting for Maggie even as she destroyed their communities.

My great love was music. I went to Rock City almost every week to see whoever was on: the Cult, Spear of Destiny, the Fine Young Cannibals, even Gene Loves Jezebel once. New Model Army were the ones though. Then everything changed.

On the last day of college, just after the last exam was over, Louise walked into the head tutor's office and collapsed. She had suffered a brain haemorrhage. After three days in a coma she had died three times. Her mother was informed by the hospital that there was no coming back. On the third day, they switched off the life support machine. I kept it together for my mam and our friends; everyone loved Louise and she had become family. I stopped drinking that summer, I can't really remember why. Around my eighteenth birthday, not long after Louise's, I sat next to the toilet in our house crying my eyes out.

I went to my audition for stage school but while there I just kept looking at everyone else trying to get on the course and thinking, *I've just lost my best mate. I don't think I can spend the next three years of my life with you bunch of cunts.* In hindsight I know that was a bit of a sweeping judgement but I went a bit strange after Lou died. The course was hard to get on, as it was the only one of its kind at the time. They said I was in if I got my grades. I failed to get the grades they asked for but they said they wanted me anyway. I couldn't be arsed.

I'd been working as a glass collector in a local fun pub, worked my first door and worked in a warehouse. I started spending more and more time following New Model Army around the country and abroad. I left the warehouse to go back to college but really it was an excuse to go to more NMA gigs.

Then I met a gorgeous lass. Her mother was from the Bahamas, she was the epitome of Eighties cool and the first woman I fell in love with. When she thought she was pregnant, I wanted to marry her. She wasn't. She was only a little older than me but the mother of a three-year-old boy, and I was still a boy myself. When it was over I was devastated.

New Model Army was my escape. I met a good set of mates and we were a tight little unit. Eventually I moved in with the band and started working with the poet Joolz and a folk singer called Revv Hammer. Joolz, Justin, Revv and Bret became my second family. Most people just assumed that Bret and I were brothers because we were so similar. Then there was Stephan, Lee, Tony, Rachel, Colin, Em and Paul and the rest of the NMA outcasts. My life revolved entirely around this group of people for four years and it was great. I was fully integrated into the life of my favourite band. We watched them perform and had the odd fight across Britain and Europe. I imagine that at times I was a self-righteous wanker but we all loved each other.

At one point I tried being a singer-songwriter. After the first time Joolz saw me perform, she saw me looking at her.

"You know, if you ask me I'll tell ya."

"I know, and I'm asking."

"You can't sing, you can't play the guitar, and your songs are terrible. But you're a great tour manager."

I smiled at this and worked as Joolz's tour manager for the next three years. I'd already been acting in that capacity for Revv, which had led to some great laughs as neither of us could drive and we had to hitch to all of his gigs. One of the reasons I got that job was because he had enough understanding of himself to know he'd get into trouble and enough faith in me that I'd keep him out of it.

Part of growing up is the passing of stages. I'd experienced grief, loved and lost, and left home. I was coming up to my twenty-first birthday and I was restless. After six years growing my hair (it was, by the way, a subject of great jealousy amongst female friends of mine who wanted that corkscrew perm look; mine was natural) I decided to mark my birthday by shaving my head.

After years of not drinking or taking drugs, Ged Mk II arrived, and he had quite an appetite. Nineteen eighty-nine was a great year to decide to experiment with drugs. Stephan took me to a house music club in Stoke called Introspective. I took my first pill at that club and was given a VIP pass on account of meeting two people almost as soon as I arrived who were to become great friends of mine. Iggy and Ring-dang introduced me to half of Stoke over the next few weeks. On that first night Tess, a local entrepreneur, gave me a pass to his club and I met the incomparable Brunty. I gave up my job with Joolz and moved out of the house I lived in in Bradford.

My only regret from those days is that my inept handling of my own restlessness led to a few wilderness years between me and people that I loved. I'm not saying that I could have explained it so that everything would have been fine, but it might have been easier if I'd tried. To this day I'm still sorry for the hurt I caused my mam and the rest of the Red Sky Coven. Red Sky was Justin, Joolz, Revv and Bret and me, a collective family of people who believed in the same things. As well as our political beliefs, we believed in the old Celtic religion of the land. I still believe in those things and still hold the same love and loyalty to those people that I did then. Thankfully I've been able to mend the bridges that fell into disrepair through my carelessness.

At the start of 1990, I was living on a sofa in a flat in Stoke. Well, if I got there first I got the sofa. There were two girls living in the two bedrooms, one boyfriend and usually five of us in the living room. We smoked skunk from when we got up, stole our food from the local supermarket and partied whenever we could. I was taking speed just about every day. I was a big lad but in three months I dropped half my body weight until I was just nine and a half stones. I moved from sofa to sofa and started working doors regular.

More than once, Iggy and Brunty sheltered me and helped me though many a bad time. They are two of the best men a man could know. Hopefully Brunty knows how much I love and respect him and that Iggy knew before he died. RIP.

For a while, Yatesey and Snigger let me live with them till they threw a surprise birthday party for me. A posse from Wolverhampton tried to gatecrash and it ended up toe to toe on the street. Two squad cars and a riot van watched until we'd won and then left. Me, Tyrone, Snigger and Scouse were the frontline, but if the Old Bill had seen the lads waiting behind us they'd have got the cameras out. Eventually I ended up on the door of the Freetown club.

I'd met Jasper at Introspective but at the Freetown we were working together most nights. We swapped stories and Jasper said I should come down to the match and that I'd enjoy it. I said that the only football casuals I'd had any dealings with were the ones I'd fought while I was following NMA and living in Bradford. He pointed out that a lot of my stories were like his except mine related to music and not football. By the time I took him up on his offer, it was near the end of the season. He'd caught my interest at one game by being more interested in me and him taking on five or six opponents in a tidy little brawl than the mass confrontation that was brewing.

That summer he was LA-bound and I was headed for the white island, my first summer in Ibiza. I worked the door for one of the coolest bars in the old town and ran a wholesale operation that many people didn't have a clue about. Due to the nature of my nefarious business activities and the fact that I was on my own, I tried to keep myself to myself. I made mates and had friends that I partied with, but during the day I stayed on my tod.

It's easy to party day after day, you just get up and do it. Casualties happen when you don't see the signs; after three months I could barely see the road. One day I came off my rented Honda Vision and bust my head open. It doesn't matter where pressure comes from, whether it's the life you live, the demons in your head or both, sooner or later it has to come out. I went on a seven-day bender. Even by my standards I was giving my metabolism a good kicking. For the last three days of it, I was followed. One of the lads I was with in the bar was a wee gay guy from London. As everyone else turned away, leaving me and the beast inside me running free, he kept track of me. He knew that a wrong wasn't far away, committed either by me or to me. I ended up safe and he got a new nickname, Nursie. He's still a good mate of mine to this day.

The bad news was that the money that had gone back to Blighty was light. I was in charge and accepted responsibility. Problem was I had no gaff, no coin and no product. On top of this I realised that I had a problem with my consumption. I'd become good friends with a firm from Leeds. I can remember the conversation with one of them very well.

"Adam, I think I've got a bit of a drink problem."

"You're not fucking wrong fella. We worked out the other day you do about two bottles of vodka a day and that's without going clubbing. When you get to the Café del Mar we can tell if you've had a drink or not. If you haven't no one talks to you till you've got a couple inside you."

Adam put me up in the apartment he shared with the rest of his lot from Leeds. They made sure I ate everyday. Word came back from England that a contract had been put on my life over the missing money. I didn't know at the time that it had been stopped by someone back home. They know who they are and that I'm grateful.

I was having two drinks a day to keep me steady in case someone turned up. One thing that touched me was the number of lads from all over who said they'd back me if anyone came looking for me. Thankfully that didn't happen. Adam loaned me the fare home and I escaped. I didn't realise at the time that I'd had or was having a nervous breakdown. That only really became clear when I was back in Stoke.

I rented a bedsit from Wilson and tried to get myself together. I only left home to work the door of the Freetown or to steal books. I didn't have a telly so I read when I wasn't trying to piece my mind and soul back together. The best way I can explain it is to liken it to a big jigsaw. I'd done the easy bit, the edges, then I sat there night after night trying to get everything else to fit.

The first night I was back, Jasper slipped me a score to get a round in. He couldn't even remember when I later reminded him of it, but to me at the time it was a massive gesture. For him it was par for the course, being there for the lads. He was organizing a trip to Poland for the England game and told me to get a photo for a visa, and that I was going. So my first ever away outing with the N40 was an international fixture behind the Iron Curtain. I missed the shenanigans on the first night as I had gone on the rob with the Stallion. Neither of us had a winter coat and it gets fucking cold in Poland in November.

Outside the ground was like a low-budget sci-fi film. There was a shanty town of food stalls in the stadium car park, all these little fairy lights twinkling from pitch to pitch through the mist and smoke. There was a petrol station off to one side. It was closed but the forecourt floodlights were on. It looked like it had just materialized.

From beyond it we could hear chanting getting louder. Then hundreds appeared through the bright mist. I was looking at this geezer at the front bouncing up and down. He was wearing some blinding kit and he had a ponytail that reached his belt, he looked cool as fuck. There were about thirty of us.

BANG! Straight into the middle of 'em. The geezer with the ponytail pulled out a truncheon and a badge, the coolest looking copper I've ever seen, and that includes Serpico. There I was, in the middle of a proper row. At first I just stood there thinking, *Right, what do I do now?* Then this big bloke in a leather jacket with a blond moustache came at me. BANG! Now I was fighting and enjoying it. I don't think Freud or Jung would approve but it definitely had a therapeutic effect on me.

I had already been intrigued, now I was hooked. When I got back the final jigsaw pieces began to fit. The same person who'd stopped the potential contract on me helped me again. I made a joke at my own expense one night and he told me to stop feeling sorry for myself. It worked. I was back.

I loved going to the match and partying. Working doors and dabbling in the black economy paid for that. There's little point in giving blow by blow accounts of this game or that. The fact is that for a number of years the most powerful drug in my life was football violence. It's more like a gambling addiction than drugs, because you aren't guaranteed a result.

When I met Lorraine I was heavily involved in the hooliganism and I have a great deal of respect for what she put up with and the fact that she gave me some stability. When we had a son I did my best to stop and be a straight goer. We split up, not for any dramatic reason; it's just the way things go sometimes. Instead of going back into the fold of the lads at the match full time I escaped into heroin and crack cocaine. I'd been doing both of them on and off for years. When they become the story of your day rather than a monthly excursion, only bad things can follow.

That was why I moved to London. Perhaps if I'd immersed myself back in the firm then my drug appetites wouldn't have gone the way they did. Other lads have been away for a while and when they need it, the firm's still there. Life is about learning.

At times, the way we lived as football casuals is mirrored in other aspects of life and that includes the dark parts. The general public views football hooligans as mindless thugs, and let's have it right, some of them are. Violence is easy to condemn, but you don't have to be violent to be cruel and malicious. You don't have to strike someone to bully them and these things are endemic in society.

People find it easy to forget that we weren't bred in a laboratory, we are a product of the society we are from. We may be its dark reflection but we're still part of the whole picture. I still have the beliefs I grew up with and still argue against right-wing politics. I still believe in trying to help rather than victimize those less fortunate than oneself and yet there was a period in my life when I used to enjoy fighting at football matches. This may be a contradiction but open your eyes, life is built on such contradictions. Many people aren't fortunate enough to have good friends who they can rely on to stand with them whenever they need it. I've been written off for various reasons five times in my life but some people had faith. Have faith and pride in who you are. And if you end up on your knees, get up and stand again.

CASUAL LIFE, CASUAL REFLECTIONS

By Ged Forrest

That's why I like it in here, all the lads know the score, this is our boozer. You get some wannabes like that tosser over there – Oi, lend us your walk, mate – wanker, he'd be the first on his toes. But in here we're all the same, we all play by the same rules.

I mean, some boozers you go into where they're supposed to be respectable and they've no fucking manners. Middle class wankers too full of themselves to be polite. Oh yeah, they've got the manners of exclusion, knowing which fork to use and all that bollocks. But you get summat wrong in their world and all you get is a cold smirk around the dinner table, get summat wrong in ours and you can get a glass smashed in your face.

You know how it starts, a little nudge, a wrong remark, ~one getting a little bit fucking fresher with your space than they ought to, know what I mean? Then it happens, that little thing that happens from time to time and in your head someone tosses a coin and the next two minutes of this cunt's life depends on how it lands.

Will it be heads, will it be tails? You take a deep breath like all those New-Age hippy wankers telling you to calm down. But the oxygen hits your lungs, adds fuel to the fire. The coin spins through the air. Heads he's dead, tails I'll leave it. Heads! I'll bust his face open and glass the first cunt who wants it, Tails! I'll down me pint and go. Will it be heads will it be tails, we'll have to wait and see.

It's nothing new, razor gangs in the Thirties, Teds, Mods. Football casuals are just like Mods further down the line, spending their money on designer gear to go down the match and have a row. All those wankers wandering around Knightsbridge, spending money they don't even notice on Armani and Dolce; we started doing that on the terraces and they don't even know it.

They live in their world and we live in ours. They talk about us like we're some sort of disease. Let me take you by the hand and lead you round the pubs and clubs of this country. I'll show you something that'll make you shit yourselves. We're the reflection of their society that they're too scared to look at.

Violence is part of this country, it's the red of the red, white and blue, it's the cross of St George. They know fuck all, we are England. They just don't live here.

Sometimes I wonder what I'd do if I stopped. I lie in the bath for ages some nights, leaving the hot tap on just enough so it doesn't get cold and I wonder what I'd do if I stopped going to the match. And I start thinking about the wolves again.

At the end of the film one of the she-wolves gets driven out of the pack. It was winter so there was a chance she might not make it as they can't hunt so well on their own. But she hooks up with this lone wolf and they go off to start their own pack. I'm not talking about having a family, but there's a big fucking world out there and I don't just wanna see it through a TV or a package holiday.

If I stopped going to the match, I'd have to move away, I don't think I could stick it around here. Then it's the morning again, and the factory, and it starts all over again. You know what I mean. It doesn't matter what job you do, it's like a snowball.

Something starts gnawing at you, a worry or something somebody's said. You don't sleep too well and the next day it's still there, whispering, and it starts to fester. There are more sleepless nights and it builds and builds as your fuse gets shorter. Then something makes you snap.

You probably take it out on your husband or your missus or your kids. For us there's the match. You see, you hurt the people you love, while we want to hurt "them" and they want to hurt us: not fellers with their kids or ordinary fans in shirts, but their firm, their top boys. The ultimate adrenalin rush.

I've been gassed, battered by the Old Bill, had fireworks, bottles, and half-enders thrown at me. I've known lads stabbed and some that have died. All that and when it's over, the fear of having your door put through with a sledgehammer on a dawn raid, even a year later.

Sometimes I wonder if it's worth it, if life would be better if my nerves were dead like every other fucker's. Senses that only work now and again just to remind them that they're still alive, instead of mine like a spring wound tight, waiting, ready.

Maybe I'll just fuck off and start afresh. Just be normal, drink in a boozer without clocking all the faces and watching the door. Go for a piss without picking the safest place in the khazi in case you get jumped. Not have to remember every face you've had a row with. No need to wonder if that car that pulls up outside is full of coppers or bad men in balaclavas looking for revenge. You know, just be normal, let life grind you down as the bastards chip away at your soul.

And then I'm back on shift, and the wanker of a foreman's trying to give me shit, or some cunt from management's talking down to me, taking the piss. They know I can do fuck all 'cos there's no work about, and I need the job 'cos my lady might be pregnant. So I have to swallow it, and it starts all over again and it's like a slow death. It's like I'm suffocating, fighting for breath.

I get to the weekend, couple of jars early doors, maybe a line, then out for some reconnaissance. There they are, fucking top boys 'n' all, they've just turned the corner. Quiet run down to the corner, no noise till we're right behind them. We don't know how many there are. There's only four of us, could be more than ten of them. They could be tooled up. Who gives a fuck, this is what we're here for. They're here. "LET'S 'AVE IT . . .!"

And I'm alive, lungs filled with air, and I unleash all that fury. And all the shit is forgotten, until next week.

It's not perfect but at least it's a laugh. That's not an excuse, it's just an observation.

WHO WANTS IT

Who wants it?
Who wants to know?
Tactical ability is secondary to heart.
There's a thing that governments and generals rely on,
When soldiers fight.
They fight for each other.

Sex, Drugs and Football Thugs

There's a code that comes with friendship,
Casuals know it in a single word,
Stand.
I stood with Jasper at one end of the bridge,
When they opened the gates to the ground,
The other end of the bridge began to swarm,
There was nowhere to go.
We don't run.
They had a bounty on Jasper from the '80s.
We stood next to each other,
An empty Budweiser bottle each,
And faith,
Faith in loyalty.
We each knew the other wouldn't run,
That we would stand,
That we were Stoke,
That was the deal.
When you enter a situation,
Knowing the extremes of its consequence,
You make a pact.
If you tell your friend that you'll stand by them,
As long as they are true,
You stand.
As they circled us it became surreal,
The fear began to ebb,
I felt a kind of calm,
I looked into their faces,
There was a lot of young lads,
Maybe carrying Stanleys,
There were fucking hundreds of 'em,
One of 'em gobbed at me.
I smiled and wiped my face,
With the sleeve of my Stone Island jumper.

"Where are your boys, Jasper?"
"Where d'you think they are, they're still in there."
After a minute they smiled,
Nodded and left.
We walked to the ground and started giggling,
"Fucking hell, Gedi, that was close."
We'd gotten away with it,
Another tale to tell,
And tell again.
When the stand off is over,
What happened matters little,
But that the deal is kept,
In a fight it's easy,
You stand.
Without the fighting,
The deal's the same,
You still,
STAND.

The Last Word

THANK YOU LADS for those priceless words and promises kept. I guess on reflection 1984 to 1994 was my very own personal decade of decadence. I enjoyed it immensely, and no, I would not change a minute of it, rough or smooth. Besides, as we know it is impossible to turn back the hands of time to change things, though I'm sure there must be many of us who wish we could.

We only get one real chance at this life, and most of us have been able to choose the roads upon which we travel. It is my belief that no matter how many roads we take, be they dark and impassable or endless and sun-drenched, they all lead to where we stand at this moment in time, period. Whether you have enjoyed them or not I suppose is down to you.

The latter part of the Nineties, after my departure from Stoke and the cutting of my physical connection to the firm, were dark to begin with. Normality had set in and I was struggling with it. As I told in *Naughty*, I had to become a hermit for a time and cut myself off from the life and people I loved, always living with the fear that the temptation of that final fix would have me returning to the fold and becoming hooked again.

But they say time is a healer and sure enough, when I eventually found the strength to have the lads back in my life without any expectation from them, or actual desire from me to participate once again, I felt that I had finally moved on. For them, the lads, the thought of "early retirement" was unthinkable, and on and on they marched. Growing in strength and stature, the N40 really did become a force to be reckoned with and stood proudly with the best of the rest. The N40 had achieved their aim of growing from a mediocre firm who were rated at home but sometimes struggled away from it, to being placed in the top three worst hooligan mobs in the country, alongside Cardiff and Millwall. For many this was the pinnacle, and I suppose rightly so as well.

No longer sick at the thought of not being with them, yet pissed off at missing the bonding and excitement of the match day experience, me the technophobe purchased my first mobile phone specifically to use on Saturdays. To a point I had got it (the buzz) back, and now match days were spent pacing the hall way of my home continuously as call after call came in from as early as six in the morning if we were at an away game, and carried on throughout the day and night, with each of the lads taking turns to call me so I could join in with the banter and share some of the love. Strange as it seems, it kept me going, although my partner at the time found it slightly bizarre that a grown man spent his entire day singing songs at the top of his voice and every now and then started punching and kicking at nothing in particular whilst using a mobile telephone. I did tell her that this behaviour was not uncommon among football fans, and the punching and kicking, well, that was a hooligan thing! She said she understood, but in the end it turned out she didn't.

Post *Naughty* it's much the same. The culture's still rife, it has just been forced underground for the time being. Nowadays you rarely see the huge numbers of the Nineties, even though they are still all out there craving the past. Fights are still commonplace, but these days are generally with Eastern Europeans and asylum seekers instead of other firms of English. A sign of the times I suppose.

The last few years for me have been slowly progressive and relatively happy, although the devastation of losing my grandmother just three months after the first book was published floored me for some time and I sorely miss the only love of my life dearly. They say as one leaves us another arrives, and during the same period the Chester side of my family eventually found me, flooring me once again. A lifetime of wishing finally over! At last I could look at my own genes and now I had no doubts where I came from.

Even better, I find out that I was not so inbred as I was led to believe throughout my childhood, although it was far too late to heal the scars given to me by my spiteful mother and grandfather. I'm not lecturing, but if you tell a child something enough times they will believe it. Ultimately it ruins their confidence, their expectations and their chances of ever finding peace. Think before you bring a child into the world, and damn you if you use that child as a weapon of revenge. Fuck all mothers who shun their responsibilities, and live and die with the guilt of watching their own mother doing it for them. Deprive a growing child of female love and nurturing and it disrupts the growth of the brain, causing chemical imbalances between the cortisone and serotonin it needs to function properly in later life. That child then becomes an adult devoid of certain important emotions, more often than not finding intimacy in adulthood a real problem.

I will be honest, my lack of love and affection as a kid didn't bother me that much that I felt the need to go out and research the facts. I just picked that information up off one of those smutty sex documentaries on Channel 5. All the same it did touch a nerve and after watching it, I pondered the fact that sexually I have always found it natural to make love to a hooker, but struggled with someone I cared for. Just a thought.

At the end of the day I'm in my forties now and self-healed, I tell myself. I've also really enjoyed writing this conclusion to my formative years' story, and some nights when I've finished writing I've sat silently at my desk. Others I've sat rolling in laughter at the memories and on the odd occasion I've been angry. Angry at the fact that I now had a family whose feelings I may have to consider all of a sudden after previously having no care in the world. But do you know what? They are Chesters and they will deal with it.

To celebrate the near completion of this book I'm going to treat myself to a bottle of vodka and a couple of Thai girls for the night. No shit! There is a place in town that has recently opened up and if you're a regular they do deliveries – and for an extra tenner they will go down on you without a rubber . . . Bloody hell here I go again. Freedom of speech, eh!

And that's it. Two books and you've had your lot. My overall summary after over thirty years of living within this phenomenon is, if you have made your commitment to that football way of life, then you have ostracized yourself from the mainstream, leaving little opportunity of slipping discreetly into the "normal" world. You become detached from reality. I don't know if that's a good thing or a bad thing, but you make that decision at an early age, when you are immature and highly impressionable. Then you grow older through the culture and eventually face the consequences of your actions. But you can't give it up; how can you? You don't know any different. You see, we are all addicts, though not your recognised ones. All of your friends are the same as you, and most are at different stages of their own reluctant retirement. None of you can relate to anybody who wants to talk about normality, you just end up drifting off mid conversation. Normality, what's that?

It is difficult to explain what is happening, as none of us knows. There is a transition period ongoing as we speak. Many people within the hooligan culture believe it has prepared them and brought a united front across the country of like-minded men who are willing to stand up and be counted. A kind of imposed destiny, they say. But they are entitled to their opinion, aren't they?

Was it all for nothing? Did we choose a hopeless lifestyle? Or did we make a bold statement? Is it all just down to fate and the writing of history? Who knows, in 100 years people may be reading this very page that have the answer to this question. Free people. People who admire and respect our legacy. Thankful people who were liberated and spawned from the determined resistance, whose forebears were the reviled and despised FOOTBALL HOOLIGANS.

Personally, and with much hindsight, I reckon we all take some time out to relax a while. Let's just smoke heaps of grass, suck greedily on a full swollen pap and swig flagons of cider on sunny English afternoons. Yeah man, SEX DRUGS and NO THUGS. None of any description whatsoever. Now wouldn't that be a much nicer world to live in?